Contemporary Perspectives on Lesbian,
Gay, and Bisexual Identities

Debra A. Hope

Editor

Contemporary Perspectives on Lesbian, Gay, and Bisexual Identities

 Springer

Editor
Debra A. Hope
Department of Psychology
University of Nebraska
Lincoln, NE
USA
e-mail: dhope1@unl.edu

ISBN: 978-0-387-09555-4   e-ISBN: 978-0-387-09556-1
DOI: 10.1007/978-0-387-09556-1

Library of Congress Control Number: 2008940910

Printed on acid-free paper

springer.com

Preface

This symposium series is supported by funds provided by the Chancellor of the University of Nebraska-Lincoln, Harvey Perlman, and by funds given in memory of Professor Harry K. Wolfe to the University of Nebraska Foundation by the late Professor Cora L. Friedline. We are extremely grateful for the Chancellor's generous support of the symposium series and for the University of Nebraska Foundation's support via the Friedline bequest. This symposium volume, like those in the recent past, is dedicated to the memory of Professor Wolfe, who brought psychology to the University of Nebraska. After studying with Professor Wilhelm Wundt, Professor Wolfe returned to this, his native state, to establish the first undergraduate laboratory in psychology in the nation. As a student at Nebraska, Professor Friedline studied psychology under Professor Wolfe.

Debra A. Hope
Series Editor

Contents

Preface v

Contributors ix

1   Introduction 1
    Debra A. Hope

2   How Many Gays are There? It Depends 5
    Ritch C. Savin-Williams

3   What is Sexual Orientation and Do Women Have One? 43
    J. Michael Bailey

4   Sexual Stigma and Sexual Prejudice in the
    United States: A Conceptual Framework 65
    Gregory M. Herek

5   An Overview of Same-Sex Couples in Relation Ships:
    A Research Area Still at Sea 113
    Esther D. Rothblum

6   Lesbian and Gay Parents and their Children:
    A Social Science Perspective 141
    Charlotte J. Patterson

7   Love, Marriage, and Baby Carriage Among
    Sexual Minorities- and Bias: Discussion of the
    54th Nebraska Symposium on Motivation 183
    Marvin R. Goldfried

Index 197

Contributors

J. Michael Bailey
Department of Psychology, Northwestern University, Evanston, IL, USA

Marvin R. Goldfried
Stony Brook University, Stony Brook, NY, USA

Gregory M. Herek
Department of Psychology, University of California, Davis, CA, USA

Debra A. Hope
Department of Psychology, University of Nebraska, Lincoln, NE, USA

Charlotte J. Patterson
Department of Psychology, University of Virginia, Charlottesville, VA, USA

Esther D. Rothblum
Women's Studies, San Diego State University, San Diego, CA, USA

Ritch C. Savin-Williams
Human Development, Cornell University, Ithaca, NY, USA

Introduction

Debra A. Hope

The Nebraska Symposium on Motivation is steeped in history and tradition. Over the years the series editors have striven to maintain the highest standards of academic excellence and to highlight some of the most important trends in psychology. Perusing the chapter titles in the first 53 volumes shows the shifting emphasis as the science of psychology developed in the latter half of the twentieth century. All of the most important topics are there — drive theory, social learning, the cognitive revolution, developing perspectives on understanding individual differences and the role of culture, and the increasing role of neuroscience. The key figures are there as well — Harry Harlow, Kenneth Spence, Raymond Cattell, George Kelly, Albert Bandura, Carl Rogers, Carroll Izard, Walter Mischel, Sandra Bem, Sandra Spence, Herbert Simon, David Barlow, and many others. In late 2004, I met with a group of interested graduate students, and together we developed a proposal to join this long and proud tradition with a volume on sexual orientation.

Our motivation stemmed, in part, from the events around us. The same-sex marriage debate was covered extensively in the media, reflecting a rapid and important discussion about sexual orientation that we were having (and are still having) as a society. Psychology and related fields have much to offer on many of the issues raised in this debate. What is sexual orientation and what determines it? How important is antigay prejudice and discrimination? What is the nature of the relationship in same-sex couples and how do their children fare? Fortunately, for us, excellent researchers had been asking and answering these questions. Our reading of the literature suggested that the body of research we were attempting to explore for the Symposium had reached a critical mass to form the basis of an entire Symposium conference and volume. Knowing that the topic of sexual orientation would not be without controversy, the steering committee, under the leadership of Richard Dienstbier, was bold enough to allow us to take it on. For that we are profoundly grateful.

This volume opens with two chapters on the nature of sexual orientation from two contrasting perspectives. Ritch Savin-Williams, well known for his ground-breaking work on the development of sexual identity, explores a variety of definitions of sexual orientation, including how youth with same-sex attraction and behavior are describing themselves. One theme in his work is the importance of how one asks a question because it often determines the answer. However much we like neat categories of "straight, " "gay, " and "lesbian, " Savin-Williams points out

D.A. Hope (ed.), *Contemporary Perspectives on Lesbian, Gay, and Bisexual Identities,*
DOI: 10.1007/978-0-387-09556-1, © Springer Science+Business Media, LLC 2009

that these categories do not capture the full range of sexual orientations as it occurs in the lives of individuals. Many youth are rejecting such labels, preferring to forge an individual sense of their own sexual identity that may well be fluid over time. Much of what we think we know from the research literature on sexual orientation is based on individuals who are willing to embrace these labels publicly, or at least for the researcher. Moving beyond the labels changes the correlates of being a sexual minority, including facts thought to be well established such as the heightened risk of suicide among gay teenagers.

One might say that Savin-Williams' research focuses on applying rigorous psychological science to what he hears when he listens to sexual minorities, especially youth. J. Michael Bailey, in contrast, asks us to move beyond self-report and self-identification in understanding sexual orientation and to focus instead on what we can learn from objective measures, defined in this case primarily as patterns of sexual arousal. For Bailey, sexual orientation is defined by the stimulus characteristics of a person that elicits a physical sexual response as measured by the penile plethysmograph in men and the vaginal plethysmograph in women and by fMRI. These patterns of response do not necessarily match the public or private labels that individuals give themselves and can include characteristics beyond the gender of the person to whom one is attracted. Never one to shy away from controversy, Bailey's chapter highlights what he sees as profound differences in how sexual orientation is expressed in men and women, with greater fluidity in women's sexual orientation, a finding that echoes other research described by Savin-Williams.

So if the first two chapters intend to answer the question, "What is sexual orientation?, " the answer must be, "it depends. " It depends on which aspect of sexual orientation is of interest. Clearly there is much discordance across physical sexual response, self-label, sexual behavior, attraction, and emotional attachment. Clearly research that purports to study sexual orientation must specify which aspect of sexual orientation is relevant to the research question, recognizing that this may correlate poorly with other aspects.

Despite the complexity of sexual orientation as discussed in the first two chapters, Chapter 3 by Gregory Herek shows that the general public has little difficulty identifying gays, lesbians, and bisexuals as a group of people about whom they have definite, often negative, attitudes. Without a doubt, Herek is the leading expert on sexual prejudice and stigma based on sexual orientation. He thoroughly reviews the literature ranging from hate crimes, to the cost of hiding one's orientation to correlates of sexual prejudice. He places this work in the political and cultural context and describes a theoretical framework for understanding the range of findings.

Chapters 4 and 5 examine same-sex couples and their families. Esther Rothblum reviews her groundbreaking work on same-sex couples in Chapter 4, based on couples who had civil unions in Vermont. Using a clever design to develop a matched comparison of heterosexual couples from siblings, Rothblum has demonstrated that sometimes the null hypothesis is the most interesting outcome in psychological research. Although there were some differences in how the same-sex and heterosexual couples organized their relationship, mostly the same-sex couples have all of the variability, strengths, and weakness of heterosexual couples.

Noting that "first comes marriage, then the baby carriage, " Charlotte Patterson delves into the experience of children raised in same-sex couples. Patterson's program of research in this area has answered critics from one study to the next, starting with convenience samples and moving to carefully matched broader samples. Patterson and others have shown repeatedly that being raised in a same-sex household is not detrimental to children — in all families the most important factors are love and support, not the gender of the parents. Clearly more research is needed on gay men as parents, but the findings for same-sex female households are clear.

The discussant at the symposium was Marvin Goldfried and he contributed the final chapter to the volume. Although Goldfried has published empirical work on sexual orientation, he also brings another perspective as the parent of a gay man. Goldfried unites his identities as an empirically oriented clinical psychologist with his real-life experience to identify what he sees as highlights of the chapters.

Each contributor was asked to include bisexuality with research on gays and lesbians. The literature on bisexuality is limited, and there are still many studies in which the bisexuals are excluded, or combined with another group, due to the small sample sizes. More research with bisexuals is needed, but we appreciate the contributors ' efforts toward inclusion.

This symposium volume was born in reaction to societal discussion about sexual orientation, especially gay marriage. As one reads this volume, however, it becomes clear that scientific research on sexual minorities enriches our understanding of all people. For example, one can better understand the nature of marital relationships when the confound of gender is removed. Patterson describes how our theories of child development have assumed crucial influences from a male and female parent that are not supported when both parents are the same gender. The healthy development of adolescents includes development of social and sexual identity. What are the possibilities for healthy development when youth can explore without the societal constraints imposed by sexual prejudice? Perhaps we can better understand the distal variables that influence important adolescent problems such as suicidality when distracting proxy variables such as self-labeled sexual minority status are better understood. In contrast to discrimination based on race and gender in which there are legal protections for civil rights, discrimination based on perceived sexual orientation has no legal consequences in many jurisdiction. In fact, overt sexual prejudice is seen as justifiable in a way that racial or gender-based prejudice is not. This creates a natural experiment in which we can examine the impact of different types of discrimination and prejudice under differing legal and cultural standards.

This volume comes out of the Nebraska Symposium on Motivation conference held in Spring 2006. For many in attendance, it was another academic conference. But for many others, especially those identifying as sexual minorities and their families and allies, there was an electrifying spirit in the air. One of the most historic and prestigious academic conferences in psychology was devoted entirely to gays, lesbians, and bisexuals. At the gala symposium dinner on the final day, Savin-Williams captured the spirit when he remarked that there was a sense of gay and lesbian psychological research having achieved some milestone of legitimacy. Many of us in attendance experienced a sense of empowerment and validation to see ourselves and our experience reflected in the presentations, not as an after-thought, not as a control group or confounding variable, but as the primary focus. Numerous nonacademics who work in clinical or advocacy positions on gay and lesbian issues in the local community attended the Symposium. They returned to their work armed with new scientific information and a renewed sense of the impor-tance of their efforts. For months afterward, findings from the Symposium were discussed in meetings both on and off campus.

A successful symposium depends upon many people. I would like to thank the doctoral students who were involved in phases of the organizing and planning: Sarah Hayes, Michelle Fortier, Andrea Perry, Jason Vogler, and Ashley Smith. Their inspiration and hard work made the event and this volume a reality. Claudia Price-Decker has been the primary staff assistant for the symposium for many years. Her experience, attention to details, and behind-the-scenes work make the event run smoothly and professionally. The realities of the climate for sexual minorities mean that we paid particular attention to security for the meeting. I am very grateful to Mario Scalora and his doctoral students who monitored potential threats prior to the event and worked with university police and building personnel to implement a security plan if any antigay protests became threatening. Thankfully, there were no disruptions. Finally, I would like to express my appreciation to the presenters and chapter contributors. Their work is important on so many levels. By being good scientists they contribute to our understanding of the human condition. By being pioneers as researchers on sexual minorities they have built a body of literature that helps sexual minorities and their advocates work toward full inclu-sion in our society.

How Many Gays Are There? It Depends

Ritch C. Savin-Williams

> *This is not a study of "homosexuals" but of participants in homosexual acts… This is the activity, and these are the actors, that I set out to study in 1965*
>
> (Humphreys, *1970, p. 18*).

Since the time of Laud Humphreys' *Tearoom Trade* and his investigation of "covert deviants," homosexuality has achieved both public and scientific visibility. Once considered by scientists to be a legal, moral, and mental abnormality, homosexuality is currently perceived by many scholars and youth as merely statistically deviant. This is not to deny that some portion of the US population still believes that same-sex sexuality is a religious and psychological aberration. It is the statistical and not the psychological health question that I address in this chapter: *How many gays are there?* In other contexts I explore whether the answer to this question matters in select (primarily clinical) domains (Savin-Williams, 2006).

Early gay scholars answered the "how many" question based on a misreading of Kinsey's findings (Kinsey, Pomeroy, & Martin, 1948; Kinsey, Pomeroy, Martin, & Gebhard, 1953), proclaiming, "10%!" Recently, sexologists have more prudently proposed a lower fraction, less than 1 in 25 (Diamond, 1993). A questionnaire study of US and Canadian college students concluded that findings did not "by all reasonable criteria" support suggestions that 10% of young adults identify as nonheterosexual. "Instead, our findings were much closer to estimates [citations] of less than 4% of males (and less than 2% of females) being predominantly non-heterosexual" (Ellis, Robb, & Burke, 2005, p. 578).

Essentially neglected in previous prevalence research are the critical, inherently logical prior questions, "Who's gay?" and "How much gayness is necessary to be gay?" I argue that estimates of the statistical standing of nonheterosexual orientation groups must first decide how relevant populations are defined. Because of dramatic changes in recent cohorts regarding the openness and possibility of nonheterosexuality (Savin-Williams, 2005), my focus, except where otherwise noted, is on data collected from adolescents and young adults growing up during the past two decades.

D.A. Hope (ed.), *Contemporary Perspectives on Lesbian, Gay, and Bisexual Identities*,
DOI: 10.1007/978-0-387-09556-1, © Springer Science+Business Media, LLC 2009

Defining Sexual Orientation

Historic Interest

The stunning findings produced by Kinsey and associates (1948, 1953) regarding the unexpected widespread engagement in homosexual behavior by a diverse and mundane populous of North Americans generated considerable scientific and political attention about the possibility of life-long homosexual individuals and their sexual activities. What Kinsey actually concluded was that 10% of males are "more or less exclusively homosexual… for at least three years" after age 16, but only 4% are "exclusively homosexual throughout their lives, after the onset of adolescence" (Kinsey et al., 1948, p. 651). Compared to males, the homosexual prevalence rate among females was about a half to a third "who were, in any age period, primarily or exclusively homosexual" (Kinsey et al., 1953, p. 475). These more stringent restrictions, largely ignored and rarely cited, correspond to modern estimates of 2–4%.

Several sexologists, however, question these approximations based on how homosexuality is conceptualized and defined. McConaghy (1999) argued that one of the unresolved issues in scientific sexology is appreciating the fact that the majority of individuals with same-sex attraction and behavior identify not as homosexual, but as heterosexual. For example, a recent study of over 4,000 New York City male adults revealed that more straight-identified than gay-identified men had sex with at least one man and no women in the past year (Pathela, Hajat, Schillinger, Blank, Sell, & Mostashari, 2006). In the Ellis study (Ellis et al., 2005), although only 2% of college men and women identified as homosexual/bisexual, 9% had exclusive same-sex sexual fantasies and an additional 4% reported 51–99% of their sexual fantasies were same-sex oriented. Is the prevalence rate of homosexuality/bisexuality 2% or 13%?

McConaghy also maintained that sexual orientation is less categorical than it is a spectrum, and points on a continuum with degrees of opposite- and same-sex attraction, desire, and behavior. At what point one demarcates "homosexual" and how much of same-sex sexuality is necessary to fall into this category are vital but unsettled considerations. Among Norwegian adolescents, 16% had some degree of same-sex attraction; the proportion was 7% if counting same-sex sexual contact and 3% if identifying those with a bisexual/gay self-label (Wichstrøm & Hegna, 2003). Among Turkish university students a similar pattern was found: 7% had sexual desire for the same sex but only 2% had an orgasmic same-sex relationship and 2% considered themselves as homosexual or bisexual (Eskin, Kaynak-Demir, & Demir, 2005).

Questions of who belongs in particular sexual groupings and on what basis are central for a viable paradigm for research on sexual orientation (Diamond, 2003a; Savin-Williams, 1990, 2001). Yet, science provides few definitive answers about the appropriate means of defining sexual orientation. In most investigations, inclusion criteria for designating homosexual populations are a crap shoot with little theoretical justification or consensus about what constitutes homosexuality. Is it a girl who consistently and unavoidably falls in love with other girls? A boy whose penis is aroused by films of naked boys? Boys who engage in same-sex behavior, regardless of their specific activities or regardless of how frequently they do it? Girls who identify themselves as lesbians or bisexuals? Most investigators simply ignore these questions and assume a practical methodological stance: whatever is prudent to insert in a questionnaire. Sometimes homosexuality is not defined and inclusion is based on such criteria as who shows up – volunteers from gay organizations or parades – or those who self ascribe a gay label. Such individuals are indeed likely to be gay, but they are also clearly not exhaustive and not necessarily representative of those with a same-sex orientation.

The historic question remains, "What is a gay?" What is it that is most essential, and to what degree, to designate such individuals? Because empirical distinctions among various operational definitions are seldom made, consumers of research are left uncertain as to how best to assess homosexuality or if those who participate in gay research are representative of gay lives. Indeed, I have argued over the past two decades that traditional gay youth research recruits are likely *not* representative of the much larger population of same-sex attracted youth, who frequently have a developmental history quite discrepant from the usual survey respondents.

Sexual Orientation Components or Expressions

Most generally, sexual orientation is defined by whether one is erotically attracted to males, females, or both (LeVay & Valente, 2006). Scientists who investigate the etiology of homosexuality usually conclude that it is present from birth, either because of genetics and/or prenatal hormonal events (Mustanski, Chivers, & Bailey, 2002). Sexual orientation is discernible from retrospective reports of prepubertal attractions/infatuations (Savin-Williams, 2005) and from childhood sex-atypical behavior and interests (Bailey & Zucker, 1995; Cohen, 2004; Ellis et al., 2005). It is during puberty and shortly thereafter when sexual orientation becomes most clearly manifested in reports and experiences of sexual arousal, romantic attraction, sexual behavior, and sexual identity (Savin-Williams & Cohen, 2004; see Box 1 for definitions).

In the biological and health sciences, sexual orientation is frequently inferred based on reports of *sexual behavior* during the past year or over a lifetime (since puberty). A single instance of same-sex activity, regardless of its normative significance for the individual's overall pattern of sexual behavior, usually places one in the homosexual category. For example, using the National Household Survey of Drug Abuse data set, Cochran and Mays (2000) defined as homosexual those who report any same-sex partners during the past year. Similarly, using interview data from the Netherlands Mental Health Survey and Incidence Study, Sandfort (Sandfort, de Graaf, Bijl, & Schnabel, 2001; Sandfort, de Graaf, & Bijl, 2003)

Box 1 Components of sexual orientation[a]

Sexual Orientation is the preponderance of erotic and romantic arousals, feelings, fantasies, and behaviors one has for males, females, or both.
Sexual orientation can be assessed by various components.

Sexual Attraction

An intense, physiological, uncontrollable erotic or sexual desire for males, females, or both sexes.

➤ "On a scale of 1–4, where 1 is very appealing and 4 is not at all appealing, how would you rate each of these activities: …having sex with someone of the same sex?" (Laumann, Gagnon, Michael, & Michaels, 1994, p. 293).

Romantic Attraction

Being or wanting to be in a primary loving, romantic relationship with males, females, or both sexes.

➤ "Have you ever had a romantic attraction to a male? Have you ever had a romantic attraction to a female?" (Udry & Chantala, 2005, p. 484).

Sexual Behavior

Involvement in (minimally) genital contact with males, females, or both sexes.

➤ "Have you ever had a relationship with someone of your own sex which resulted in sexual orgasm?" (Eskin et al., 2005, p. 188).
➤ "Here, by 'sex' or 'sexual activity,' we mean any mutually voluntary activity with another person that involves genital contact and sexual excitement or arousal, that is, feeling really turned on, even if intercourse or orgasm did not occur" (Laumann et al., 1994, p. 67).

Sexual Identity

Personally selected, socially and historically bound labels attached to the perceptions and meanings individuals have about their sexuality.

➤ "Pick from these six options: gay or lesbian; bisexual, but mostly gay or lesbian; bisexual, equally gay/lesbian and heterosexual; bisexual, but mostly heterosexual; heterosexual; and uncertain, don't know for sure" (D'Augelli, Hershberger, & Pilkington, 2001, p. 252).
➤ "Do you think of yourself as heterosexual, homosexual, bisexual, or something else?" (Laumann et al., 1994, p. 293).

[a]Based in part on Savin-Williams (2006)

linked mental health and sexual orientation by defining as homosexual anyone who reported same-sex behavior in the preceding year. Others make a higher demand, defining homosexuality as engaging in *exclusive* same-sex behavior (Durant, Krowchuk, & Sinal, 1998; Faulkner & Cranston, 1998). Yet, same-sex oriented youth may have limited opportunities to find desired sexual partners (few identifiable peers willing to engage in same-sex behavior), yearn for sexual experimentation or pleasure with opposite-sex peers, or desire to fit in and appear heterosexual. For some youth, of course, sex with both sexes is simply an expression of their bisexuality. Unexamined in these data sets are the contexts in which the same-sex activity takes place (whether in a prison, rectory, boarding school, the bedroom), the frequency of sexual behavior (once, occasionally, daily), or the motivations for the behavior (lust, curiosity, love, money, friendship). Thus, a young woman who has among her daily sexual encounters with men a single, mutual masturbation experience with a best female friend is in the same category as a young man who has exclusive, daily oral/anal intercourse with multiple male partners. Seldom do investigators record or consider these extenuating variables.

Also unexamined is what constitutes sex for the subjects (for a more general discussion of this issue, see Savin-Williams & Diamond, 2004). When Norwegian students were asked about their "homosexual experiences," 27% of the girls and 7% of the boys responded affirmatively. If asked specifically for particular sexual behaviors, 26% of the girls and 4% of the boys engaged in French kissing; if, however, the category was genital experiences the proportions dropped to 5% and 3%, respectively (Hegna & Larsen, 2005).

By contrast, in the psychological and social sciences, sexual orientation is usually determined by a self-reported description of sexuality, usually referred to as *sexual identity*. In most cases, the single-choice options are limited to gay, lesbian, bisexual, and heterosexual; occasionally, "not sure," "uncertain," or "something else" is included, but then discarded in analyses because of its low frequency. For example, the Massachusetts Youth Risk Behavior Survey posed the question, "Which of the following best describes you?" Subjects selected one of the following: "heterosexual (straight)," "gay/lesbian," "bisexual," or "not sure" (Garofalo, Wolf, Wissow, Woods, & Goodman, 1999). In other studies, questionnaire stems include phrases such as "think of yourself as" or "nominate yourself as." A second strategy is to give participants a 5-point scale from exclusive heterosexual to exclusive homosexual and instruct them to select one of the five descriptors (e.g., "mostly heterosexual"). Investigators seldom define these terms or agree about how to group the response options, such as how far along the continuum is to be counted as gay. For example, in one of the most productive data sources on the lives of gay youth, participants were to "describe yourself." Available responses included:

1. Gay or lesbian
2. Bisexual, but mostly gay or lesbian
3. Bisexual, equally gay/lesbian and heterosexual
4. Bisexual, but mostly heterosexual
5. Heterosexual
6. Uncertain, don't know for sure

Terms such as gay, bisexual, mostly, and uncertain were not defined; the relevant domains of sexuality to be described were not specified; only individuals in the first three groups were included in the study (the true gays and bisexuals); and data analyses treated the three groups as one ("lgb") (D'Augelli, Hershberger, & Pilkington, 2001).

The other two components of sexual orientation, *sexual attraction* (sometimes named arousal, desire, fantasy) and *romantic attraction/relationship*, are the least frequently assessed. Indeed, a study less than a decade old on "homosexual demography" (Hewitt, 1998, p. 390) noted that homosexuality "can be defined behaviorally or in terms of an individual's sexual identity" – with no indication that same-sex attraction or love might be a method of assessing homosexuality. Recent inclusions of romantic or sexual attraction are often practically or politically motivated: questions that explicitly ask minors about their sexual identity, especially when terms such as gay and lesbian are included, and sexual activities are too controversial and threaten parental consent (Caldwell, Kivel, Smith, & Hayes, 1998). Political reservations contributed to the definitions of sexuality in the National Longitudinal Survey of Adolescent Health (Add Health) (Udry & Bearman, 1998a, b). Although the third wave of data collection (when participants were young adults) asked about sexual identity, the first two waves, primarily given to adolescent minors, queried about the gender of sexual behavior and romantic attraction. Participants' attraction and behavior were classified as opposite-sex, same-sex, both-sex, or none. In early analyses of the data set, the middle two categories were perceived to capture "a broad range of youths, both those who might identify themselves as gay, lesbian, or bisexual and those who would not," but who might eventually come out (Russell & Joyner, 2001, p. 1277). For other researchers as well, romantic/sexual attraction was considered to be a surrogate, an acceptable proxy for sexual identity, the apparent sine qua non sexual orientation component (Caldwell et al., 1998, p. 345; see also Ellis et al., 2005).

By contrast, international investigators have been more willing to assess sexual/ romantic attraction as a legitimate measure of sexual orientation. Norwegian youth were asked "Are you sexually interested in men or in women (sexually attracted to, sexual fantasies about)?" and given a 7-point response scale mimicking the Kinsey range (Wichstrøm & Hegna, 2003, p. 145). Similar questions have been asked in Australia (Dunne, Bailey, Kirk, & Martin, 2000; Smith, Rissel, Richters, Grulich, & de Visser, 2003), New Zealand (Dickson, Paul, & Herbison, 2003; Fergusson, Horwood, Ridder, & Beautrais, 2005; Skegg, Nada-Raja, Dickson, Paul, & Williams, 2003), Switzerland (Narring, Stronski Huwiler, & Michaud, 2003), Turkey (Eskin et al., 2005), and the United Kingdom (Warner et al., 2004; Wellings, Field, Johnson, & Wadsworth, 1994).

Most striking about both the national and international literatures is the failure of investigators to ask participants what they believe constitutes sexual orientation. With this in mind, a group of researchers asked mixed-sex and mixed-orientation adolescent focus groups to develop a definition of sexual orientation (Friedman et al., 2004). The youth's consensus best measure did *not* include the traditional sexual orientation components sexual identity and sexual behavior because, the youth believed, too many people lie about their sexual activities and misunderstand what their sexuality means when they label themselves with a sexual identity. Their recommendation was to highlight two aspects:

- Whether one is or desires to be in a primary loving, sexual, and romantic relationship with a particular sex
- Whether one has an intense, physiological response for one or both sexes

The latter component, one not generally made by social scientists, can be assessed by physiological genital arousal expressions of sexual orientation – penile plethysmography (changes in the circumference of the penis) and vaginal photoplethysmography (changes in vaginal vasocongestion) (Chivers, Rieger, Latty, & Bailey, 2004; Rieger, Chivers, & Bailey, 2005). The assumption is that such assessments do not easily lie; it might also be possible to measure a continuum of responses (e.g., perhaps how erect the penis becomes). Other less intrusive biologic possibilities not yet adequately developed or tested include brain scans, eye tracking or pupil dilation in response to visual stimuli, differential attention given to male/female stimuli, body odor preference (pheromones), and anatomical variations (e.g., digit length ratio, handedness, otoacoustic emissions, sex-role motor behavior, and sex-atypical behavioral characteristics such as voice and body movement). Many of these assessments have unknown psychometric properties and may elicit unacceptably high levels of error.

Regardless of which sexual orientation component is assessed, little is known about its stability over time or its concurrent and longitudinal consistency – that is, do various sexual orientation components relate to themselves and to one another?

Stability and Consistency of Sexual Orientation

Stability

The extent to which sexual orientation is stable over time is essentially unknown, a surprising fact given the presumption of its stability by behavioral scientists and the critical nature of these data for issues such as whether sexual orientation is a matter of choice or destiny. Youth maintain that sexual identity (gay today, straight tomorrow) and sexual behavior (it was only a one-time thing) are by their very nature subject to change, especially during adolescence and young adulthood (Friedman et al., 2004). Is sexual attraction and romantic feeling so vulnerable? The stability data for all components are relatively meager and inconsistent.

In a short-term longitudinal study of sexual questioning among pre- and early adolescents, the stability over a school year was relatively high, 0.75 (Carver, Egan, & Perry, 2004). By contrast, among the 14% of Dutch adult men who reported ever having physical attraction to males, about half noted that these feelings disappeared later in life (Sandfort, 1997). Diamond's (2003b, 2008) 10-year longitudinal study of young women is one of the few to assess long-term stability in same-sex sexuality. Nearly two-third of the young women changed their identity label at least once, often because the identity categories did not adequately capture the diversity of their sexual and romantic feelings for female and male partners. Over time, lesbian and bisexual identities lost the most adherents and heterosexual and unlabeled gained the most. What remained relatively unchanged were reports of sexual and romantic attraction. That is, a young woman might change her identity from bisexual to heterosexual to unlabeled without undergoing a comparable change in her attraction to females.

Several retrospective studies provide support for an instability conclusion, at least for nonheterosexual populations. Among community and college youth, nearly two-third of gay/bisexual-identified individuals thought at one time during their development that they were in the other category (Rosario et al., 1996) – although it is not clear whether the reference to "change" captures identity, attraction, behavior, or some combination of these three. A recent study of adults attempted to clarify this issue by assessing on a 7-point Kinsey scale (from exclusively heterosexual to exclusively homosexual) multiple components of sexuality, including sexual fantasy, romantic attraction, sexual behavior, and sexual identity (Kinnish, Strassberg, & Turner, 2005). Change scores were derived by asking participants to rate themselves on these components for every 5-year period beginning with ages 16–20 years. In general, women and nonheterosexuals were more likely than men and heterosexuals to report changes in their sexuality. Even though each identity category step represented a significant alteration in self-presentation, over time many gays, lesbians, and bisexuals changed their identity label (especially women and bisexuals). Summarized in Table 1 is how various identity groups changed. For example, most gay men always identified as gay; only about one-third of lesbians had always identified as lesbian. The dimensional assessments of fantasy, attraction, and behavior reflected similar trends. Even though roughly 90% of heterosexually identified individuals had a 0- or 1-point change during their lifetime, the majority of gay (52%), lesbian (80%), and bisexual (90%) identified individuals had multiple changes on the dimensional variables. Reports of sexual behavior changed more often than romantic attraction.

Two additional longitudinal data sets provide unique opportunities to assess the stability of sexual orientation measures over time. Comparing sexual attraction at two

Table 1 Changes among identity groups over time in identification

Identity	Heterosexual (%)	Gay (%)	Lesbian (%)	Bisexual (%)	Multiple (%)
Heterosexual	97	0	0	3	1
Gay	11	61	–	19	9
Lesbian	39	–	35	10	16
Bisexual male	50	12	–	34	4
Bisexual female	63	–	6	23	8

time periods in a New Zealand birth cohort, first when participants were 21 years old and 5 years later as 26 year olds, Dickson et al. (2003) found that the proportion of young men who reported at least occasional same-sex attraction increased from 4 to 6%; among young women, from 9 to 16%. Although nearly all heterosexual men (98%) kept their opposite-sex attraction, 12% of opposite-sex attracted young women experienced at least occasional same-sex attraction. The migration among sexual orientations was bidirectional. The proportion of nonheterosexuals switching to heterosexuality was far greater than the reverse (as might be expected given their lower numbers): one-half and one-third of 21-year-old women and men, respectively, who experienced occasional same-sex attraction only had opposite-sex attraction as 26 year olds. Nearly 80% of 21-year-old men who reported exclusive same-sex attraction kept the attraction; however, 20% moved into the "occasional" same-sex attraction group 5 years later. Again, young women appeared more fluid: only 38% of exclusive same-sex attracted young women stayed in this group with the rest moving into "occasional" same-sex attraction (38%) or "exclusive" opposite-sex attraction (25%).

In the ongoing Add Health longitudinal study, romantic attraction and sexual behavior proved to be significantly stable over 6 years in three waves of data collection, largely because of the stability of opposite-sex attraction and behavior (Savin-Williams & Ream, 2007). However, youth who reported being romantically attracted to their own sex or engaging in same-sex behavior were seldom the ones who reported same-sex attraction or behavior 1 or 6 years later. For example, of the 69 Wave I boys who indicated that they had *exclusive* same-sex romantic attraction, only 11% reported exclusive same-sex attraction 1 year later (6% to both sexes); 48% had only opposite-sex attraction and 35% had no attraction to either sex (Udry & Chantala, 2005). Of the Wave 1 girls with exclusive same-sex romantic attraction, over half reported exclusive opposite-sex attraction 6 years later as 22 year olds (Savin-Williams & Ream, 2007). Yet, these Wave 1 reports of romantic attraction have been used to define "gay youth" (Russell & Joyner, 2001).

Components of same-sex sexuality are more stable among males than females and heterosexuals than nonheterosexuals. It is not possible, however, to state with confidence which sexual orientation component is more or less stable over time. In part this is due to the large variety of definitions used to encapsulate the components. It is safe to conclude that the available data indicate relatively low levels of stability across all same-sex components, especially during adolescence and young adulthood. This might have less to do with individuals' sexuality than with our assessments of sexual orientation.

Consistency

Data documenting consistency among sexual orientation components (one predicting the others within a time period or across time periods) are rare but now less elusive, largely because recently several investigators have included more than one expression of sexual orientation in their research design. Despite this, conclusions are difficult to reach; correlations between components within a time frame range from extremely low (0.10) to high (0.79) (Ellis et al., 2005; Eskin et al., 2005; van Griensven et al., 2004). Longitudinal consistency data – a component at one point in time predicting another component at another point in time – are largely absent. Before reviewing the adolescent/young adult literature, findings from adults are presented.

A study of Dutch adult men illustrates the discrepancies among sexual orientation components (Sandfort, 1997). More than half of the men who reported ever having physical attraction to other males never sexually acted on their attraction, less than half reported ever being in love with a man, and nearly all said they had at one time been in love with a woman. Even among the Dutch men who reported sex with another male, one-third said they were not attracted to males and just half of these same-sex behaving men identified as gay/bisexual or had ever been in love with a male. In a study of adult British women who have had a female sex partner, 96% also had a male partner; of British men, 90% had an opposite-sex partner (Wellings et al., 1994). Among US adults, only about 20% of those who were gay on one component reported being gay on the other two; 70% reported being gay on only one of the three components (Laumann, Gagnon, Michael, & Michaels, 1994).

Among adolescents and young adults, the empirical evidence is similarly inconsistent. One of the most telling was an anonymous questionnaire study conducted with a representative sample of Minnesota junior and senior high school students. The youth rarely reported agreement among their same-sex fantasy, attraction, behavior, and identity (Remafedi, Resnick, Blum, & Harris, 1992). The relationship between pairs of the components is reviewed here.

First, a substantial body of literature supports the finding that the vast majority of those who *identify* as gay also engage in same-sex *behavior*. The one exception is an Internet study which found that nearly one-third of young men and one-half of young women who self-ascribed a same-sex identity had not engaged in same-sex behavior (Kryzan, 1997). Less convincing, however, is the transposition: although a higher proportion of gay than heterosexual-identified youth engages in same-sex behavior, the sexual partners of gay youth usually identify as heterosexual. Indeed, in terms of pure numbers, similar to Pathela et al.'s (2006) study of adult men, most adolescents with a same-sex experience do not identify as gay but as heterosexual – three-quarters in the Remafedi et al. (1992) study. The reverse is also true: a heterosexual encounter is as likely or more likely to be reported by a gay- as a heterosexual-identified youth (DuRant et al., 1998; Garofalo, Wolf, Kessel, Palfrey, & DuRant, 1998). This seeming contradiction, that a majority of gay-identified youth report opposite-sex behavior, is reflected in the finding that exclusive same-sex behavior within adolescent and young adult populations is relatively rare (<1%) (D'Augelli, 1991; D'Augelli & Hershberger, 1993; Garofalo et al., 1999; Remafedi et al., 1992; Savin-Williams, 1998). These findings are supported by crosscultural data. Among Swiss adolescents, 87% of girls and 77% of boys with same-sex activity identified as heterosexual (Narring et al., 2003). Among Turkish college students, the correlation (0.36) between same-sex behavior and identity was significant but low (Eskin et al., 2005). Slightly over 4% of heterosexually identified Thai adolescents first had sex with a same-sex partner (van Griensven et al., 2004).

Second, the association between same-sex *attraction* and *behavior* is also weak. Among Norwegian 17- to 18-year olds, Hegna and Larsen (2005, p. 1) found that only a minority of those with homosexual sex also had homosexual attraction, except among males when the homosexual experiences were defined as oral and anal intercourse. They concluded, "Hence, most homosexual experiences among Norwegian youth are not unequivocally tied to homosexual attractions and possible homosexual self-identity." This discrepancy was especially true for females; their same-sex behavior appeared to the authors as exploratory rather than an explicit statement about their sexuality. Another study also found this sex difference: same-sex attracted young Australian women more often engaged in exclusive sex with males than they did with females or with both sexes, whereas same-sex attracted young men were more likely to be exclusively same-sex focused (Hillier et al., 1998). Among Turkish college students, the correlation (0.24) between same-sex attraction and behavior was significant but of a low order (Eskin et al., 2005). Just over one-third of Minnesota students with homosexual sexual fantasies had a same-sex experience (Remafedi et al., 1992).

Finally, the consistency between same-sex *attraction* and *identity* is also weak, at best. Minnesota public school students were four times more likely to report same-sex attraction than a same-sex identity and only 5% of those with same-sex attraction identified as gay; the correlation between same-sex attraction and a gay identity was strikingly low, especially for girls (0.10) compared to boys (0.30) (Remafedi et al., 1992). Among Swiss adolescents, the relationship between sexual identity and attraction was generally low. For girls, 73% of those with same-sex attraction (83% of those with same-sex fantasies) identified not as lesbian/bisexual but as heterosexual. For boys, the proportions were lower but in the same direction: 71% and 61% (Narring et al., 2003). Among Turkish college students, the correlation (0.37) between same-sex attraction and a same-sex identity was significant but low (Eskin et al., 2005). Counter to these results were the correlations between sexual identity and attraction among Thai adolescents (0.79 for boys and 0.64 for girls) (van Griensven et al., 2004) and of self-descriptions of being homosexual, bisexual, or heterosexual among US college students with self-reported fantasies about same-sex romantic relationships (Schmitt & Buss, 2000).

The weak relationships among sexual orientation components are also illustrated by the Add Health longitudinal data set (Savin-Williams & Ream, 2006). For example, during Wave 3 when the average participant was 22 years old, less than 2% of the young woman who reported having exclusive same-sex romantic attraction or having exclusive same-sex behavior identified as exclusively or mostly gay; among young men, 13% and 3%, respectively. Of those who had *both* exclusive same-sex attraction and behavior, 41% of women and 82% of men identified as mostly or exclusively gay. The effect of same-sex sexual behavior was subsumed over time with the effect of same-sex romantic attraction such that past sexual behavior *only* had implications for a young adult's sexual identity if it "meant something" in terms of romantic attraction. That is, attraction plus behavior was better than either alone in predicting eventual sexual identity. Same-sex behavior per se had little predictive power for young women. Of adolescents who engaged in same-sex behavior at Wave 1, fewer than one in 25 males and one in five females identified as nonheterosexual as Wave 3 young adults. Of those who reported exclusive same-sex romantic attraction when they were 16 years old, more reported future opposite- than same-sex behavior.

Summary

Based on the available data, sexual orientation components tend to be unstable over time and inconsistent with each other. Changes can be bidirectional, multiple, and seemingly unpredictable. Individuals leave and enter nonheterosexuality, perhaps once or several times, and at different rates and times across the components. Although nearly all individuals who identify as gay also report same-sex attraction, arousal, and behavior (except for gay virgins), a relatively small minority of those with same-sex attraction, arousal, or behavior identify as gay. Considerably more adolescents report same-sex attraction than engage in same-sex behavior or identify as gay/bisexual. Whether this instability and inconsistency uniquely reflect adolescent developmental phenomena is doubtful because the same trends are also found among adult populations (Dunne et al., 2000; Laumann et al., 1994; Pathela et al., 2006; Savin-Williams & Ream, 2006, 2007; Smith et al., 2003).

Several investigations indicate that there is more of an alignment among males than females in sexual orientation components. Among young women, these inconsistencies have been interpreted as manifestations of "sexual fluidity" (Diamond, 2003a) or "erotic plasticity" (Baumeister, 2000). For example, compared to young men, young women in the Add Health data set were relatively more inconsistent in their romantic attraction and sexual behavior and in their opposite-sex attraction and sexual identity; they also expressed lower levels of stability in opposite-sex attraction, same-sex behavior, and opposite-sex behavior. One task for researchers is to explain the finding that young women who engage in exclusive sexual behavior with other women are more likely to report that they are exclusively attracted to males than to both sexes or only to females (Savin-Williams & Ream, 2006).

How or why individuals transform their sexuality or their understanding of their sexuality, or remain stable and consistent, is unknown. Yet, when considering the real-life experiences of adolescents, these instabilities and inconsistencies do not seem surprising. A young woman may be romantically attracted to women, but she does not thus necessarily give up her enjoyment of sex with men. How to identify her sexuality? Perhaps she identifies as lesbian as a means to bond with a community of women, as heterosexual to please her parents, or as unlabeled because she does not want to be pigeon-holed. A young man may have consistent and persistent longings for sex with males, falls deeply in love with a woman, has sexual experiences with both sexes, and identifies as heterosexual as a means to secure his chosen career. Developmental movements over time from assumed heterosexuality to nonheterosexuality and back to heterosexuality characterize lives in which an individual has a singular idealized, hero-worship infatuation with a coach, teacher, or older peer that is interpreted as a romantic crush; engages in a curiosity-driven sexual experience that may be a one-time event, sporadic, or continuous; or says gay or bisexual to be "in" or to fit the image of the rebellious teen. Youth want to be "acceptable" and the moving target of popularity may motivate various sexual identifications or behaviors. Movements among heterosexuality and nonheterosexuality may also be understood as "finally" recognizing one's true or authentic self, even if that acknowledgment is merely temporary.

These real-life developmental experiences are seldom investigated by behavioral scientists who struggle to explain the stability or predictive failure of sexual orientation components. Worthy research pursuits would be to test whether different components have a different meaning or salience at various ages or for the sexes. In the Add Health data set, for example, consistency between attraction and behavior increased with age for both sexes such that by young adulthood same-sex attracted individuals were more likely to engage in behavior consistent with their attraction (Savin-Williams & Ream, 2006). This developmental trend might be the result of the greater opportunities afforded young adults in college or the work world to sexually act on their attraction or their greater realization over time about the permanence, meaning, and significance of their attraction and behavior.

An early study conducted with college women in the 1970s (Goode & Haber, 1977) provides data that guide us in understanding both the relative instability and inconsistency in sexual orientation components. Of the 160 young women in the study, 10% reported that they had sex with a woman. Nearly all these women, however, also had intercourse with a man, with many reporting that they enjoyed it. What most clearly distinguished these women from the collegiate women without same-sex contact were the details – the spectrum or continuum of same-sex sexuality. They had half as many male partners, had a narrower range of sexual activities with men, were half as likely to "almost always" have an orgasm with a man, were more likely to have had sex with a man they did not love, were half as likely to usually enjoy fellatio with a man, and were far less likely to have had their most pleasurable orgasm during intercourse with a man. Thus, rather than pursuing absolutes (e.g., women who have exclusive same-sex behavior), it was in the degree, proportion, and level of sex that most clearly distinguished the women. Yes, they had sex with men, but they had it less often, they had it later, and they enjoyed it less. These findings help us understand sexual orientation – especially prevalence rates.

Prevalence of Gays

In reviewing the demographics of gay and lesbian populations over the past decade, Black, Gates, Sanders, and Taylor (2000, p. 141) noted that the "incidence rate of homosexuality varies greatly depending on how homosexuality is defined" and that the correlations between definitions are frequently lower than "one might think." They contrasted various measures of sexual behavior and found over twice as many women and men reported having at least one same-sex encounter since the age of 18 as having exclusive same-sex behavior during the past year. By either time frame, the proportion of those identifying as gay or bisexual was far smaller – often by a factor of at least one-half – than those engaging in same-sex behavior. Thus, which sexual orientation component is assessed and how much of a component matters are critical when reporting prevalence rates (Table 2).

Depends on Which Measure

When researchers determine who is gay, they usually base their estimate on a single component of sexual orientation at one point in time. Yet, this strategy excludes many same-sex oriented individuals and misidentifies some heterosexuals as gay. If gay is defined as engaging in same-sex behavior, all virgins are omitted, heterosexuals who engage in same-sex behavior are miscounted, and gays who have only opposite-sex behavior are excluded. If gay is defined by self-identification, the much larger number of individuals who become aroused by those of the same sex, who report same-sex romantic relationships or sexual attraction, or who engage in same-sex behavior but who, for whatever reason, do not identify as gay is eliminated. If gay is defined by having same-sex attraction or a romantic relationship, then questions such as how intense do same-sex attraction or love need to be and what proportion of attraction or relationships must be same-sex oriented before counting as gay matter. Together these excluded individuals constitute a sizeable number. Clearly, individuals classified as gay in one study might not be so designated in another study that uses a different component or a different time frame. The result is differential prevalence rates.

These definitional dilemmas are not restricted to one age group or one culture. In the United States, the United Kingdom, and France, exclusive same-sex behavior rarely characterized more than 1% of the adult population (Sell, Wells, & Wypij, 1995). If the definition was broadened to include individuals who had both same- and opposite-sex behavior, who had some degree of same-sex attraction, or at least one of the two, then the proportion of gays expanded considerably – nearly one-fifth of the population of men and women (Table 3). Sell and associates, consistent with the adolescent focus groups (Friedman et al., 2004), suggested that researchers should *not* use homosexual behavior alone to define sexual orientation.

Similar conclusions characterize crosscultural research among adolescent and young adult populations. Empirical investigations consistently reveal wide variations within and across studies regarding the prevalence of sexual orientation groups based on definitional considerations (Table 2). Although it is not possible to systematically compare cohorts or cultures because of the relatively few intragroup studies, the various ways in which sexual orientation has been defined, and the multiple groupings of subjects (often within wide age ranges; sexes are separated or combined), requesting information about sexual attraction or

Table 2 Studies assessing prevalence rates of same-sex orientation among adolescents and young adults

Data collected	Source	Sample characteristics	Measure	Female	Both	Male
1970	Fay, Turner, Klassen, and Gagnon (1989)	US Kinsey, 21–29 years old, $n = 270$ men	Sexual experience with climax (yes/no)			14% rare 8% occ/often
1974	Asayama (1976)	Japan, 16–21 years old, $n =$ 2,101 women, 2,574 men	Homosexual contact (kiss, pet, mutual masturbation; yes/no)	4% yes		7% yes
1975, 1981, 1987	Diamond (1993)	Japan, 10–22 years old, $n =$ 2,236 women, 2,764 men; n = 2,485 women, 2,505 men; n=? women, 4,317 men	Homosexual body contact for 3 years (yes/no)	4% 1975 5% 1981 3% 1987		7% 1975 6% 1981 4% 1987
1986–1987	Remafedi et al. (1992)	Minnesota grades 7–12, n = 18,444 women, 18,077 men	Think/daydream about sex (with male/ female)	3% both 1% same		2% both 1% some
			Attracted only, strongly, equally and sexual with same or opposite sex (5-pt. scale)	5% both 1% same		4% both 1% same
			Sexual experience, any kind (yes/no)	1% some		2% some
			Sexual identity (5-pt. scale: 100% homo, most homo, bisexual, most het, 100% het)	1% bisexual 0.5% homo		1% bisexual 1% homo

(continued)

Table 2 (continued)

Data collected	Source	Sample characteristics	Measure	Female	Both	Male
1987, 1989, 1991, 1993	Breakwell and Fife-Schaw (1992)	United Kingdom schools, n = 1,315 women, 856 men (four cohorts, age range = 16–20)	Deep kissing	2%		1%
				1%		3%
				2%		2%
				2%		3%
			Stimulating genitals	1%		2%
				1%		7%
				1%		3%
				1%		3%
			Oral sex	1%		1%
				1%		4%
				2%		3%
				0.4%		2%
			Anal sex	-		0%
				-		1%
				-		1%
				-		2%
1988, 1989	Rogers and Turner (1991)	Combined US NORC General Social Surveys, n = 486, 21–29 year old men	Same-sex partners since age 18 (yes/no)			6% yes
1989	Rogers and Turner (1991)	Dallas County, TX survey, n = 265, 21–29 year old men	Same-sex partners since 11 years ago			7% yes

Date	Study	Sample	Measure		
1990?	Wellings et al. (1994)	National survey of Britain, 16–24 years old, n = 2,246 women, 1,984 men	Sexually attracted, interview (5-pt.) scale, only females to only males)	5% any att.	7% any att.
			Sexual experience, interview (kiss, touch, intercourse, other on 5-pt. scale, only females to only males)	2% any exp.	5% any exp.
			Sexual experience or contact with same sex booklet	3% any exp.	4% any exp.
			Genital contact with same sex, booklet	1% any contact	2% any contact
			Homosexual partner, at least 1, booklet	1% ever; 1% last 5 years; 1% last 2 years; 1% last year	3% ever; 2% last 5 years; 1% last 2 years; 1% last year
1991	Billy, Tanfer, Grady, and Klepinger (1993)	US National Survey of Men, n = 3,321, two groups: 20–24 & 25–29 year olds	Sexual activity in past 10 years (5-pt. scale, exclusively het to exclusively homo)		3% any act.; 2% homo
1992?	Papadopoulos, Stamboulides, and Triantafillou (2000)	Greece university students, 17–23 + age range, n = 2,275 women, 1,309 men	Sexual interest	8%	
			Sexual experiences	3%	

(continued)

Table 2 (continued)

Data collected	Source	Sample characteristics	Measure	Female	Both	Male
1991–1997	Ellis et al. (2005)	US, Canada college students, mean age = 22, n = 5,253 women, 2,653 men	Sexual attractions to same and opposite sex, 100-pt. scale	8% 1–10% 4% 11–50% 1% 51–99% 1% 100%		6% 1–10% 3% 11–50% 1% 51–99% 1% 100%
			Sexual fantasies during sexual interactions to same and opposite sex, 100-pt. scale	10% 1–10% 3% 11–50% 4% 51–99% 7% 100%		8% 1–10% 2% 11–50% 3% 51–99% 9% 100%
			Intimate sexual interactions if had sex (intercourse or to climax with proportion of same to opposite sex)	1% 1–10% 6% 11–50% >1% 51–99% 1% 100%		1% 1–10% 9% 11–50% >1% 51–99% 1% 100%
			Describe sexual orientation	1% bisexual 1% homosexual 1% uncertain		1% bisexual 1% homo- sexual 1% uncertain

1992, 1994	Orenstein (2001)	Massachusetts high schools $n = 2,946$	Sexual thoughts/romantic feelings (yes/no) (sexes combined)	7% yes 3% not sure
			Sexual experiences	2% yes 1% not sure
			Identity label	2% bisexual 1% homo-sexual 4% not sure
			Worry being gay	4% some-times/seldom 2% always/often
			Worry treated differently because gay or bisexual	4% some-times/seldom 2% always/often
			Percentage who have the above 5 indicators	1 = 11% 2 = 3% 3 = 2% 4 = 1% 5 = 0.5%

(continued)

Table 2 (continued)

Data collected	Source	Sample characteristics	Measure	Female	Both	Male
1992, 1994, 1999	Wichstrøm & Hegna (2003)	Norway schools, grades 7–12, n = 2,924	Sexually interested, attracted to, sexual fantasies (7-pt. scale; scale; only, predominantly, equally men/women)	21% some	3% bisexual/ homo 1% exclusive homo	9% some
			Sexual contact since 12 (yes/no)	7% yes		6% yes
			Sexual identity (7-pt. scale; exclusively hetero to gay)	14% nonhet	5% bisexual/ homo 1% exclusive homo	9% nonhet
1993	Bagley & Tremblay (1998)	Calgary, Canada community survey, 18–27 age range, n = 750 men	Sexual identity (homo, bi) and/or sexual activity (in last 6 months)			11% homo/bi 9% behavior 15% id/beh
1993–1994	Lock & Steiner (1999)	California high school, n = 841 women, 914 men	Wonder might be gay/bi (frequent, sometimes, no, know I am)	17% freq/some 6% know		9% freq/some 6% know
1993, 1995	Berg-Kelly (1995)	Sweden schools, grades 9 & 11, n = 886, 477 women, 854, 413 men	Definitely or possibly homosexual	2% 1%		1% 2%
1994	Caldwell et al. (1998)	Four Southeast US high schools, n = 1,488 women, 1,268 men	Sexual feelings (yes, no, both, none, not sure)	1% both 0.5% same 2% unsure 2% none		1% both 2% same 2% unsure 2% none

Date	Study	Sample	Measure		
1994–1995	Savin-Williams & Ream (2007)	US Add Health, mean 16 years, n = 20,747	Romantic attraction (male/female)	4% both; 1% same; 1% both	6% both; 1% same; 1% both
			Sexual activities (intercourse, partners)	0.5% same	0.5% same
1995–1996	Narring et al. (2003)	Switzerland students, 17 years old, n = 2,075 women, 2,208 men	Sexual attraction (5-pt. scale; only own sex and be sexual to own sex to opposite sex; also not sure)	1% both sexes; 2% only/strong; 1% not sure	1% both sexes; 3% only/strong; 1% not sure
			Sexual fantasies, daydreams (males, females, both)	5% both sexes	3% both sexes; 1% same sex
			First same-sex experience (sexual = kiss, caress, physical or sexual intimacy, intercourse)	0.4% same sex; 2% yes	1% same sex; 3% yes
			Sexual self identification (5- pt. scale, hetero to homo, & not sure)	1% bisexual; 0.3% homo; 4% not sure	1% bisexual; 1% homo; 2% not sure
1996	Savin-Williams & Ream (2007)	US Add Health, mean 17 years, n = 14,738	Romantic attraction (male/female)	4% both; 1% same; 1% both	3% both; 1% same; 1% both
			Sexual activities (intercourse, partners)	1% same	1% same

(continued)

Table 2 (continued)

Data collected	Source	Sample characteristics	Measure	Female	Both	Male
1993	Paul, Fitzjohn, Eberhart-Phillips, Herbison, and Dickson (2000)	New Zealand birth cohort, 21 years old, n = 453 women, 470 men	Sexually attracted to (5-pt. scale; opposite to same sex), current and ever	7%, 9% most het 1%, 1% equal 1%, 1% most homo 0.4%, 0.2% homo 2%, 2% no one		3%, 5% most het 0.2%, 1% equal 0.4%, 0.2% most homo 0.4%, 1% homo 1%, 0.2% no one
			Same-sex sexual contact (oral, anal, or other)	3% last year 10% ever		4% last year 9% ever
1998	Dickson et al. (2003)	New Zealand birth cohort, 26 years old, n = 473 women, 485 men	Sexually attracted to (5-pt. scale; opposite to same sex), current and ever	14%, 23% more het 1%, 1% equal 0.4%, 1% more homo 1%, 0% homo 0.2%, 1% no one		4%, 9% more het 0.2%, 0.4% equal 0.2%, 1% more homo 1%, 1% homo 0%, 0% no one
			Same-sex sexual contact (oral, anal, or other)	3% last year 10% ever		4% last year 9% ever
	Lippa (2000)	California college students, n = 434 women, 287 men	Sexually attracted male/female (7-pt. scale; strongly agree/ strongly disagree)	24% "any" (2–7 response) 12% "mostly" (4–7 response)		19% "any" (2–7 response) 10% "mostly" (4–7 response)
			Identity label	2% bisexual 1% lesbian		3% bisexual 2% gay

1998	Fergusson et al. (2005)	New Zealand birth cohort, mean = 21 and 25 years, n = 498 women, 469 men	Sexual attractions (age 25 yrs.) (5-pt. scale; only attracted to and sexual with opp. sex to only attracted to and sexual with same sex)	12% strg opp 1% equal att 1% strg same 1% only same	4% strg opp 0.2% equal att 1% strg same 1% only same
			Sexual relationship same sex (21 years) (yes/no)	3% yes	2% yes
			Sexual relationship same sex (25 years) (yes/no)	4% yes	1% yes
			Nominate sexual orientation (age 21 years)	0.4% homo/lesbian 1% bisexual	0.2% homo/gay 2% bisexual
			Nominate sexual orientation (age 25 years) (5-pt. scale; 100% hetero to 100% homo)	12% most het 1% bisexual 1% most homo 1% homo/lesbian	5% most het 0.2% bisexual 1% most homo 0.2% homo/gay
1999	van Griensven et al. (2004)	Thailand vocational students, mean = 18 years, n = 832 women, 893 men	Sexual feelings (females only, males only, both)	7% both 3% females 5% bisexual	4% both 4% males 3% bisexual
			Sexual identity group (heterosexual, bisexual, homosexual)	3% homosexual	5% homosexual

(continued)

Table 2 (continued)

Data collected	Source	Sample characteristics	Measure	Female	Both	Male
1999–2002	Williams, Connolly, Pepler, and Craig (2005)	Canada high schools, urban area, m = 16 years, n = 814 women, 784 men	Describe sexual orientation	4% questioning		3% questioning
				3% bisexual		2% bisexual
				0.1% lesbian		1% gay
2001–2002	Savin-Williams & Ream (2007)	US Add Health, mean 22 years, n = 15,170	Romantic attraction (male/female) Sexual relations (intercourse, oral, anal)	12% both		4% both
				1% same		1% same
				3% both		1% both
				1% same		1% same
			Sexual identity; 100%, mostly, equal hetero/gay (5-pt.scale)	11% most het		3% most het
				3% bisexual		1% bisexual
				1% most homo		1% most homo
2001–2002	Smith et al. (2003)	Australia national sample, n = 9134 women, 10,173 men, two groups: 16–19 and 20–29 years old	Sexually attracted (5-pt. scale, only opp. sex, more often opp. sex with at least one same sex, equal, etc.)	1% homo		1% homo
				4%, 3% het att, homo exp		1%, 1% het att, homo exp
				7%, 11% homo		2%, 3% homo
			Sexual experience (5-pt. scale, same as above)	att, het exp 10%, 10% homo		att, het exp 1%, 6% homo
			Sexual identity, think of self: hetero, homo, bisexual, queer, not sure, something other	att, homo exp 0.3%, 3% bi		att, homo exp 0.2%. 1% bi
				0%, 0.3% homo		1%, 2% homo
2002	Eskin et al. (2005)	Turkey university students, mean 21 years, n = 683 women, 579 men	Sexual desire same sex (yes/no); ever/ now	3% current		3% current
				7% ever		6% ever
			Intimate with sexual arousal (yes/no)	4% yes		5% yes
			Relationship with orgasm (yes/no)	1% yes		3% yes
			Consider self-sexually attracted (hetero, bisexual, homo)	2% bisexual		1% bisexual
				0.1% homo		1% homo
			Overall: one of above		10% yes	

2002	Mosher et al. (2005)	US national survey, n = 12,571, three age grps: 18–19, 20–24, 25–29 years Old	Sexual attraction (5-pt. scale, only, mostly, equal, mostly, only females/males)	13%, 13%, 14% most males 5%, 2%, 2% equal 0%, 0%, 1% most females 0%, 1%, 1% females	3%, 5%, 4%, most females 2%, 1%, 1% equal 0%, 1%, 1% most males 0%, 1%, 1% males
			Sexual behavior (females: any kind; males: oral/anal)	11%, 14%, 14%	5%, 5%, 6%
			Sex identity (think of self, bi, homo, something else)	7%, 4%, 3% bi 1%, 1%, 2% homo 6%, 4%, 3% SE	1%, 2%, 1% bi 2%, 2%, 3% homo 4%, 4%, 6% SE

Table 3 Proportion of men and women in three countries with exclusive and some same-sex behavior, same-sex attraction, and either same-sex behavior or attraction

Measure	Men			Women		
	US	United Kingdom	France	US	United Kingdom	France
Exclusive same-sex behavior	<1%	1%	<1%	<1%	<1%	<1%
Some same-sex behavior	6%	5%	11%	4%	2%	3%
Same-sex attraction	9%	8%	9%	11%	9%	12%
Same-sex behavior or attraction	21%	16%	19%	18%	19%	18%

romantic desires nearly always elicits the greatest prevalence rate of same-sex sexuality across multiple cultures. It can double or triple the number of individuals who report same-sex behavior or a gay/bisexual identity. For example, among US youth a prevalence rate of 9% was calculated if counting same-sex romantic attraction, but 3% if counting same-sex behavior and 4% if counting a bisexual or gay identity (Savin-Williams & Ream, 2007). In one high school, 11% of students self-ascribed one or more attributes of a same-sex sexuality; however, congruent with the overall trend, fewer than 3% identified as gay (Orenstein, 2001).

These findings also hold among adults, with two exceptions. First, there is a greater prevalence among adults than adolescents of same-sex behavior, perhaps because of the greater length of time in which they have to experience such an event (Sell et al., 1995). In a national, representative survey of US adults, 8% percent reported attraction for others of their sex, 7% had same-sex behavior since puberty, and 2% identified as gay/bisexual (Laumann et al., 1994). Of Dutch men, nearly the same proportion reported feeling physical attraction toward men and having sex with a man; however, less than half as many, 6%, identified as gay/bisexual (Sandfort, 1997).

The second difference between adult and adolescent populations is the much greater tendency of young vs. adult women to report same-sex romantic or sexual attraction. For example, 21% of Norwegian adolescent girls were interested in, attracted to, or had fantasies about other girls (Wichstrøm & Hegna (2003); 23% of New Zealand young women was sexually attracted to other women (Dickson et al., 2003); 12% of US college women were mostly sexually attracted to other females (Lippa, 2000); and 13–14% of US young adult women reported having some sexual attraction to other females (Mosher, Chandra, & Jones, 2005). Adult women and adult and adolescent men seldom report such high prevalence rates of sexual and romantic interest or attraction to same-sex others.

One of the most revealing studies of same-sex sexuality distinguished sexual orientation components in a national sample of adult Australian twins (Dunne et al., 2000). Eight groups were identified based on yes/no answers to questions about attraction, sexual behavior, and sexual identity. As might be expected, the vast majority (80%) of adults was opposite-sex oriented on all three components and 95% of the total population identified as heterosexual – but this still left a significant percentage of twins who had either same-sex attraction (16%) or same-sex behavior (men: 16%; women: 8%). Only 6% of men and 3% of women were same-sex oriented on all three components. Nearly two-thirds of individuals who reported same-sex behavior identified not as gay or bisexual but as heterosexual; many men (46%) and most women (70%) with same-sex attraction identified as heterosexual. Men were more likely than women to have same-sex behavior in the absence of same-sex attraction or identity; women, to have same-sex attraction but without same-sex behavior or identity. The disjuncture between attraction and behavior is more prevalent among women than men (Smith et al., 2003; Wellings et al., 1994). These studies suggest that it is the identification of oneself as gay/bisexual rather than its practice or the feeling of it per se that is avoided.

Prevalence rates are also affected by the cohort assessed, with modern increases in reports of same-sex sexuality (Savin-Williams, 2005). For example, Berg-Kelly (2003) noted that the number of Swedish adolescents who responded positively to the question, "Have you had thoughts about being homosexual?" went from 2% in 1994 to more than double in 1998 for girls and somewhat less so for boys. In addition, 14% of the 1998 17-year-old Swedes reported same-sex experiences, a substantial increase from previous studies. The number of Thai male adolescents self-identifying as homosexual/bisexual or reporting same-sex attraction was threefold greater than in a study conducted a decade earlier; the proportion reporting same-sex behavior, however, was comparable to previous cohorts (van Griensven et al., 2004).

Depends on Degree of Measure

Decisions about "how much" of a same-sex component is necessary to count as gay can affect prevalence rates. Kinsey et al. (1948) argued against a dichotomous construction of sexual orientation, demonstrating that sexuality existed along a continuum. Several large data sets encourage a sexual dimensionality approach (Dunne et al., 2000; Johnson, Wadsworth, Wellings, Field, & Bradshaw, 1994; Laumann et al., 1994; Savin-Williams & Ream, 2007; Sell et al., 1995). Dunne et al. (2000, p. 556) concluded from their data that there was "little evidence for true bipolarity in sexual orientation." Although most sexologists articulate a Kinsey-like dimensionality perspective, at least in regard to sexual and romantic attraction, and easily acknowledge a sexual continuum as evidently true, implicit in the resolutions they implement in assembling research participants into sexual orientation groups is the assumption of the alternative categorical perspective. In large part this is due to constraints of data analysis – the low frequencies of same-sex sexuality impose a need, they believe, for a categorical approach. However, unresolved issues remain regarding how even that pie should be sliced to create categorical sexual orientation groupings. The relevant research questions raised by Sell et al. (1995, p. 245) are, "How frequent should sexual behavior with one or the other sex be, and/or how strong or frequent should sexual attraction to one or the other sex be in order to classify a respondent as homosexual, bisexual, or heterosexual?" They might also have added that which sexual identity terms qualify as homosexual or bisexual is also an important question – do bi-curious, unlabeled, and questioning labels count as nonheterosexual? In most studies they do not.

Although individuals with a significant amount of homosexuality (however defined) are usually treated as belonging to the class identified as gay, the critical consideration is, does having "any" same-sex sexuality the sine qua non to qualify one as belonging to the gay club? Does being attracted to one same-sex peer, falling in love once with a same-sex other, or engaging in one same-sex encounter sufficient to tip the scales from a heterosexual to a homosexual sexual orientation? Research about sexuality usually omits individuals who have "a little bit" of same-sex attraction, behavior, or identity; they are neither heterosexual nor homosexual, just deleted. Subjects who are "bisexual leaning toward the heterosexual side" are nearly always excluded from the sample (e.g., D'Augelli et al., 2001), while a "bisexual leaning toward the homosexual side" is nearly always considered gay. Hence, Cochran and associates (Cochran & Mays, 2000; Cochran, Sullivan, & Mays, 2003) combined bisexuals and homosexuals, whether defined by their sexual behavior or their self-description. Two groups were created: an "any same-gender partner reported" and the remainder (heterosexual) (Cochran & Mays, 2000, p. 519).

One consequence is that a unique bisexual orientation grouping is often omitted in investigations. This has been justified for statistical power reasons or because initial analyses revealed no differences between bisexual and homosexual populations on variables of interest (e.g., Sandfort et al., 2003) – how they might differ on other variables is left to the imagination. The fact that relatively little is known about bisexuals (the work of Rodríguez Rust, 2000, 2002, is a notable exception) is thus not surprising. One is gay or not gay, perhaps bisexual, but, if so, then grouped with gays to form an LGB group. Even more recently and intriguing is the possibility of a new nonheterosexual group, the "mostly straight" (Thompson & Morgan, 2008; see also, Busseri, Willoughby, Chalmers, & Bogaert, 2008; Savin-Williams, 2006). These individuals frequently reject a sexual identity label because they do not view themselves as totally heterosexual; they have real but not overwhelming same-sex attraction

The repercussions of these decisions are readily apparent when considering prevalence rates for homosexuality. In several investigations, the proportion of nonheterosexual participants dropped steeply as the inclusion criteria became more singularly same-sex focused. The 16% of Norwegian youth who reported some attraction to the same sex was reduced to 5% if only those with bisexual and same-sex attraction were included and to 1% if only those with exclusive same-sex attraction was the criterion. Similarly, in terms of identity, the proportion dropped from 11% to 3% to 0.5% if the criteria were "not exclusively heterosexual," "bisexual or homosexual identity," and "exclusive homosexual identity," respectively (Wichstrøm & Hegna, 2003). Two percent of New Zealander adults were classified as "persistent major same-sex attraction" because of their equal or only attraction to the same sex (Skegg et al., 2003). A second group, individuals with "minor same-sex attraction" (primarily attracted to the opposite sex but with some same-sex attraction), was considerably larger: 11% among men and 26% among women.

Another study with New Zealander adults (Fergusson et al., 2005, p. 978) similarly concluded that the construction of same-sex groups depended on "the stringency of the criteria applied" (a spectrum model of sexual orientation). Especially noteworthy was the finding that women were far more likely than men to be included in the nonheterosexual groups: 14% vs. 5% in the predominantly heterosexual group and 4% vs. 2% in the predominantly homosexual group. Nearly 20% of women had some same-sex inclination or experience compared to 6% of men. Among Australian adults, when sexual attraction and behavior were placed on a 5-point continuum, significant relationships between the two and sexual identity were reported for both sexes (Smith et al., 2003). Considering the 3–5 points on the continuum for attraction and behavior, both sexes averaged 1% for each point. It was at the number 2 location ("mostly heterosexual") at which women were twice as prevalent as men: 11% vs. 5% (attraction) and 8% vs. 4% (behavior). This sex difference – women more likely than men to report minor degrees of same-sex sexuality – is a common finding (see Table 2). US young women had a greater likelihood than men of selecting the midpoints of identity ("mostly heterosexual" or "bisexual") (Savin-Williams & Ream, 2007) – a finding replicated among Thai adolescents for both sexual attraction and identity (van Griensven et al., 2004). When Lippa (2000) asked college students about their sexual identity, 5% of men and 3% of women described themselves as gay/bisexual. When asked if they were "sexually attracted to men/women" on a 7-point scale from strongly agree to strongly disagree, twice as many men (10%) and four times as many women (12%) were classified as "mostly attracted" to the same sex. If classified as showing "any attraction" to same-sex others (from disagree to strongly agree), the proportions increase to 19% of college men and 24% of college women.

Lippa's (2000) results emphasize that at what point along an opposite- to same-sex attraction continuum an individual is counted as "no longer heterosexual" is a critical one. What is someone if she is "neutral" or does not "disagree strongly" regarding being sexually attracted to same-sex others? As with current attitudes toward race, is a "little bit" of same-sex attraction or arousal sufficient to make one gay? Indeed, most individuals with same-sex attraction report equal or predominant attraction to the other sex (McConaghy, 1999). Is intensity of attraction or arousal important? On the penile plethysmography, what percentage of change in the circumference of the penis is necessary to make one gay? Or, what are individuals who "frequently or sometimes wonder whether I am homosexual," as did 13% of high school students in one study (Lock & Steiner, 1999)? Should these youth, a significant proportion of the whole, be considered heterosexual or nonheterosexual?

In terms of sexual behavior, what is the appropriate ratio of opposite- to same-sex partners necessary to tip the balance to "gay" or as no longer heterosexual?

Omitting the issue of what constitutes sex (see review in Savin-Williams & Diamond, 2004), the vast majority of same-sex oriented individuals have had sex with opposite-sex members. How should they be classified – perhaps as bisexual because they have had sex with both sexes? Can one have sex exclusively with opposite-sex partners and still be gay? Can one be a gay virgin? That is, if one forsakes sexual behavior does one thus forsake a sexual orientation (Sell et al., 1995). Because investigators often use some version of the sexual behavior question stem "during the past 12 months" or "since the age of puberty," what if an individual has a "dry spell?" Is this person no longer gay? Why is it only sex after puberty or age 16 or 18 that counts, and what are the assumptions made about pre-pubertal sexual activities (i.e., they do not indicate sexual orientation)? Perhaps of greater importance than the number or ratio of sexual partners is how much one enjoyed the sexual encounters. Yet, this pleasure or delight in sex is seldom assessed by behavioral scientists. It is the count and not the experience that is registered. If two women have sex with each other and for one the sex is just "okay" and for the other it was absolutely erotic, are both equally "gay" (both, after all, had same-sex behavior)? Finally, if 7% of Americans report that they would like to have sex with someone of their biologic sex (Euro RSCG, cited in Fetto, 2002), should they be counted as gay?

Regarding another component of sexual orientation, I have previously discussed the problem that many same-sex oriented individuals have with designating their sexuality with a label (Savin-Williams, 2005). This has become increasingly acute during the past few years because current cohorts of same-sex oriented teenagers are resisting identifying themselves with sexual terms, for personal, political, and philosophical reasons. Some identify as gay and have no same-sex attraction or behavior, while others have only same-sex attraction and behavior and do not identify as gay because the concept does not fit their experience.

Questions posed in this section are largely uninvestigated yet highly significant. McConaghy (1999, p. 300) argued that most research is not about "homosexuality but identification as homosexual... The majority of men and women with homosexual feelings are aware of predominant heterosexual feelings and those with homosexual experience have predominant heterosexual experience." The percentage of a country's population with less than 100% heterosexuality is certainty large, often exceeding by several-fold those who identify as homosexual or bisexual.

Conclusions

Perhaps most helpful in calculating the prevalence rate of homosexuality are investigations that assess the dimensionality of sexuality and that resist translating the reported dimensionality into groupings – to maintain its true state. In data that I am currently collecting among college students, when given the opportunity to rate themselves on both heterosexuality and homosexuality scales, a number of both sexes report that they are neither exclusively one nor the other, but some of both – as they are with femininity and masculinity. Individuals consider themselves low or high on both; others as high on one and low on the other; and, of course, some rate themselves as high on one and nonexistent on the other. Deciding whether and, if so, how to distribute these individuals might well determine the outcome of many investigations.

Indeed, Sell (1997) critiqued the tendency to treat sexual orientation as a single dichotomous dimension (heterosexual or homosexual) rather than as a multidimensional, continuous construct. Subjects are typically given one question with an unclear reference as to which component of sexual orientation is being measured. Even investigators who use multiple measures of sexual orientation seldom report how they are related to each other, presenting instead a composite measure that sums responses to various measures. The Self Scale includes not only which sex one is attracted to and has sex with but also how often the attraction/behavior occurs and the degree of attraction/behavior. Sexual identity is assessed using not culturally loaded singular terms such as gay or straight but a continuum for *both* homosexuality and heterosexuality. Of particular significance is the unique possibility that asexuality (without a sexual orientation) can be ascertained. However, this ideal solution, multiple measures with permutations of sexual orientation dimensions, is seldom incorporated by behavioral scientists in their assessment of sexual orientation.

The other extreme, an inclusive definition that rules out youth without all three components, would admit few individuals as qualified to be same-sex oriented. Four studies provide the available data – the proportion of individuals who report one, two, or three components of a same-sex sexuality (Dunne et al., 2000; Laumann et al., 1994; Savin-Williams & Ream, 2007; Smith et al., 2003). Of the seven combination possibilities, three rarely occurred (about 1% of the same-sex population):

- Same-sex behavior and gay/bisexual identity without same-sex attraction
- Gay/bisexual identity without same-sex attraction or same-sex behavior
- Gay/bisexual identity and same-sex attraction without same-sex behavior (more prevalent among adolescent than adult populations)

The most common groupings were the following:

1. Same-sex attraction alone without same-sex behavior or gay/bisexual identity (women: over half; men: one-third)
2. All three components (women: one-eighth; men: about one-quarter)
3. Same-sex attraction and same-sex behavior without gay/bisexual identity (women: one-fifth; men: one-eighth)
4. Same-sex behavior without same-sex attraction or gay/bisexual identity (women: one-tenth; men: one-fifth)

The other extreme, defining a same-sex population based solely on assessing one component of sexual orientation at one point in time, is clearly problematic and results in widely disparate estimates of "gayness" across time, cultures, and genders. It could be as low as 1% if counting exclusive same-sex behavior or as high as 24% if counting young adult women with any sexual attraction to other females.

These patterns present a dilemma for researchers who portray same-sex sexuality as a stable trait of individuals or assume consistency among sexual orientation components. Consistency is weakest between sexual attraction and sexual identification or behavior (many with same-sex attraction do not identify as gay or engage in same-sex behavior) and between sexual behavior and attraction or identity (many with same-sex behavior do not report same-sex attraction or identity) and strongest between sexual identity and attraction or behavior (most of those with a gay identity have same-sex attraction and engage in same-sex behavior) (Savin-Williams, 2005).

It must also be recognized that measures of sexual orientation can elicit characteristics of individuals that are merely temporary. Same-sex behavior may result from a spur of the moment event or thought, a gay label may be refused as a reaction against being reduced to a category, and words to describe sexual orientation might be vague or off-putting. A woman might not say "I'm gay" if she is only in love with a particular woman or "Yes, I've had same-sex intercourse" if she does not know what that implies. Gayness may also be fluid or plastic for some individuals – lesbian in college, bisexual until marriage, straight in career. Thus, depending on the way in which individuals are asked about their sexuality, a different conclusion can be drawn about their representation in the population, perhaps by a factor of three or four.

Researchers would be best assured of a primarily same-sex oriented young adult sample if they included youth with same-sex attraction and behavior over multiple times who also seldom or weakly report opposite-sex attraction and behavior – that is, individuals who consistently and reliably report multiple aspects of a same-sex orientation. There is a problem, however, with this approach: few data sets offer these amenities. One exception is the Add Health data set that provides information about romantic attraction and sexual behavior over two waves; unfortunately, only once the youth graduated from high school was sexual identity assessed. Another approach is to forsake the general notion of sexual orientation altogether and assess only those components relevant for the research question. For example, to assess HIV transmission, measure sexual behavior; to assess interpersonal attachments, measure sexual/ romantic attraction; and to assess political ideology, measure sexual identity.

The largest task, however, may be convincing researchers to believe their own data and to move away from positing either same-sex behavior or identity as the only meaningful measures of sexual orientation. For example, a recent study used the now typical self-description of orientation as the standard (Ellis et al., 2005). Although considerable inconsistencies were apparent in the data – heterosexually identified students claiming same-sex attraction, fantasy, or behavior – the data were not framed as indicating a continuum of sexuality. Instead, the discrepancy among the 200 males and 400 females who identified as heterosexual yet nevertheless reported that over 90% of their sexual fantasies were same-sex oriented was explained as an indication that inconsistencies in reports of sexuality are not uncommon, that the fantasy reports were referencing as "ever having" rather than as "predominant," and that the length of the questionnaire generated errors. Another option, not taken, would be to believe the reports: heterosexually identified individuals with same-sex fantasies exist.

The instability and inconsistency of sexual orientation components do not imply that adolescents should not be asked about their sexual orientation – merely that as researchers we need to ask better questions and to ask them more frequently. We need to better explain our terms, listen to youth about how they define terms, allow sexuality to be dimensional and not categorical, and assess multiple and not singular components. Depending on the way in which adolescents are asked about their sexuality, different conclusions can be drawn about their sexuality – and hence the prevalence rate of nonheterosexual adolescents and young adults in the general population.

References

Asayama, S. (1976). Sexual behavior in Japanese students: Comparisons for 1974, 1960, and 1952. *Archives of Sexual Behavior, 5*, 371–390.

Bagley, C., & Tremblay, P. (1998). On the prevalence of homosexuality and bisexuality, in a random community survey of 750 men aged 18 to 27. *Journal of Homosexuality, 36*, 1–18.

Bailey, J. M., & Zucker, K. J. (1995). Childhood sex-typed behavior and sexual orientation: A conceptual analysis and quantitative review. *Developmental Psychology, 31*, 43–55.

Baumeister, R. F. (2000). Gender differences in erotic plasticity: The female sex drive as socially flexible and responsive. *Psychological Bulletin, 126*, 247–374.

Berg-Kelly, K. (2003). Adolescent homosexuality: We need to learn more about causes and consequences. *Acta Pædiatric, 92*, 141–144.

Billy, J. O. G., Tanfer, K., Grady, W. R., & Klepinger, D. H. (1993). The sexual behavior of men in the United States. *Family Planning Perspectives, 25*, 52–60.

Black, D., Gates, G., Sanders, S., & Taylor, L. (2000). Demographics of the gay and lesbian population in the United States: Evidence from available systematic data sources. *Demography, 37*, 139–154.

Breakwell, G. M., & Fife-Schaw, C. (1992). Sexual activities and preferences in a United Kingdom sample of 16 to 20-year-olds. *Archives of Sexual Behavior, 21*, 271–293.

Busseri, M. A., Willoughby, T., Chalmers, H., & Bogaert, A. R. (2008). On the association between sexual attraction and adolescent risk behavior involvement: Examining mediation and moderation. *Developmental Psychology, 44*, 69–80.

Caldwell, L. L., Kivel, B. D., Smith, E. A., & Hayes, D. (1998). The leisure context of adolescents who are lesbian, gay male, bisexual and questioning their sexual identities: An exploratory story. *Journal of Leisure Research, 30*, 341–355.

Carver, P. R., Egan, S. K., & Perry, D. G. (2004). Children who question their heterosexuality. *Developmental Psychology, 40*, 43–53.

Chivers, M. L., Rieger, G., Latty, E., & Bailey, J. M. (2004). A sex difference in the specificity of sexual arousal. *Psychological Science, 15*, 736–744.

Cochran, S. D., & Mays, V. M. (2000). Relation between psychiatric syndromes and behaviorally defined sexual orientation in a sample of the US population. *American Journal of Epidemiology, 151*, 516–523.

Cochran, S. D., Sullivan, J. G., & Mays, V. M. (2003). Prevalence of mental disorders, psychological distress, and mental health services use among lesbian, gay, and bisexual adults in the United States. *Journal of Consulting and Clinical Psychology, 71*, 53–61.

Cohen, K. M. (2004). Etiology of homoeroticism. *Current Problems in Pediatric and Adolescent Health Care*, 34, 355–359.

D'Augelli, A. R. (1991). Gay men in college: Identity processes and adaptations. *Journal of College Student Development, 32*, 140–146.

D'Augelli, A. R., & Hershberger, S. L. (1993). Lesbian, gay, and bisexual youth in community settings: Personal challenges and mental health problems. *American Journal of Community Psychology, 21,* 421–448.

D'Augelli, A. R., Hershberger, S. L., & Pilkington, N. W. (2001). Suicidality patterns and sexual orientation-related factors among lesbian, gay, and bisexual youths. *Suicide and Life-Threatening Behavior, 31,* 250–264.

Diamond, L. M. (2003a). New paradigms for research on heterosexual and sexual-minority development. *Journal of Clinical Child and Adolescent Psychology, 32,* 490–498.

Diamond, L. M. (2003b). Was it a phase? Young women's relinquishment of lesbian/bisexual identities over a 5-year period. *Journal of Personality and Social Psychology, 84,* 352–364.

Diamond, L. M. (2008). *Sexual fluidity: Understanding women's love and desire.* Cambridge, MA: Harvard University Press.

Diamond, M. (1993). Homosexuality and bisexuality in different populations. *Archives of Sexual Behavior, 22,* 291–310.

Dickson, N., Paul, C., & Herbison, P. (2003). Same-sex attraction in a birth cohort: Prevalence and persistence in early adulthood. *Social Science and Medicine, 56,* 1607–1615.

Dunne, M. P., Bailey, J. M., Kirk, K. M., & Martin, N. G. (2000). The subtlety of sex-atypicality. *Archives of Sexual Behavior, 29,* 549–565.

DuRant, R. H., Krowchuk, D. P., & Sinal, S. H. (1998). Victimization, use of violence, and drug use at school among male adolescents who engage in same-sex sexual behavior. *Journal of Pediatrics, 132,* 113–118.

Ellis, L., Robb, B., & Burke, D. (2005). Sexual orientation in United States and Canadian college students. *Archives of Sexual Behavior, 34,* 569–581.

Eskin, M., Kaynak-Demir, H., & Demir, S. (2005). Same-sex sexual orientation, childhood sexual abuse, and suicidal behavior in university students in Turkey. *Archives of Sexual Behavior, 34,* 185–195.

Faulkner, A. H., & Cranston, K. (1998). Correlates of same-sex sexual behavior in a random sample of Massachusetts high school students. *American Journal of Public Health, 88,* 262–266.

Fay, R. E., Turner, C. F., Klassen, A. D., & Gagnon, J. H. (1989). Prevalence and patterns of same-gender sexual contact among men. *Science, 243,* 338–348.

Fergusson, D. M., Horwood, L. J., Ridder, E. M., & Beautrais, A. L. (2005). Sexual orientation and mental health in a birth cohort of young adults. *Psychological Medicine, 35,* 971–981.

Fetto, J. (2002, May). Gay friendly? *American Demographics, 24,* 6.

Friedman, M. S., Silvestre, A. J., Gold, M. A., Markovic, N., Savin-Williams, R. C., Huggins, J., et al. (2004). Adolescents define sexual orientation and suggest ways to measure it. *Journal of Adolescence, 27,* 303–317.

Garofalo, R., Wolf, R. C., Kessel, S., Palfrey, J., & DuRant, R. H. (1998). The association between health risk behaviors and sexual orientation among a school-based sample of adolescents. *Pediatrics, 101,* 895–902.

Garofalo, R., Wolf, R. C., Wissow, L. S., Woods, E. R., & Goodman, E. (1999). Sexual orientation and risk of suicide attempts among a representative sample of youth. *Archives of Pediatric Adolescent Medicine, 153,* 487–493.

Goode, E., & Haber, L. (1977). Sexual correlates of homosexual experience: An exploratory study of college women. *Journal of Sex Research, 13,* 12–21.

*Hegna, K., & Larsen, C. J. (2005). Straightening out the queer? Norwegian young people's homosexual experiences and same-sex attractions in a population-based study. Paper in preparation.

Hewitt, C. (1998). Homosexual demography: Implications for the spread of AIDS. *Journal of Sex Research, 35,* 390–396.

*Hillier, L., Dempsey, D., Harrison, L., Beale, L., Matthews, L., & Rosenthal, D. (1998). *Writing themselves in: A national report on the sexuality, health and well-being of same-sex attracted young people* (Monograph series 7, Australian Research Centre in Sex, Health and Society, National Centre in HIV Social Research, La Trobe University) Carlton, Australia.

Humphreys, L. (1970). *Tearoom trade*. Chicago, IL: Aldine.

Johnson, A. M., Wadsworth, J., Wellings, K., Field, J., & Bradshaw, S. (1994). *Sexual attitudes and lifestyles*. Oxford: Blackwell Scientific.

Kinnish, K. K., Strassberg, D. S., & Turner, C. W. (2005). Sex differences in the flexibility of sexual orientation: A multidimensional retrospective assessment. *Archives of Sexual Behavior, 34*, 173–183.

Kinsey, A. C., Pomeroy, W. B., & Martin, C. E. (1948). *Sexual behavior in the human male*. Philadelphia: W. B. Saunders.

Kinsey, A. C., Pomeroy, W. B., Martin, C. E., & Gebhard, P. H. (1953). *Sexual behavior in the human female*. Philadelphia: W. B. Saunders.

Kryzan, C. (1997). OutProud/Oasis Internet Survey of Queer and Questioning Youth. Sponsored by OutProud, The National Coalition for Gay, Lesbian, Bisexual and Transgender Youth and Oasis Magazine. Contact survey@outproud.org.

Laumann, E. O., Gagnon, J., Michael, R. T., & Michaels, S. (1994). *The social organization of sexuality: Sexual practices in the United States*. Chicago: University of Chicago Press.

LeVay, S., & Valente, S. M. (2006). *Human sexuality* (2nd ed.). Sunderland, MA: Sinauer Associates.

Lippa, R. A. (2000). Gender-related traits in gay men, lesbian women, and heterosexual men and women: The virtual identity of homosexual-heterosexual diagnosticity and gender diagnosticity. *Journal of Personality, 68*, 899–926.

Lock, J., & Steiner, H. (1999). Relationships between sexual orientation and coping styles of gay, lesbian, and bisexual adolescents from a community high school. *Journal of the Gay and Lesbian Medical Association, 3*, 77–82.

McConaghy, N. (1999). Unresolved issues in scientific sexology. *Archives of Sexual Behavior, 28*, 285–318.

Mosher, W. D., Chandra, A., & Jones, J. (2005). Sexual behavior and selected health measures: Men and women 15–44 years of age, United States, 2002. *Advance Data from Vital and Health Statistics* (number 362). Hyattsville, MD: National Center for Health Statistics.

Mustanski, B. S., Chivers, M. L., & Bailey, J. M. (2002). A critical review of recent biological research on human sexual orientation. *Annual Review of Sex Research, 13*, 69–140.

Narring, F., Stronski Huwiler, S. M., & Michaud, P. (2003). Prevalence and dimensions of sexual orientation in Swiss adolescents: A cross-sectional survey of 16 to 20-year-old students. *Acta Pædiatric, 92*, 233–239.

Orenstein, A. (2001). Substance use among gay and lesbian adolescents. *Journal of Homosexuality, 41*, 1–15.

Papadopoulos, N. G., Stamboulides, P., & Triantafillou, T. (2000). The psychosexual development and behavior of university students: A nationwide survey in Greece. *Journal of Psychology and Human Sexuality, 11*, 93–110.

Paul, C., Fitzjohn, J., Eberhart-Phillips, J., Herbison, P., & Dickson, N. (2000). Sexual abstinence at age 21 in New Zealand: the importance of religion. *Social Science and Medicine, 51*, 1–10.

Remafedi, G., Resnick, M., Blum, R., & Harris, L. (1992). Demography of sexual orientation in adolescents. *Pediatrics, 89*, 714–721.

Rieger, G., Chivers, M. L., & Bailey, J. M. (2005). Sexual arousal patterns of bisexual men. *Psychological Science, 16*, 579–584.

Rodríguez Rust, P. C. R. (2000). *Bisexuality in the United States: A social science reader*. New York: Columbia University Press.

Rodríguez Rust, P. C. R. (2002). Bisexuality: The state of the union. *Annual Review of Sex Research, 13*, 180–240.

Rogers, S. M., & Turner, C. F. (1991). Male-male sexual contact in the U.S.A.: Findings from five sample surveys, 1970–1990. *Journal of Sex Research, 28*, 491–519.

Rosario, M., Meyer-Bahlburg, H. F. L., Hunter, J., Exner, T. M., Gwadz, M., & Keller, A. M. (1996). The psychosexual development of urban lesbian, gay, and bisexual youths. *Journal of Sex Research, 33*, 113–126.

Russell, S. T., & Joyner, K. (2001). Adolescent sexual orientation and suicide risk: Evidence from a national study. *American Journal of Public Health, 91*, 1276–1281.

Sandfort, T. G. M. (1997). Sampling male homosexuality. In J. Bancroft (Ed.), *Researching sexual behavior: Methodological issues* (pp. 261–275). Bloomington, IN: Indiana University Press.

Sandfort, T. G. M., de Graaf, R., & Bijl, R. V. (2003). Same-sex sexuality and quality of life: Findings from the Netherlands Mental Health Survey and Incidence Study. *Archives of Sexual Behavior, 32,* 15–22.

Sandfort, T. G. M., de Graaf, R., Bijl, R. V., & Schnabel, P. (2001). Same-sex sexual behavior and psychiatric disorders. *Archives of General Psychiatry, 58,* 85–91.

Savin-Williams, R. C. (1990). *Gay and lesbian youth: Expressions of identity.* Washington, DC: Hemisphere.

Savin-Williams, R. C. (1998). *"... and then I became gay." Young men's stories.* New York: Routledge.

Savin-Williams, R. C. (2001). A critique of research on sexual-minority youth. *Journal of Adolescence, 24,* 15–23.

Savin-Williams, R. C. (2005). *The new gay teenager.* Cambridge, MA: Harvard University Press.

Savin-Williams, R. C. (2006). Who's gay? Does it matter? *Current Directions in Psychological Science, 15,* 40–44.

Savin-Williams, R. C., & Cohen, K. M. (2004). Homoerotic development during childhood and adolescence. *Child and Adolescent Psychiatric Clinics of North America: Sex and Gender.* M. Diamond & A. Yates (Eds.), *Volume 13,* 529–549.

Savin-Williams, R. C., & Diamond, L. M. (2004). Sex. In R. M. Lerner & L. Steinberg (Eds.), *Handbook of adolescent psychology* (2nd ed.) (pp. 189–231). New York: Wiley.

*Savin-Williams, R. C., & Ream, G. L. (2006). *Consistency of Sexual Orientation during Adolescence and Young Adulthood.* Paper in preparation, Cornell University, Ithaca, NY.

Savin-Williams, R. C., & Ream, G. L. (2007). Prevalence and stability of sexual orientation components during adolescence and young adulthood. *Archives of Sexual Behavior, 36,* 385–394.

Sell, R. L. (1997). Defining and measuring sexual orientation: A review. *Archives of Sexual Behavior, 26,* 643–658.

Sell, R. L., Wells, J. A., & Wypij, D. (1995). The prevalence of homosexual behavior and attraction in the United States, the United Kingdom and France: Results of national population-based samples. *Archives of Sexual Behavior, 24,* 235–248.

Skegg, K., Nada-Raja, S., Dickson, N., Paul, C., & Williams, S. (2003). Sexual orientation and self-harm in men and women. *American Journal of Psychiatry, 160,* 541–546.

Smith, A. M. A., Rissel, C. E., Richters, J., Grulich, A. E., & de Visser, R. O. (2003). Sexual identity, sexual attraction and sexual experience among a representative sample of adults. *Australian and New Zealand Journal of Public Health, 27,* 138–145.

Thompson, E., & Morgan, E. M. (2008). "Mostly straight" young women: Variations in sexual behavior and identity development. *Developmental Psychology, 44,* 15–21.

Udry, J. R., & Bearman, P. S. (1998a). *The national longitudinal study of adolescent health.* Retrieved April 30, 2003, from http://www.cpc.unc.edu/projects/addhealth/

Udry, J. R., & Bearman, P. S. (1998b). New methods for new research on adolescent sexual behavior. In R. Jessor (Ed.), *New perspectives on adolescent risk behavior* (pp. 241–269). New York, NY: Cambridge University Press.

Udry, J. R., & Chantala, K. (2005). Risk factors differ according to same-sex and opposite-sex interest. *Journal of Biosocial Science, 37,* 481–497.

Van Griensven, F., Kilmarx, P. H., Jeeyapant, S., Manopaiboon, C., Korattana, S., Jenkins, R. A., et al. (2004). The prevalence of bisexual and homosexual orientation and related health risks among adolescents in Northern Thailand. *Archives of Sexual Behavior, 33,* 137–147.

Warner, J., McKeown, E., Griffin, M., Johnson, K., Ramsay, A., Cort, C., et al. (2004). Rates and predictors of mental illness in gay men, lesbians and bisexual men and women: Results from a survey based in England and Wales. *British Journal of Psychiatry: The Journal of Mental Science, 185,* 479–485.

Wellings, K., Field, J., Johnson, A. M., & Wadsworth, J. (1994). *Sexual behaviour in Britain: The national survey of sexual attitudes and lifestyles.* London: Penguin.

Wichstrøm, L., & Hegna, K. (2003). Sexual orientation and suicide attempt: A longitudinal study of the general Norwegian adolescent population. *Journal of Abnormal Psychology, 112,* 144–151.

Williams, T., Connolly, J., Pepler, D., & Craig, W. (2005). Peer victimization, social support, and psychosocial adjustment of sexual minority adolescents. *Journal of Youth and Adolescence, 34,* 471–482.

What is Sexual Orientation and Do Women Have One?

J. Michael Bailey

Recent research has focused increased attention on sex differences in the expression of sexuality, including sexual orientation (e.g., Baumeister, 2000; Diamond, 2003). There is an emerging consensus that women's sexual partner choices are sometimes made for different reasons than men's. For example, women are thought to have greater erotic plasticity than men, meaning that their sexual behavior is more apt to be shaped by sociocultural factors (Baumeister). Furthermore, women's sexual desire may be more "fluid" than men's, less rigidly directed toward persons of a particular sex and more changeable over time, depending on relational factors such as romantic attachment (Diamond, 2008).

One strong candidate for a primary mechanism underlying these differences is a striking sex difference in sexual arousal patterns (Chivers, Rieger, Latty, & Bailey, 2004; Chivers, Seto, & Blanchard, 2007). Men, but not women, have a category specific sexual arousal pattern, one that is usually directed much more strongly to members of one sex than to those of the other. For example, almost all men who identify as homosexual are more sexually aroused by men than by women. In contrast, the arousal pattern of heterosexual women tends to be bisexual, and thus irrelevant to most women's partner choices. That is, women who identify themselves as heterosexual tend to be similarly aroused by male and female sexual stimuli. The category specific male sexual arousal pattern is the primary sexual motivation that directs male sexual activity to certain kinds of individuals (most often women, but sometimes men) rather than others. Indeed, I contend that a man's category specific sexual arousal pattern *is* his sexual orientation. Most women lack this strong directional motivation, and so it is not surprising that their sexual behavior is more malleable and sexually fluid.

In this chapter I begin by proposing some definitional distinctions in order to clarify what sexual orientation is *not*. I review research on the male sexual arousal pattern and argue for equating sexual arousal pattern with sexual orientation. Next I review recent findings on the sexual arousal patterns of women and address some methodological concerns. I conclude with a reconsideration of the idea of women's sexual orientation.

D.A. Hope (ed.), *Contemporary Perspectives on Lesbian, Gay, and Bisexual Identities,*
DOI: 10.1007/978-0-387-09556-1, © Springer Science + Business Media, LLC 2009

What is Male Sexual Orientation?

Sexual behavior pattern refers to one's history of sexual and romantic relationships with men vs. women. *Private sexual identity* refers to how one conceives of oneself, and *public sexual identity* refers to how one wishes to be considered by others. *Sexual preference* refers to the ultimate choice that one would make, on whatever grounds, regarding the sex of an erotic partner. (Note that here I do not consider "sexual preference" to be synonymous with sexual orientation.)

To clarify these classifications, it is useful to consider how they might differ within a single individual. For example, a man married to a woman but who engages in secret sexual relationships with other men might consider himself bisexual; this would be his private sexual identity. He might well want his wife to consider him heterosexual, and if so, this would be his public sexual identity, at least with respect to her. He may claim a different sexual identity with his male partners. (Public sexual identity can vary across contexts.) This hypothetical man's sexual preference might conceivably be heterosexual, bisexual, or homosexual. For example, he may strongly prefer female partners due to religious beliefs that homosexuality is morally wrong and hence have a heterosexual preference. He may strongly prefer male partners due to intense sexual attraction and thus have a homosexual preference. Or he may have difficulty deciding and have a bisexual preference.

The concepts I have introduced so far can be applied similarly to both men and women. They are all potentially malleable. Any of them might be complexly determined, that is, may reflect the influence of more than one factor. Indeed, sexual feelings need not be the primary determinant of any of them. Finally, although only one of them, public sexual identity, is defined in terms of some kind of self-report, all of them depend on self-report. Unless and until we have major advances in lie detection, that is all we have.

The term *sexual orientation* connotes a mechanism, analogous to a compass, that directs our sexuality. Furthermore, sexual orientation is generally considered to reflect sexual feelings rather than other factors, such as social constraints. Sexual orientation is commonly described in terms of sexual desire, arousal, fantasy, and attraction. Of these, only one, arousal, can be measured directly and independent of self-report. In the next section, I argue that for men, sexual orientation should be conceived of as a sexual arousal pattern.

The Measurement of the Male Sexual Arousal Pattern

Heterosexual men are much more sexually arousable by attractive women than by attractive men, and feelings of sexual arousal are often accompanied by penile erections, which can be measured. Homosexual men show an opposite pattern, with greater arousal to attractive men. These assertions seem obvious, and they have also been demonstrated repeatedly in the laboratory using psychophysiological studies (e.g., Chivers et al., 2004; Freund, 1963; Mavissakalian, Blanchard, Abel, & Barlow, 1975). In these studies, experimenters present different kinds of erotic stimuli to homosexual and heterosexual men and measure their genital response. The relative arousal to different types of stimuli is an objective, but imperfect, measure of a man's sexual arousal pattern.

In these studies stimuli typically consist of pictures, audiotaped narratives (sometimes presented with pictures), or video clips. Men typically find video clips to be the most arousing stimuli (Julien & Over, 1988). Furthermore, video clips of couples engaged in explicit sex acts are generally more arousing than videos of individuals (Chivers et al., 2007). An effective combination of stimuli to assess male sexual arousal patterns includes videos of attractive male couples, and of attractive female couples, engaged in explicit sexual activity (Chivers et al., 2004, 2007; Mavissakalian et al., 1975; Sakheim, Barlow, Beck, & Abrahamson, 1985). Homosexual men show much greater arousal to videos of the male couples, and heterosexual men to the female couples. Although at first it may seem that the most appropriate stimuli to assess heterosexuality would depict heterosexual couples, this is not so. A heterosexual couple consists of a man and a woman, and thus, both homosexual and heterosexual men can be aroused by watching such a couple, presumably by focusing on the actor of their preferred sex. Indeed, homosexual and heterosexual men tend to experience similar degrees of arousal to videos of heterosexual couples (e.g., Chivers et al., 2004).

Men's erections to each stimulus are measured using penile plethysmography (PPG). There are two general types of PPG. Volumetric PPG relies on changes in air pressure in a small glass cylinder that contains the penis (Freund, 1963). Circumferential PPG measures change in penile girth most commonly using a stretch-sensitive metal-in-rubber gauge; a weak electrical current runs through the metal and changes when penile erection changes its shape (Bancroft, Jones, & Pullan, 1966). Volumetric PPG is more sensitive at low levels of genital arousal (Kuban, Barbaree, & Blanchard, 1999). This is because in the early stages of erection, the penis tends both to lengthen and also to decrease in circumference, with volume increasing. Unfortunately, the volumetric device is expensive and invasive (it must be attached by an experimenter), and it is used in only a few laboratories worldwide. The circumferential PPG, in contrast, is common, and it is the technique used by my lab.

I have gotten this far without defining sexual arousal. Most researchers conceive of sexual arousal as having physiological, affective, and cognitive components, and these components can be dissociated (e.g., Janssen, Everaerd, Spiering, & Janssen, 2000; Wiegel, Scepkowski, & Barlow, 2007). Sexual arousal is an emotion and hence depends on more than penile erection. In men who are awake, penile erection is usually accompanied by sexual arousal; indeed, penile erection usually requires such arousal. (Healthy men who are asleep often experience spontaneous "nocturnal" erections, and it is doubtful that this represents sexual arousal as I mean it.) The converse is not always true, however. Men are capable of feeling sexual arousal without a measurable erection. This is particularly true of older men and of men with erectile dysfunction. The main point here is, again, that a sexual arousal pattern is not equivalent to relative erection to different kinds of sexual stimuli. Most men who do not become genitally aroused to any stimuli in a laboratory assessment report that they do feel such arousal to at least some of the stimuli. And presumably all such men have some kind of sexual orientation. As I conceive of it, male sexual arousal is an imperfectly measured latent variable, and erectile measures are good, albeit imperfect, objective indicators of it.

Not all men produce erections in the laboratory, and those who do not do so cannot be accurately classified with respect to arousal pattern. One cost of using circumferential PPG is that depending on one's selection criteria, a high percentage of men may have to be excluded due to insufficient responding. Such men are called nonresponders. It is common to require at least a 2.5-mm increase in circumference to at least one sexual stimulus, relative to response to neutral stimuli. Experimenters using this criterion in a recent study excluded only 4% (2/46) of their sample (Chivers et al., 2007). In a similar study using more stringent exclusion criteria, one-third (23/69) of men were excluded (Chivers et al., 2004). The best criteria for demarcating nonresponders depend on one's purpose, but it is clear that the more men respond, the more accurately they are measured. For example, in the aforementioned study with high exclusion rates (Chivers et al., 2004), three men's genital arousal patterns did not match their self-reported sexual orientation. Although these men met the cut-off criteria for responding, they barely did so; on average their response indices were substantially lower than those of the 43 other included men. With respect to their subjective, self-reported, sexual arousal, each of the three poorly measured men reported that he felt more sexually aroused by the stimuli consistent with his self-reported sexual orientations, and I believe their self-reports. As I have noted, sexual arousal patterns are not identical to genital arousal patterns produced in the laboratory. The latter are objective, often very good, measures of the former, but they contain measurement error.

PPG is not the only possible objective way to measure male sexual arousal patterns. As with all other emotions, sexual arousal is dependent upon the brain for its realization. Advances in neuroimaging techniques allow the possibility of assessing sexual arousal by observing brain activity. In principle, this would be a more direct measure compared with PPG, and it would also be more sensitive. The psychological experience of sexual arousal typically precedes, and can occur without, erection. Thus, fewer men may be nonresponders with brain imaging techniques compared with PPG.

Another scientific advantage of brain imaging as a tool for assessing sexual arousal patterns concerns its multidimensionality. Penile measures are unidimensional – the penis only gets larger or smaller (if it responds at all). In contrast, sexual arousal is undoubtedly complexly determined, the sum of excitatory inputs (e.g., strength of erotic stimulus) and inhibitory inputs (e.g., fatigue, conscious suppression of arousal). Because neurological data are multidimensional, they may be more useful for unraveling the complex determinants of sexual arousal. They are certainly more useful in exploring relevant brain systems. This multidimensionality is an advantage for long-term scientific progress, but it is a disadvantage in the short term. PPG measures are straightforward and uncontroversial as measures of sexual arousal.

We have not yet mapped out the relevant neural architecture, and so assessing sexual arousal patterns with fMRI is less straightforward and more controversial.

My lab has conducted an fMRI study of sexual arousal and male sexual orientation (Safron et al., 2007). We recruited 11 homosexual men and 11 heterosexual men, classified based on their self-reported identities. They viewed erotic and control stimuli in an fMRI scanner. Erotic stimuli consisted of pictures of either single nude men or women or of male or female couples engaged in explicit sexual interactions. Control stimuli consisted of pictures of men or women playing sports, again either singly or in pairs. There were four experimental blocks during which a man saw 100 randomly ordered stimuli. Each picture was presented for 3.5 s followed by a 1.5-s interstimulus interval. Participants also pressed buttons to indicate their subjective appraisal of each stimulus.

Analysis of fMRI data consists of determining differences in brain activation between different conditions or contrasts. We were especially interested in the contrasts of activation to preferred erotic stimuli (i.e., male sexual stimuli for homosexual men and female sexual stimuli for heterosexual men) vs. control (i.e., sports) stimuli as well as activation to nonpreferred erotic stimuli (i.e., male sexual stimuli for heterosexual men and female sexual stimuli for homosexual men) vs. control stimuli. We were also interested in whether these contrasts differed between homosexual and heterosexual men.

For the most part, homosexual and heterosexual men showed very similar patterns of activation (albeit to different erotic stimuli). One possible exception was the amygdala, in which homosexual men showed greater activational differences between preferred and nonpreferred erotic stimuli compared with heterosexual men. However, this difference was not hypothesized a priori, was not large, and was the only group difference found out of many tested. Thus, this finding needs replication.

When preferred erotic stimuli were compared with neutral stimuli, we saw widespread greater brain activation to the former; that is, much of the brain is activated to a greater degree by preferred erotic stimuli than by neutral sports stimuli (Fig. 1a). Areas showing this pattern include the primary and higher-order visual processing areas, regions associated with directed attention (e.g., the anterior and posterior cingulate), regions associated with motivation and reward (e.g., the basal ganglia, the medial orbital frontal cortex, and the ventrial striatum). Although fMRI is not the most powerful way to image these structures, the dorsal amygdala and hypothalamus also showed greater activation to preferred sexual stimuli.

The contrast of nonpreferred erotic stimuli vs. neutral stimuli looks much different (Fig. 1b). There is much less significant activational difference across brain regions, and what activational differences there are tend to favor the neutral (sports) stimuli. We had hypothesized that the insula might show greater activation to nonpreferred sexual stimuli than to control stimuli, because some research has suggested that the insula plays a role in processing disgust (e.g., Phillips et al., 1997). This hypothesis was not confirmed, however.

We selected brain regions of interest – areas that should be active during sexual arousal – based on available literature on imaging and sexual arousal, and were able to determine that 16 of the 22 participants showed significantly greater activation

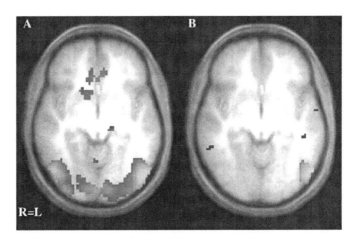

Fig. 1 Areas of differential activity to preferred vs. nonpreferred stimuli ((**a**): increased activity to preferred stimuli shown in *orange*) and nonpreferred vs. sports stimuli ((b): increased activity to sports stimuli shown in *blue*). Sports images contained actors of the participants' preferred sex. Axial slices are at Z = −3 (right = left, according to standard radiological convention)

in these areas to erotic stimuli of one sex than to erotic stimuli of the other sex. (The six participants who did not show significantly greater activation can be thought of as neural nonresponders in our study.) Of these 16 men, 15 had brain activity that matched their stated sexual orientation. The exception was a man who reported that he was heterosexual. This man, however, had an unusual pattern of ratings of the erotic stimuli. He was much more likely than other heterosexual men to admit that he liked male erotic stimuli, and he was much less likely to say that he disliked or strongly disliked it. Our results suggest that fMRI is a promising technique for measuring sexual arousal patterns, even at the level of individual men.

A Man's Sexual Arousal Pattern is his Sexual Orientation

Recall that I described *sexual orientation* as a mechanism that directs a person's sexual desire, fantasies, and attractions. To see that a man's sexual arousal pattern is the best contender for the meaning of *sexual orientation*, consider the following hypothetical, not unrealistic, person. A heterosexually married man insists that he is attracted only to women and tells people he is heterosexual. But in the laboratory he gets erections to male sexual stimuli, and he does not get erections to female sexual stimuli. What is his sexual orientation? No matter what he truly believes (i.e., no matter what his private sexual identity), no matter whom he prefers to have sex with (i.e., regardless of sexual preference), and no matter whom he chooses as his sex partners, I contend that his sexual orientation is homosexual. A man who experiences sexual arousal for men but not for women cannot plausibly be considered *sexually* oriented to women.

Sexual arousal patterns have the advantage of being objectively measurable, but it is not objective measurement that privileges sexual arousal pattern as the meaning of sexual orientation. Rather, it is because a man's sexual arousal pattern is the sexual input that orients his sexual preference. For example, the much stronger sexual arousal that a homosexual man feels for attractive men than for attractive women is strong motivation for him to pursue men as sex partners, despite the disincentive of occasional societal approbation. It induces approach motivation, inspires sexual fantasies, and facilitates sexual interactions. If a man with a homosexual arousal pattern decides to pursue sex with women, then he does so for nonsexual reasons.

Predominant sexual arousal for women is the most common male sexual arousal pattern, and it is evolutionarily adaptive. Obviously in evolutionary history men who had a heterosexual arousal pattern (hence a heterosexual orientation) had a reproductive advantage over men with arousal patterns which motivated them to pursue sexual interactions with people (and things) other than fertile women. A heterosexual arousal pattern motivates men to seek women as sex partners, and it facilitates sexual intercourse with (and hence fertilization of) them. Only slightly less obviously, men with a heterosexual arousal pattern had an advantage over men with indiscriminate arousal patterns, or with no sexual arousal at all. The existence of male sexual arousal patterns producing maximum arousal to people (or things) other than fertile women remains evolutionarily mystifying. Of course, this fact is irrelevant to how socially acceptable nonheterosexual arousal patterns are; to assume otherwise is to commit the naturalistic fallacy. Some putative evolutionary adaptations are not at all admirable (e.g., the propensity to be sexually unfaithful under certain circumstances), and most (such as a heterosexual arousal pattern, compared with a homosexual arousal pattern) are morally neutral.

I do not mean to suggest that sexual arousal is the only motivational factor that attracts heterosexual men to women, or homosexual men to each other. For example, attachment in a long-term relationship is often much more important than sexual desire. I continue to insist, however, that one's sexual arousal pattern has the best claim on the meaning of sexual orientation. A sexual arousal pattern is both sexual and orienting.

One consequence of the view that a man's sexual orientation is equivalent to his sexual arousal pattern is that answers to questions about male sexual orientation may ultimately require the objective assessment of sexual arousal. One example is whether male sexual orientation can be changed. Perhaps the best-known investigation of this question was conducted by Spitzer (2003), who interviewed 143 men (as well as 57 women) who had sought help in changing their sexual orientations. Spitzer concluded that indeed, many men (and women) were capable of genuine changes in their sexual orientation. Spitzer regretted that employing PPG measures was "not feasible" in the study. In my view, claims that male sexual orientation can be changed should be viewed with great skepticism unless and until a study using PPG (or perhaps eventually, fMRI) shows this quite clearly.

Pedophilia: A Case Study of the Motivating Force
of a Sexual Arousal Pattern

Arguably, the motivational aspects of a sexual arousal pattern can be most clearly observed in an example in which sexual arousal pattern is dysfunctional: pedophilia. Pedophiles are men who are more sexually aroused by children than they are by adults of either sex. That is, their sexual orientation is toward children. Not all men who have sexually molested children are pedophilic in this sense (Seto, 2007, Chapter 2). Among child molesters, a PPG-assessed arousal pattern consistent with pedophilia is a good predictor of recidivism (Hanson & Morton-Bourgon, 2005), which is a good indicator of the motivation to molest children. Although there has been interesting historical variation in the degree to which adult–child sexual interactions are tolerated (e.g., Jenkins, 1998), intolerance of pedophilic acts has been most common and often severe. Pedophiles risk societal disapproval and their own freedom, if they act on their arousal pattern. The fact that some act anyway suggests that for some men, at least, sexual arousal pattern is strongly motivating indeed.

Castration lowers sex drive and erectile capacity, both aspects of sexual arousal. During the twentieth century some European countries (especially Germany and the Netherlands) surgically castrated certain types of sex offenders, including pedophiles. Follow-up studies suggest that this intervention was highly successful. The best study compared recidivism in castrated sex offenders (most but not all of whom were pedophilic) with that in sex offenders who agreed to be castrated but then changed their minds. This 11-year follow-up study yielded a recidivism rate of 3% for 99 castrated offenders, compared with a rate of 46% for 35 uncastrated men (Wille & Beier, 1989). These rates are consistent with those of larger, but less well-controlled studies (Bailey & Greenberg, 1998). Chemical castration is also effective, especially using powerful Gonadotropin-Releasing Hormone (GnRH) agonists such as leuprolide acetate (Lupron). These chemicals reduce testosterone levels even further than surgical castration. While treated with Lupron, 30 men with anomalous sexual orientations (25 of whom were pedophilic) experienced dramatic reductions in sexual fantasies about children, erectile capacity, and masturbation frequency (Rosler & Witzum, 1998). No man committed a sexual offense during treatment. Thus, pedophiles' sexual arousal pattern is motivating enough to encourage some to seek sexual interactions with children, despite the threat of prison. Reducing their sexual arousal to children is enough to discourage the large majority of pedophiles from such interactions.

Sexual Arousal Patterns vs. the Kinsey Scale: The Case
of Male Bisexuality

One of Alfred Kinsey's most famous contributions was the Kinsey Scale, a seven-point scale intended to measure sexual orientation. (Kinsey did not use the term "sexual orientation," and I am uncertain whether he would have agreed with my equating sexual orientation with arousal pattern. Nevertheless, the Kinsey scale has become the most widely used measure of sexual orientation.) Kinsey believed that sexual orientation in men was graded rather than dichotomous, and he proposed the Kinsey scale as an appropriate measure:

> Males do not represent two discrete populations, heterosexual and homosexual. The world is not to be divided into sheep and goats. It is a fundamental of taxonomy that nature rarely deals with discrete categories... The living world is a continuum in each and every one of its aspects (Kinsey, Pomeroy, & Martin, 1948, p. 639).

While emphasizing the continuity of the gradations between exclusively heterosexual and exclusively homosexual histories, it has seemed desirable to develop some sort of classification which could be based on the relative amounts of heterosexual and homosexual experience or response in each history... An individual may be assigned a position on this scale, for each period in his life.... A seven-point scale comes nearer to showing the many gradations that actually exist (Kinsey et al., 1948, p. 656).

By Kinsey's scale a score of "0" represents complete heterosexuality, "7" complete homosexuality, and"3" perfect bisexuality, with "1," "2," "4," and "5" representing the gradations therein. The scale can be employed to ask about different aspects of sexual behavior or feelings, such as partner choice ("As an adult, have your sex partners tended to be the other sex or your own sex?"), sexual attraction ("Are you attracted to members of the other sex or those of your own sex?"), sexual fantasy, or sexual arousal. One clear limitation to Kinsey's approach is that it is based on self-report. Of course that limitation is shared with almost all other methods for assessing sexual orientation.

Kinsey's contention that male sexual orientation is fundamentally continuous rather than discrete is challenged by the observation that in large representative samples of men, the distribution of Kinsey scores tends to be bimodal (e.g., Bailey, Dunne, & Martin, 2000; Diamond, 1993; Laumann, Gagnon, Michael, & Michaels, 1994). Men who report scores in the bisexual range of the Kinsey scale (2–4) are rarer than men who report homosexual scores (5–6). Furthermore, bisexuality is often a transitional phase for men. One survey found that 40% of gay men had identified as "bisexual" during some point of their coming out process (Lever, 1994). The eminent sexologist Kurt Freund, who invented PPG, used to remark that he had looked without success for many years to find a man who showed a bisexual arousal pattern (to adults; bisexual pedophilia is not uncommon).

It was this context that led my lab to conduct a study of the sexual arousal patterns of bisexual men. We recruited 33 men who identified themselves as bisexual. Consistent with the notion that bisexuality is a relatively rare phenomenon among men, it took us much longer to recruit our bisexual subsample than it did to recruit the 30 heterosexual and 38 homosexual participants who also participated in this study. We asked all men about their sexual attraction patterns using the Kinsey scale, and all seven points of the Kinsey scale were well represented. Bisexually identified men indeed reported bisexual attraction patterns.

In the lab, the men watched sexually explicit videos of male couples, female couples, and heterosexual couples, as well as neutral stimuli (i.e., nature films). Again, the key stimuli are the same-sex couples. PPG was assessed circumferentially, and 22 bisexual men responded sufficiently to meet our criteria for adequate measurement of their sexual arousal pattern, as did 21 heterosexual men and 25 homosexual men. In addition, men reported their subjective level of sexual arousal to each stimulus.

We were primarily interested in the question of whether bisexual men (that is, men who identified as bisexual and reported attraction patterns on the Kinsey scale in the bisexual range) would have a bisexual arousal pattern. But what would a bisexual arousal pattern look like? We reasoned as follows: A bisexual arousal pattern does not necessarily imply very similar levels of arousal to both men and women. A bisexual man might, for example, have more arousal to men than to women. But if he has a bisexual arousal pattern, his arousal to women should be appreciable. That is, a bisexual arousal pattern implies substantial arousal to both men and women, and to both male and female erotic stimuli. Furthermore, a man with a bisexual arousal pattern should be more aroused by men than heterosexual men are, and he should be more aroused by women than homosexual men are.

Thus, in our first and most important analysis, we created a variable "Minimum Arousal" representing the minimum of arousal to male stimuli and arousal to female stimuli. That is, we looked at each person's average level of arousal to the male stimuli and his average level of arousal to the female stimuli; whichever of these was lower was his "Minimum Arousal" score. Separate variable were created for subjective and genital arousal (Minimum Subjective Arousal and Minimum Genital Arousal, respectively). The specific hypothesis tested was that men with bisexual (i.e., middle) Kinsey scores should have higher Minimum Arousal than men with heterosexual or homosexual Kinsey scores. Specifically, the regression of Minimum Arousal on Kinsey scores should be negatively quadratic. For Subjective (i.e., self-reported) Minimum Arousal, this is exactly the pattern that we found (Fig. 1a). For Minimum Genital Arousal, however, we did not find this (Fig. 1b). Instead, we found that bisexual men's Minimum Genital Arousal was statistically indistinguishable from heterosexual and homosexual men's. Thus, we found no evidence that bisexual men had a *uniquely* bisexual arousal pattern – that is, any more than heterosexual and homosexual men do. To be sure, heterosexual and homosexual men showed more genital arousal to their nonpreferred erotic stimuli (male and female erotic stimuli, respectively) than to neutral stimuli, and one might thus argue that *all* men, regardless of sexual orientation, are somewhat bisexual. I am skeptical of this argument, however, because arousal to the nonpreferred sexual stimuli was much less than arousal to the preferred stimuli. Furthermore, our fMRI study suggested that patterns of activation to preferred and nonpreferred sexual stimuli were different in kind and not just degree (e.g., Fig. 2b).

In a second analysis we examined whether bisexual men's arousal patterns tend to be more similar to that of homosexual men than to heterosexual men. This would be consistent with the observation that many bisexually identified men eventually identify as homosexual. Indeed, we found that bisexual men tended to be more genitally and subjectively aroused to the male stimuli than to the female stimuli. There were exceptions, however. Thus, most bisexual men in our study had a homosexual arousal pattern, but a few had a heterosexual pattern.

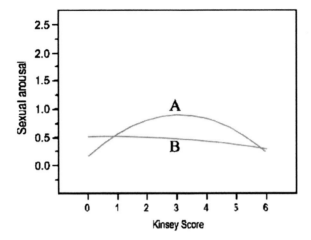

Fig. 2 Quadratic regression curves obtained by regressing Minimum Subjective Arousal (**a**) and Minimum Genital Arousal (**b**) onto Kinsey score. Kinsey score was assessed as self-reported relative attraction to men and women

Our study failed to find good evidence for a bisexual arousal pattern (and hence, a bisexual orientation) among men with bisexual identities and self-reported bisexual feelings. To use the terms introduced at the beginning of this chapter, bisexual behavior patterns certainly exist. In addition, many men publicly identify as bisexual and, to the best of our ability to measure, also seem privately to think of themselves as bisexual. Many men insist that their sexual feelings are bisexual, and many choose partners of both sexes; thus by the aforementioned definition, their sexual preferences are bisexual. However, our findings suggest that their sexual arousal patterns are not bisexual. It is possible that bisexual arousal patterns exist among men, but that we failed to detect them. For example, perhaps male bisexual arousal patterns occur but are rare. Perhaps we did not have a sufficient number of such men to detect bisexual arousal patterns. Our study did show a clear dissociation between genital arousal patterns and self-reports using the Kinsey scale. I like to think that Kinsey would feel challenged by our data, and that in light of it, he would consider it an open, scientific, question whether homosexual and heterosexual men represent two separate populations, like "sheep and goats."

Female Sexual Arousal Patterns and Sexual Choices

What about women? Is a woman's sexual orientation her sexual arousal pattern? Research on women's sexual arousal patterns has lagged far behind that on men's. In part this undoubtedly reflects scientific privileging of male concerns, perhaps especially in the sexual sphere. In part, however, it reflects measurement difficulty. Genital arousal assessment is much more difficult to do in women than in men. Thus, our discussion of women's arousal patterns begins with their measurement.

Measurement of Female Genital Arousal

Genital arousal is a more complex phenomenon in women than in men. Rather than a single observable output (i.e., penile erection), women have three main responses: clitoral erection, vasocongestion (engorgement of blood) of the labia and vaginal walls, and lubrication of the vagina. So far, psychophysiologists have had success measuring only one of these, namely vaginal vasocongestion.

Vasocongestion causes a darkening of vaginal tissue, as the pooled blood loses its oxygen. The primary method of measuring female sexual arousal exploits this color change. The vaginal photoplethysmograph consists of a clear acrylic tampon-sized tube that contains both a light source and a light detector (Geer, Morokoff, & Greenwood, 1974). The device outputs two signals, one of which is thought to measure vaginal blood volume (VBV) and the other of which is thought to measure vaginal pulse amplitude (VPA), or the phasic changes in the vascular walls due to pressure changes. VPA has greater construct validity than VBV as a measure of genital arousal, and it is used far more often (Geer & Janssen 2000; Janssen 2001; Laan, Everaerd, & Evers, 1995). Obviously, VPA is a more indirect and complex measure of genital sexual arousal compared with PPG in men.

Evidence for construct validity of VPA includes the fact that VPA reliably increases in most women as they process erotic stimuli (typically, erotic videos). Furthermore, VPA increases as stimuli become more explicit (Laan & Janssen, 2007). The far greater consumption of visual pornography by men compared with women (e.g., Hald, 2006) has led researchers to examine whether women's genital arousal is provoked by different stimulus media compared with men's. This does not appear to be the case, however. For example, women have more genital arousal while watching sexually explicit videos than they do reading erotic stories or engaging in erotic fantasy (van Dam, Honnebier, van Zelinge, & Barendregt, 1976), and romantic content does not appear to enhance genital arousal (Heiman, 1977). Like men, they have more genital arousal watching videos of couples interacting sexually compared with videos of nude exercising or masturbating individuals (Chivers et al., 2007).

One striking difference between female and male genital arousal data is that there is a much lower concordance between genital and self-reported subjective arousal measures for women than for men (Chivers, Seto, Lalumiere, Laan, & Grimbos, 2006). That is, when men are genitally aroused, they usually report that they are subjectively aroused as well. This is substantially less true for women. We do not currently understand why this unlinking of genital and subjective sexual arousal occurs in women.

Female Sexual Arousal Patterns

In 1996 Ellen Laan and colleagues reported the surprising results of a study on the arousal patterns of self-identified heterosexual and homosexual women. Participants watched sexually explicit videos of heterosexual couples and of lesbian couples, while their genital arousal (VPA) was assessed, and while providing ratings of their subjective arousal. Neither genital nor subjective arousal pattern differed between the two groups. Both groups showed highest arousal to the stimuli featuring the heterosexual couple (Laan, Sonderman, & Janssen, 1996). This was quite surprising in view of male findings. The analogous result for men would be for homosexual and heterosexual men to have similar arousal patterns to sexually explicit videos of heterosexual couples and homosexual male couples. Such a result is unheard of in the male literature.

With some methodological modifications my lab attempted to replicate this surprising finding using a sample of women recruited from the Chicago area (Chivers et al., 2004). For example, we collected extensive self-report dataconcerning participants' sexual feelings. This allowed us to make sure that participants who identified as lesbian also reported much stronger sexual feelings for women than for men, and that participants who identified as heterosexual showed the opposite pattern. Most importantly, we included erotic stimuli featuring male couples. As I have noted, arousal to sexual stimuli featuring heterosexual couples is less informative in studies of sexual orientation, because such couples contain both a man and a woman.

With respect to genital arousal (VPA), the heterosexual women showed a strikingly flat profile. That is, VPA was similar for the three kinds of stimuli (videos of the male–male couples, female–female couples, and male–female couples). Lesbians were somewhat more genitally aroused by the female–female stimuli than by the male–male stimuli, although this difference was much less than the analogous differences seen in male arousal patterns. Figure 3 shows the sex difference in patterns of genital arousal (figure adapted from Chivers et al., 2004). This figure combines homosexual and heterosexual men, who had very similar arousal patterns, but it separates homosexual and heterosexual women, whose sexual arousal patterns differed somewhat. The figure plots participants' average genital arousal to stimuli featuring their preferred sex (for heterosexual men and homosexual women, this is women; for homosexual men and heterosexual women, this is men) and their nonpreferred sex (for heterosexual men and homosexual women, this is men; for homosexual men and heterosexual women, this is women). Men showed a substantial difference in genital arousal to stimuli depicting their preferred sex compared with stimuli depicting their nonpreferred sex. Overall, women showed a small, nonsignificant difference. Furthermore, women's slightly greater arousal to stimuli featuring their preferred sex was entirely due to the lesbian participants.

What about women's self-reported subjective arousal patterns (Figure 4)? Lesbians' results showed a similar pattern to men's. Specifically, they reported far greater arousal to their preferred sex than to their nonpreferred sex (with arousal to

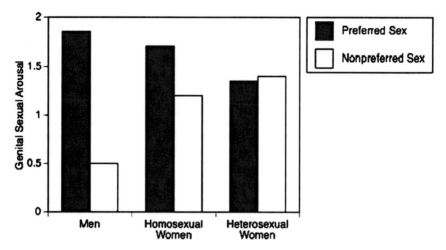

Fig. 3 Genital sexual arousal to sexually explicit videos containing same-sex couples of participants' preferred sex or nonpreferred sex. Arousal to neutral stimuli has been subtracted. Units are within-subjects standard deviations. Adapted from Chivers et al. (2004)

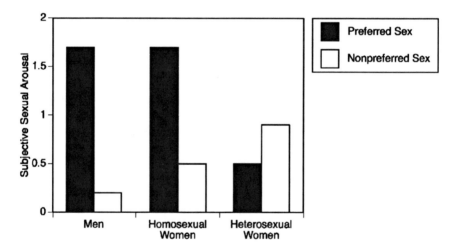

Fig. 4 Subjective self-reported sexual arousal to sexually explicit videos containing same-sex couples of participants' preferred sex or nonpreferred sex. Arousal to neutral stimuli has been subtracted. Units are within-subjects standard deviations. Adapted from Chivers et al. (2004)

the mixed-sex videos intermediate). However, heterosexual women reported the *least* arousal to videos featuring only their preferred sex (i.e., the male couples). They reported greatest arousal to the mixed-sex couple (Chivers et al., 2004). Across all our female participants, the correlation between their subjective and genital male–female contrasts (i.e., the difference between arousal to the male–male and female–female films) was 0.48; the analogous correlation for men was 0.88.

Thus, most women's sexual arousal patterns seemed profoundly different than men's. Although lesbians' arousal pattern might be viewed as a much-attenuated version of the male pattern (i.e., with highest arousal to stimuli containing the preferred sex), heterosexual women's arousal pattern was nothing like men's. With respect to genital arousal pattern, heterosexual women appeared almost perfectly bisexual. With respect to subjective arousal pattern, heterosexual women's response to the same-sex stimuli was opposite that of men's. Men's sexual arousal is *category specific*, meaning that it is highest to sexual stimuli featuring the category of person that men are most attracted to. Women's sexual arousal does not appear to be category specific.

One possible methodological concern is that volunteers for our female arousal study were unusual women from whom generalization is risky (Morokoff, 1986). In general, most women are reluctant to consider participating in a study requiring them to watch pornography in a laboratory with a gauge inserted in their vaginas. Perhaps those willing to do so are different in ways that include their sexual arousal patterns. To address this concern, we recruited a group of young heterosexual women through university psychology classes. Recruitment was phased, with an initial information session, followed by an assessment of both willingness to participate in a sexual arousal study and aspects of their sexual behavior and attitudes. Finally, women who agreed to proceed had their sexual arousal patterns assessed in the laboratory.

Women who agreed to participate in the sexual arousal assessment (Volunteers) did in fact differ from women who did not (Refusers) in several respects. The former had more lifetime sexual partners, masturbated more frequently, achieved orgasm more frequently via masturbation, and consumed erotica more frequently. Among the Volunteers, however, there was considerable variability in all these predictors. For example, two of the Volunteers were virgins. We examined whether variation in these predictors was associated with sexual arousal pattern (i.e., subjective or genital arousal to male–male, female–female, or male–female sexual stimuli). It was not, and so we concluded that volunteer bias probably did not account for our participants' sexual arousal patterns. What was the average sexual arousal pattern of this young, heterosexual female sample? Just as in our older, more experienced, community sample of heterosexual women, the genital arousal pattern was nearly flat, with similar levels of genital arousal to videos featuring male–male, female–female, and male–female couples. The two samples also had very similar subjective arousal patterns, with highest arousal to videos featuring the heterosexual couple and lowest arousal to those featuring the male couple.

A second methodological concern we have addressed involves the limitations of vaginal photoplethysmography. In general, sex researchers are considerably less satisfied with female genital assessment than with male genital assessment (e.g., Levin, 1998). Vaginal photoplethysmography is a less direct measure, and its construct validity is much less well established. Perhaps it cannot detect a category specific sexual arousal pattern even if one exists. To examine this concern, we recruited a group of women whom we believed might indeed have a category specific sexual arousal pattern:postoperative male-to-female transsexuals. These *new women* had surgically constructed neovaginas, and so assessing their genital arousal would require vaginal photoplethysmography. Because the transsexuals had all been born male, and because men have category specific arousal patterns, we thought they might as well. Furthermore, we capitalized on the fact that there are two types of male-to-female transsexuals, one type primarily attracted to men and the other type primarily attracted to women (Bailey, 2003; Blanchard, 1989). The transsexuals could be perfectly classified according to their genital sexual arousal patterns. All six who preferred men had greater genital arousal to the male–male videos, and all five who preferred women had greater arousal to the female–female videos. This shows that vaginal photoplethysmography is not to blame in our failure to find category specific genital arousal in natal women.

Another interesting conclusion from this study concerns the sensitivity of vaginal arousal assessment. Every single transsexual became sufficiently aroused genitally to be counted as a responder and to have her genital arousal pattern correctly assessed, despite having been castrated and taking female hormones. Both of these drastically reduce the level of testosterone, which is necessary for male sexual arousal. A castrated man on female hormones would stand little chance of attaining enough genital arousal to meet minimum PPG criteria. This suggests that VPA is a far more sensitive measure of genital arousal compared with PPG. Another interesting conclusion from this study concerns the development of category specificity of male sexual arousal. Male-to-female transsexuals who are attracted to men are in many respects extraordinarily feminine (Bailey, 2000, 2003). Yet, their sexual arousal patterns show the male-typical, category specific, pattern. Evidently, whatever has feminized some parts of their minds and brains has left untouched the mechanisms that direct their sexual arousal (Chivers et al., 2004, Lawrence, Latty, Chivers, & Bailey, 2005).

The nonspecific sexual arousal patterns of natal women do not appear to be due to methodological artifacts of sampling or measurement. And it has been recently replicated yet one more time, using additional stimuli unlike those employed previously (Chivers et al., 2007). This study included videos of individual men and women who were either masturbating or exercising in the nude, as well as sexually explicit videos of couples, as in the prior studies of this topic. Both men and women were most sexually aroused by the sexually interacting couples and least sexually aroused by the nude exercise videos. However, men were substantially aroused only to videos featuring actors of their preferred sex. Women showed the same basic arousal pattern as earlier research. Heterosexual women showed a genital arousal pattern that can only be described as bisexual, and their subjective arousal pattern was if anything opposite what one would expect based on their self-reported identity and attractions (i.e., they reported more arousal to female than to male stimuli). Homosexual women did show significant genital and subjective bias toward female rather than male sexual stimuli, but their genital bias was less than that found among the men in the study. Still, it seems that homosexual women are more category specific than heterosexual women in their sexual arousal pattern. Perhaps homosexual women's minds and brains have been masculinized to some degree, on average, and this masculinization has encompassed sexual arousal.

Do Most Women Have Sexual Orientations?

I have argued that a man's sexual orientation is precisely his sexual arousal pattern. If we insist that women have sexual orientations and that *sexual orientation* must have the same mechanism for both sexes, this leads us to the odd conclusion that most women with heterosexual identities and preferences have a bisexual orientation. (Some lesbians appear to have sexual arousal patterns that match their partner preferences, so I focus on the difficulty of understanding heterosexual women, who comprise the large majority of women.) It would also follow that for heterosexual women, sexual identity and preference have little to do with sexual orientation. This is a logically defensible position, but it is not one that I favor.

An alternative possibility is that laboratory studies have suggested a highly misleading picture of female sexual arousal patterns, which are truly category specific. It would certainly be useful to explore whether other methods (e.g., other kinds of sexual stimuli) might lead to different conclusions. But I do not think it is likely that they will. When I have discussed our findings with women, they have not complained that our results are invalid or misleading, and they have not insisted that they have a sexual arousal pattern that is analogous to that of men. Certainly no one has offered a promising alternative methodology to reveal a category specific sexual arousal pattern in women.

Another alternative is that for most women sexual orientation – the orienting of sexual feelings and behavior toward certain targets and not others – is not about a sexual arousal pattern. In contrast to the male heterosexual arousal pattern, the female heterosexual arousal pattern does not appear to have been designed by evolution to motivate women to seek opposite-sex partners. For most women, their sexual arousal pattern is an ineffective orienting device indeed. One problem with this position is that it requires us to define the same concept, sexual orientation, differently for men and women. A second problem is that if we take this route, we have no good idea what female sexual orientation is. That is, female sexual orientation is a hypothesized mechanism whose existence is unproven and whose nature is unknown. The flip side to this position is that most women may have nothing like a sexual orientation, if sexual orientation is conceived of as a well-designed sexual mechanism that strongly motivates women to select sexual partners of one sex or the other (or both).

At least one other alternative exists: reject my claim that a man's sexual orientation is the same as his sexual arousal pattern, and continue to use the term to mean the same thing in both sexes, such as the propensity to be attracted to men or to women or to both. This approach has at least two problems, however. First, it obscures the importance of arousal patterns in men's sexuality. Second, it implies similarity between the sexes where there may be fundamental difference.

If heterosexual women had no sexual orientation, how might they manage to wind up with male partners? Even if they had the potential to enjoy sex with men and women, most women might choose men due to overwhelming socialization pressures. From early childhood most people are exposed to a largely heterosexual world, are encouraged in various ways to behave heterosexually, and discouraged from behaving homosexually. Even if women's sexuality is potentially very socially malleable (Baumeister, 2000) and flexible (Diamond, 2008), current social forces in most of the world work to mold heterosexual lives.

The possibility that women do not have sexual orientations is consistent with the observation that few if any women have paraphilias such as pedophilia (American Psychiatric Association, 2000). Pedophilia occurs in men despite immense societal pressure and stigma. Although a few women have sexual fantasies about children, and some even molest them (e.g., Federoff, Fishell, & Federoff, 1999), these women are quite rare. Furthermore, there is no persuasive evidence that such women are motivated by an arousal system directed much more strongly toward children than adults. Perhaps because most women do not have sexual arousal patterns directed at a particular kind of person, they cannot easily develop misdirected sexual arousal patterns and dysfunctional sexual orientations.

The best evidence that women may have a sexual orientation analogous to men's is indirect. There is striking similarity between the sexes in the development of sexual preference. Both male and female homosexuality is associated with gender nonconformity in both childhood and adulthood. Gender nonconformity is manifested differently at different developmental stages. In childhood it may include preferences for play behavior more typical of the other sex, for opposite-sex playmates, and for clothing of the other sex. Retrospective studies of both sexes have shown that homosexual individuals recall substantially more childhood gender nonconformity compared with heterosexual individuals (Bailey & Zucker, 1995). The retrospective studies have been confirmed by prospective studies (e.g., Green, 1987; Zucker et al., 2008). In adulthood relevant behavior includes recreational and occupational interests somewhat typical of the other sex (Lippa, 2000, 2002) as well as superficial overt behavior including patterns of speech, dress, and movement (Ambady, Hallahan, & Conner, 1999; Johnson, Gill, Reichman, & Tassinary, 2007; Rieger, Linsenmeier, Gygax, & Bailey, 2008). These highly robust findings suggest symmetry between the sexes in the development and causes of sexual preference. It seems less likely in this light that men have a sexual orientation mechanism that has no close analog in women. If women possess such a mechanism, however, we have little idea what it is.

Let me be clear that I am not asserting that most women have no sexual orientation; I am merely raising the possibility that this might be so. My main point has been to clarify the meaning of sexual orientation in men, and to show that for most women, sexual orientation cannot plausibly mean the same thing. In her insightful attempt to explain how some apparently heterosexual women fall in love with other women, Lisa Diamond (2003) asked: "What does sexual orientation orient?" Asking this question about women seems premature to me. Diamond's observations about sexual fluidity – the degree to which some women's partner choices, sexual feelings, and sexual identities can shift back and forth over time, from men to women – are consistent with the idea that women are less constrained than men by a focused sexual arousal pattern. Before asking what sexual orientation orients, we should first ask whether *anything* sexually orients women.

References

Ambady, N., Hallahan, M., & Conner, B. (1999). Accuracy of judgments of sexual orientation from thin slices of behavior. *Journal of Personality and Social Psychology, 77*, 538–547.

American Psychiatric Association. (2000). *Diagnostic and statistical manual of mental disorders* (4th ed., Text Revised). Washington, DC: Author

Bailey, J. M. (2000). *Homosexual Male-to-Female Transsexualism.* Paper presented at the 26th Annual Meeting of the International Academy of Sex Research, June 21–24, Paris France.

Bailey, J. M. (2003). *The man who would be queen: The science of gender-bending and transsexualism.* Washington, DC: Joseph Henry Press.

Bailey, J. M., Dunne, M. P., & Martin, N. G. (2000). Genetic and environmental influences on sexual orientation and its correlates in an Australian twin sample. *Journal of Personality and Social Psychology, 78*, 524–536.

Bailey, J. M., & Greenberg, A. S. (1998). The science and ethics of castration: Lessons from the *Morse* case. *Northwestern Law Review, 92*, 1225–1245.

Bailey, J. M., & Zucker, K. J. (1995). Childhood sex-typed behavior and sexual orientation: A conceptual analysis and quantitative review. *Developmental Psychology 31*, 43–55.

Bancroft, J., Jones, H. G., & Pullan, B. P. (1966). A simple transducer for measuring penile erection with comments on its use in the treatment of sexual disorder. *Behavior Research and Therapy, 4*, 239–241.

Baumeister, R. F. (2000). Gender differences in erotic plasticity: The female sex drive as socially flexible and responsive. *Psychological Bulletin, 126*, 347–374.

Blanchard, R. (1989). The concept of autogynephilia and the typology of male gender dysphoria. *Journal of Nervous and Mental Disease, 177*, 616–623.

Chivers, M. L., Seto, M. C., & Blanchard, R. (2007). Gender and sexual orientation differences in sexual response to sexual activities versus gender of actors in sexual films. *Journal of Personality and Social Psychology, 93*, 1108–1121.

Chivers, M. L., Seto, M. C., Lalumiere, M. L., Laan, E., and Grimbos, T. (2006). Agreement of genital and subjective measures of sexual arousal: A meta-analysis. Poster presented at the 32nd Annual Meeting of the International Academy of Sex Research, July 12–15, 2006, Amsterdam, the Netherlands.

Chivers, M. L., Rieger, G., Latty, E., & Bailey, J. M. (2004). A sex difference in the specificity of sexual arousal. *Psychological Science, 15*, 736–744.

van Dam, F. S. A. M., Honnebier, W. J., van Zelinge, E. A., & Barendregt, J. T. (1976). Sexual arousal measured by photoplethysmography. *Behavioral Engineering, 3*, 97–101.

Diamond, M. (1993). Homosexuality and bisexuality in different populations. *Archives of Sexual Behavior, 22*, 291–310.

Diamond, L. M. (2003). What does sexual orientation orient? A biobehavioral model distinguishing romantic love and sexual desire. *Psychological Review, 110*, 173–192.

Diamond, L. M. (2008). *Sexual fluidity: Understanding women's love and desire.* Cambridge, MA: Harvard University Press.

Dworkin, S. H. (2001). Treating the bisexual client. *Journal of Clinical Psychology, 57,* 671–680.

Federoff, J. P., Fishell, A., & Federoff, B. (1999). A case series of women evaluated for paraphilic sexual disorders. *Canadian Journal of Human Sexuality, 8,* 127–140.

Freund, K. (1963). A laboratory method for diagnosing predominance of homo- or hetero-erotic interest in the male. *Behaviour Research and Therapy, 1,* 85–93.

Geer, J., & Janssewn, E. (2000). The sexual response system. In J. T. Cacioppo, L. G. Tassinary, & G. G. Berntson (Eds.), *Handbook of psychophysiology* (pp. 315–341). New York: Cambridge University Press.

Geer, J. H., Morokoff, P., & Greenwood, P. (1974). Sexual arousal in women: The development of a measurement device for vaginal blood volume. *Archives of Sexual Behavior, 3,* 559–564.

Green, R. (1987). *The "sissy boy syndrome" and the development of homosexuality.* New Haven, CT: Yale University Press.

Hanson, R. K., & Morton-Bourgon, K. (2005). The characteristics of persistent sexual offenders: A meta-analysis of recidivism studies. *Journal of Consulting and Clinical Psychology, 73,* 1154–1163.

Heiman, J. R. (1977). A psychophysiological exploration of sexual arousal patterns in females and males. *Psychophysiology, 14,* 266–274.

Janssen, E. (2001). Psychophysiological measures of sexual response. In M. W. Wiederman & B. E. Whitley (Eds.), *Handbook for conducting research on human sexuality* (pp. 139–171). Mahwah, NJ: Erlbaum.

Janssen, E., Everaerd, W., Spiering, M. & Janssen, J. (2000). Automatic processes and the appraisal of sexual stimuli: Toward an information processing model of sexual arousal. *Journal of Sex Research, 37,* 8–23.

Jenkins, P. (1998). *Moral panic: Changing concepts of the child molester in modern America.* New Haven, CT: Yale University Press.

Johnson, K. L., Gill, S., Reichman, V., & Tassinary, L. G. (2007). Swagger, Sway, and Sexuality: Judging Sexual Orientation from Body Motion and Morphology. *Journal of Personality and Social Psychology, 93,* 321–334.

Kinsey, A. C., Pomeroy, W. B., & Martin, C. E. (1948). *Sexual behavior in the human male.* Philadelphia, PA: W.B. Saunders

Kuban, M., Barbaree, H. E., & Blanchard, R. (1999). A comparison of volume and circumference phallometry: Response magnitude and method agreement. *Archives of Sexual Behavior, 28,* 345–359.

Laan, E., & Everaerd, W. (1995). Determinants of female sexual arousal: Psychophysiological theory and data. *Annual Review of Sex Research, 6,* 32–76.

Laan, E., Everaerd, W., & Evers, A. (1995). Assessment of female sexual arousal: Response specificity and construct validity. *Psychophysiology, 32,* 476–485.

Laan, E., & Janssen, E. (2007). How do men and women feel? Determinants of subjective experience of sexual arousal. In E. Janssen (Ed.), *The psychophysiology of sex* (pp. 278–290). Bloomington, IN: Indiana University Press.

Laan, E., Sonderman, M., & Janssen, E. (1996). *Straight and lesbian women's sexual responses to straight and lesbian erotica: No sexual orientation effects.* Poster presented at the 22nd Annual Meeting of the International Academy of Sex Research, Rotterdam, Netherlands.

Laumann, E. O., Gagnon, J. H., Michael, R. T., & Michaels, S. (1994). *The social organization of sexuality: Sexual practices in the United States.* Chicago, IL: University of Chicago Press.

Lawrence, A. A., Latty, E. M., Chivers, M. L., & Bailey, J. M. (2005). Measurement of sexual arousal in postoperative male-to-female transsexuals using vaginal photoplethysmography. *Archives of Sexual Behaviour, 34,* 135–145.

Lever, J. (1994). Sexual revelations: The 1994 Advocate survey of sexuality and relationships: The men. *The Advocate,* August 23.

Levin, R. J. (1998). Assessing human female sexual arousal by vaginal plethysmography: A critical examination. *Sexologies, European Journal of Medical Sexology, 6,* 26–31

Lippa, R. A. (2000). Gender-related traits in gay men, lesbian women, and heterosexual men and women: The virtual identity of homosexual-heterosexual diagnosticity and gender diagnosticity. *Journal of Personality, 68*, 899–926.

Lippa, R. A. (2002). Gender-related traits of heterosexual and homosexual men and women. *Archives of Sexual Behavior, 31*, 83–98.

Lippa, R. A. (2005). *Gender, nature, and nurture*. Mahwah, NJ: Erlbaum.

Julien, E., & Over, R. (1988). Male sexual arousal across five modes of erotic stimulation. *Archives of Sexual Behavior, 17*, 131–143.

Mavissakalian, M., Blanchard, E. B., Abel, G. C., & Barlow, D. H. (1975). Responses to complex erotic stimuli in homosexual and heterosexual males. *British Journal of Psychiatry, 126*, 252–257.

Morokoff, P. J. (1986). Volunteer bias in the psychophysiological study of female sexuality. *Journal of Sex Research, 22*, 35–51.

Phillips, M. L., Young, A. W., Senior, C., Brammer, M., Andrew, C., Calder, A. J. et al. (1997). A specific neural substrate for perceiving facial expressions of disgust. *Nature, 389*, 495–498.

Rieger, G., Chivers, M. L. & Bailey, J. M. (Aug 2005). Sexual arousal patterns of bisexual men. *Psychological Science, 16*, 579–584.

Rieger, G., Linsenmeier, J. A. W., Gygax, L., & Bailey, J. M. (2008). Sexual orientation and childhood gender nonconformity: Evidence from home videos. *Developmental Psychology, 44*, 46–58.

Rosler, A., & Witzum, E. (1998). Treatment of men with paraphilia with long-acting analogue of gonadotropin-releasing hormone. *New England Journal of Medicine, 338*, 416–422.

Safron, A., Barch, B., Bailey, J. M., Gitelman, D. R., Parrish, T. B., & Reber, P. J. (2007). Neural correlates of sexual arousal in homosexual and heterosexual men. *Behavioral Neuroscience, 121*, 237–248.

Sakheim, D. K., Barlow, D. H., Beck, J. G., & Abrahamson, D. J. (1985). A comparison of male heterosexual and male homosexual patterns of sexual arousal. *Journal of Sex Research, 21*, 183–198.

Seto, M. C. (2007). *Pedophilia and sexual offending against children*. Washington, DC: American Psychological Association.

Spitzer, R. L. (2003). Can some gay men and lesbians change their sexual orientation? 200 participants reporting a change from homosexual to heterosexual orientation. *Archives of Sexual Behavior, 32*, 403–417.

Wiegel, M., Scepkowski, L. A., & Barlow, D. H. (2007). Cognitive-affective processes in sexual arousal and dysfunction. In E. Janssen (Ed.), *The psychophysiology of sex* (pp. 141–165). Bloomington, IN: Indiana University Press.

Wille, R., & Beier, K. M. (1989). Castration in Germany. *Annals of Sex Research, 2*, 103–133.

Sexual Stigma and Sexual Prejudice in the United States: A Conceptual Framework

Gregory M. Herek

In 1972, psychologist George Weinberg's book, *Society and the Healthy Homosexual*, introduced readers to a new term, *homophobia*, and to the then-novel idea that hostility to homosexuality, rather than homosexuality itself, posed a threat to mental health (Weinberg, 1972; see also Herek, 2004). The following year, the American Psychiatric Association's Board of Directors declared that homosexuality is not inherently associated with mental illness and voted to remove it from the *Diagnostic and Statistical Manual of Mental Disorders*, or DSM (Bayer, 1987; Minton, 2002). The American Psychological Association quickly endorsed the psychiatrists' action and further urged mental health professionals "to take the lead in removing the stigma of mental illness that has long been associated with homosexual orientations" (Conger, 1975, p. 633). Thus, a major cultural institution renounced its longstanding role in legitimating society's stigmatization of homosexuality just when the psychological manifestations of such stigma were beginning to be redefined as a social problem. This historic confluence of events provides an appropriate starting point for the present chapter.

The term homophobia has gained widespread usage since 1972, even as its limitations have become increasingly apparent. Chief among these is its construction of prejudice as an individual pathology. As I have explained elsewhere (Herek, 2004), this clinically derived perspective limits our ability to understand hostility toward sexual minorities, both among individuals and in society at large. I have argued instead for the value of framing heterosexuals' negative responses to sexual minorities in terms of *sexual prejudice* and of conceptualizing sexual prejudice as the internalization of societal stigma (Herek, 2000a, 2004, 2007; Herek, Chopp, & Strohl, 2007).

In the present chapter, I elaborate on these points and provide a more detailed framework than I have previously presented for conceptualizing both societal and individual reactions to homosexuality and sexual minorities in the United States.[1] A central aim of this discussion is to integrate insights relevant to sexual orientation from the sociological literature on *stigma* with findings from psychological research

---

[1] The framework described here may have applicability across national and cultural boundaries, as suggested by the fact that some of its key underlying constructs have been developed outside the United States (e.g., Scambler & Hopkins, 1986). Because most of the data I discuss (including my own empirical research) are derived from US samples, however, I restrict my generalizations to American culture.

D.A. Hope (ed.), *Contemporary Perspectives on Lesbian, Gay, and Bisexual Identities*, DOI: 10.1007/978-0-387-09556-1, © 2009 Gregory M. Herek

on *prejudice*. Although the terms stigma and prejudice have often been used interchangeably, distinguishing between the two constructs permits a more refined understanding of the status and experiences of sexual minorities than is possible from either a sociological or psychological research perspective alone. In addition to incorporating institutional and individual levels of analysis, the framework described here suggests a rethinking of some existing constructs (e.g., internalized stigma, felt stigma) in ways that are amenable to describing the experiences of both the nonstigmatized majority and the stigmatized minority group. It also considers points of intersection between structural and individual stigma.

I begin by briefly introducing the construct of stigma and discussing its structural manifestations in the institutions of society. Then, consistent with the theme of the present volume, I focus mainly on manifestations of stigma among individuals. After discussing three such manifestations, I consider how individuals' attitudes can affect structural stigma and how cultural events can create conditions that are conducive to the diminution of individual prejudice.

A Framework for Conceptualizing Sexual Stigma

Like most contemporary discussions in this area, the present chapter draws from Goffman's (1963) seminal account for a basic definition of stigma. While acknowledging that the term historically referred to a mark or bodily sign "designed to expose something unusual and bad about the moral status of the signifier" (Goffman, 1963, p. 1), he focused attention on the socially constructed meaning of the mark. By virtue of the mark (or characteristic or group membership), an individual is regarded by society as diverging in a disfavored way from its understanding of normalcy. Thus, he used stigma to refer to "an undesired differentness" (p. 5) and "an attribute that is deeply discrediting" (p. 3). A particular attribute can be discrediting in one context but desired or expected in another, although Goffman noted that "there are important attributes that almost everywhere in our society are discrediting" (p. 4). Other writers have similarly emphasized that stigma is very much about the socially constructed meanings associated with a characteristic and have noted that these meanings can vary across situations (e.g., Crocker, Major, & Steele, 1998; Jones et al., 1984). Moreover, the meanings are grounded in society's power relations (Link & Phelan, 2001). Compared to the nonstigmatized, individuals who inhabit a stigmatized role enjoy less access to valued resources, less influence over others, and less control over their own fate.

With these insights as a foundation, stigma is used here to refer to the negative regard and inferior status that society collectively accords to people who possess a particular characteristic or belong to a particular group or category. Inherent in this definition is the fact that stigma constitutes shared knowledge about which attributes and categories are valued by society, which ones are denigrated, and how these valuations vary across situations.

Sexual stigma is a particular instance of this phenomenon. It is the stigma attached to any nonheterosexual behavior, identity, relationship, or community. In other words, it is socially shared knowledge about homosexuality's devalued status relative to heterosexuality. Like other stigmas, it creates social roles and expectations for conduct that are understood and shared by the members of society, regardless of their own sexual orientation or personal attitudes. Most people in the United States know that homosexual desires and conduct are regarded negatively relative to heterosexuality, and they are aware of the malevolent stereotypes that are routinely attached to individuals whose personal identities are based on same-sex attractions, behaviors, relationships, or membership in a sexual minority community.

Stigma-based differentials in status and power are legitimated and perpetuated by society's institutions and ideological systems in the form of structural or institutional stigma (e.g., Link & Phelan, 2001). Structural stigma "is formed by sociopolitical forces and represents the policies of private and governmental institutions that restrict the opportunities of stigmatized groups" (Corrigan et al., 2005, p. 557). An example is institutional racism (Carmichael & Hamilton, 1967), that is, "accumulated institutional practices that work to the disadvantage of racial minority groups even in the absence of individual prejudice or discrimination" (Link & Phelan, 2001, p. 372).

Similarly, the power differential at the heart of sexual stigma is perpetuated by structural sexual stigma, which is referred to here as *heterosexism*. By embedding sexual stigma in society's institutions – including religion, the law, and medicine – heterosexism ensures that sexual minority individuals have less power than heterosexuals. It accomplishes this through at least two general processes. First, it promotes a heterosexual assumption (i.e., all people are presumed to be heterosexual) which renders gay, lesbian, and bisexual people invisible in most social situations. Second, when sexual differences become visible, heterosexism perpetuates the assumption that heterosexuals, heterosexual behavior, and different-sex relationships are normal and natural, whereas nonheterosexuals, homosexual behavior, and same-sex relationships are abnormal and unnatural and, therefore, inferior. Heterosexuals are regarded as prototypical members of the category *people*, whereas homosexuals and bisexuals are considered deviants and thus require explanation (Hegarty & Pratto, 2004). This deviant status serves to legitimate hostility, discrimination, and even aggression against sexual minorities (for a more detailed discussion of heterosexism in religion, law, and medicine, see Herek et al., 2007).

Heterosexism serves as the foundation and backdrop for individual manifestations of sexual stigma. The present chapter focuses principally on three such manifestations (a) individual behaviors that express stigma, (b) individuals' awareness of stigma and its consequences, and (c) individuals' acceptance of stigma's legitimacy, whether it is aimed at them or at others. These manifestations – labeled *enacted stigma, felt stigma*, and *internalized stigma*, respectively – are each discussed now.

Enacted Stigma

In his classic work on prejudice, Allport (1954) described a continuum of negative actions through which prejudice might be expressed, ranging from antilocution through avoidance, discrimination, and physical attack, and culminating in extermination of the outgroup. Consistent with Allport's conceptualization, sexual stigma is overtly expressed through actions ranging from antigay comments and the use of antigay epithets, to shunning and ostracism of sexual minority individuals, to overt discrimination and violence. In some societies during certain historical eras, such as twentieth century Nazi Germany, state-sponsored persecution and violence has resulted in the imprisonment and death of many sexual minority individuals (Micheler, 2002).

Although most enactments of stigma target sexual minority individuals, some are directed at the friends and family members of sexual minorities, and at "allies," that is, heterosexuals who take a public stand against sexual stigma. Such individuals experience stigma by association – what Goffman (1963) called a *courtesy stigma* – because of their connections with sexual minorities (Neuberg, Smith, Hoffman, & Russell, 1994; Sigelman, Howell, Cornell, Cutright, & Dewey, 1991). Moreover, because of sexual orientation's concealability, any heterosexual can be mistakenly labeled homosexual or bisexual. Thus, everyone is potentially vulnerable to enactments of sexual stigma.

Violence is arguably the most extreme form taken by such enactments. Reflecting the hegemony of sexual stigma in the United States, violent victimization was long considered the inevitable price that homosexual people paid when they became visible to heterosexuals. Perpetrators were rarely arrested or prosecuted. Indeed, victims were routinely blamed for having invited their attacks (Herek & Berrill, 1992). In the 1980s, however, the gay community allied itself with the civil rights, feminist, and crime victim movements to challenge the legitimacy of this worldview. Community advocates had considerable success in arguing that antigay attacks – like other instances of murder, assault, robbery, and vandalism – should rightly be regarded as crimes and that blame and punishment should be directed at the perpetrators, not the victims (Herek & Sims, 2008).

In response, policymakers began to redefine antigay violence in the 1980s, recognizing it as a social problem (Jenness & Grattet, 2001). Antigay attacks came to be included under the general rubric of *hate crimes*, which are commonly defined as criminal actions intended to inflict physical injury, property damage, or emotional suffering because of the victim's perceived race, sexual orientation, religion, or other comparable group membership (Herek, 1989; Levin & McDevitt, 1993). One important outcome of this effort was the enactment of the 1990 Hate Crimes Statistics Act (Public Law 101–275, 104 Stat. 140), which directed the federal government to collect statistics on hate crimes based on race, ethnicity, religion, and sexual orientation.

Between 1991 and 2004, the FBI recorded more than 14,800 incidents based on sexual orientation, representing approximately 17,000 victims. In any given year, sexual orientation incidents have comprised about 11–17% of all bias crimes reported to the FBI (Herek & Sims, 2008). However, these figures under-state the true incidence of antigay crimes because reporting by law enforcement agencies is voluntary and the quality of data varies widely from one jurisdiction to another. In addition, many victims never report their experiences to the police because they fear further harassment or believe that their assailants will never be apprehended (Herek, Cogan, & Gillis, 2002). Data from the National Crime Victimization Survey (NCVS) indicate that only about 42% of hate crime inci-dents motivated by the victim's perceived sexual orientation were reported to police authorities from July 2000 to December 2003 (Herek & Sims, 2008; Harlow, 2005). Using NCVS data, the Bureau of Justice Statistics estimated that more than 37,800 hate crime victimizations motivated by the victim's sexual orientation occurred in the United States during that period – considerably more than the FBI has recorded since the Hate Crimes Statistics Act was first enacted. These incidents constituted roughly 18% of all hate crime victimizations recorded by the NCVS (Harlow, 2005).

Estimates of the prevalence of hate crime experiences in the sexual minority population have typically utilized data from samples recruited through commu-nity groups and venues (Berrill, 1992; D'Augelli & Grossman, 2001; D'Augelli, Grossman, & Starks, 2006; Herek, Gillis, & Cogan, 1999; Huebner, Rebchook, & Kegeles, 2004; Pilkington & D'Augelli, 1995). These studies have demonstrated that victimization is widespread but, because they used convenience samples, the extent to which their results are generalizable cannot be determined. Population prevalence can be estimated, however, from a recent study reporting data from a national probability sample of self-identified lesbian, gay, and bisexual adults (Herek, in press). In that sample (N=662), 13% of the respondents had experi-enced violence against their person based on their sexual orientation at least once during their adult life, and 15% had experienced a property crime. Approximately 1 in 5 reported experiencing one or both types of crime. Gay men were signifi-cantly more likely than other respondents to report having been the victim of antigay violence (25%) and property crimes (28%). In all, about 38% of gay men reported experiencing one or both types of crimes, compared to 13% of lesbians, 11% of bisexual men, and 13% of bisexual women (Herek, in press).

Hate crime victimization exacts a serious toll. In addition to physical harm, hate crimes appear to inflict greater psychological trauma on victims than other kinds of violent crime. In one study, gay men and lesbians who had experienced a crime against their person based on their sexual orientation manifested significantly higher levels of anxiety, anger, depressive symptoms, and traumatic stress symptoms com-pared to lesbians and gay men who had experienced comparable crimes during the same time period that were unrelated to their sexual orientation (Herek et al., 1999). Other studies have similarly found that sexual minority victims of hate crimes have elevated levels of psychological distress (Mills et al., 2004; Szymanski, 2005).

In addition to violence, members of sexual minority groups routinely encounter other forms of enacted stigma because of their sexual orientation. In the previously cited national survey, for example, 13% of respondents reported having objects thrown at them because of their sexual orientation, 23% had been threatened with violence, and 49% had experienced verbal abuse (Herek, in press). As with criminal assault and property crimes, gay men were the group most likely to report such attacks: 21% had objects thrown at them, 35% had been threatened, and 63% had experienced verbal abuse. In addition, 11% of respondents had experienced housing or employment discrimination because of their sexual orientation. Such discrimination was significantly more likely to be experienced by gay men and lesbians (reported by 18% and 16%, respectively) compared to bisexual men and women (reported by 4% and 7%, respectively).

Felt Stigma

As used here, felt stigma refers to an individual's expectancies about the probability that stigma will be enacted in different situations and under various circumstances. Felt stigma is based on an awareness of the existence of sexual stigma and beliefs about how and when society condones its enactment. Because individuals are motivated to avoid being the target of stigma enactments, this awareness often affects behavior. The pervasiveness of sexual stigma in the United States, coupled with the fact that everyone is a potential target, means that virtually all Americans experience some degree of felt sexual stigma, regardless of their own sexual orientation.

Scambler and Hopkins (1986) proposed that the emotion of fear underlies felt stigma. Whereas fear may indeed be a common response to the anticipation of enacted stigma, such an expectation might more usefully be considered a potential stressor that can elicit various emotional responses in different individuals and situations. Conceptualized as a potential stressor, felt stigma can be understood in terms of psychological theories of stress and coping (Lazarus & Folkman, 1984; Meyer, 2003; Miller & Major, 2000). From this perspective, felt stigma is seen as stimulating an individual to make ongoing appraisals of the possibilities for stigma enactments in social situations. This process includes appraising both the threat posed by the situation and the options and resources available for avoiding harm. If a situation is evaluated as stressful – that is, if the threat exceeds the individual's available resources for responding to it – the individual engages in some form of coping behavior.

Past accounts of felt stigma have generally focused on how it motivates stigmatized individuals to engage in preemptive, protective coping to avoid situations in which stigma enactments are possible (Scambler, 1989; Scambler & Hopkins, 1986). Such behaviors include, for example, attempting to pass as a member of the nonstigmatized majority and isolating oneself from that majority. To the extent that individuals accurately assess the likelihood of stigma enactments in their social environment, such coping strategies can reduce their risks for discrimination and attack. In this sense, felt stigma can lead to highly adaptive behavior. However, trying to avoid stigma can also significantly disrupt one's life, restrict one's options, and heighten one's psychological distress (Herek, 1996; Lewis, Derlega, Griffin, & Krowinski, 2003).

Moreover, whereas instances of enacted stigma might occur relatively infrequently, felt stigma may be experienced by the stigmatized on a continuing basis. Thus, it can play a more pervasive role in shaping their daily lives.[2]

One way to operationally define felt stigma is to ask sexual minority group members about their expectations that nonheterosexual individuals will encounter discrimination or differential treatment in various situations. When questions of this type were posed in the previously cited national survey of lesbian, gay, and bisexual adults (Herek, in press), most respondents manifested some degree of felt stigma. More than one-third agreed with the statement, "Most people where I live think less of a person who is [gay/lesbian/bisexual]."[3] About one-fourth *disagreed* that "Most employers where I live will hire openly [gay/lesbian/bisexual] people if they are qualified for the job." Roughly 40% agreed that "Most people where I live would *not* want someone who is openly [gay/lesbian/bisexual] to take care of their children." Overall, 55% of respondents gave at least one response symptomatic of felt stigma.

Felt stigma can also be observed in the phenomenon of stereotype threat (Steele & Aronson, 1995). As with other stigmatized groups, when sexual minority individuals find themselves in situations that make stereotypes about their group salient, their performance can be impaired. For example, the stereotype that gay men (and, to a lesser extent, lesbians) prey on children has been widespread in the United States at least since the World War II era (Chauncey, 1993; Freedman, 1989). Although most heterosexual Americans today do not believe that gay men and women are child molesters (Herek, 2002a), the stereotype continues to be invoked in antigay discourse (e.g., Family Research Institute, 2006, "Molestation and Incest" section). It also can still play a role in felt stigma, as illustrated by a study comparing childcare skills among gay and heterosexual men (Bosson, Haymovitz, & Pinel, 2004). In that experiment, independent raters judged the gay men as displaying somewhat better childcare skills overall than the heterosexual men. However, the subgroup of gay men whose sexual orientation had been made salient to them prior to the task performed more poorly than did other gay men, and this difference was due mainly to the former group's higher levels of nonverbal anxiety during the interaction. The researchers concluded that making the gay men's sexual orientation salient increased stereotype threat for them, and subsequently had negative effects on their performance in the child care task (Bosson et al., 2004).

---

[2] Felt stigma can be distinguished from stigma consciousness, which refers to the extent to which stigmatized individuals are chronically self-conscious of their own stigmatized status and expect to be stereotyped by others because of it (Pinel, 1999). Stigma consciousness can be understood as a manifestation of felt stigma, but the latter construct more broadly encompasses awareness of the general effects of stigma — enacted not only against oneself but also against others who manifest the stigmatized characteristic. In addition, felt stigma is experienced by nonstigmatized individuals as well as the stigmatized.

[3] The item wording matched the respondent's preferred self-label.

In response to felt stigma, many sexual minority individuals carefully manage information about themselves in order to prevent potential attackers from knowing about their sexual orientation (Herek, 1996). This coping strategy can lead them to chronically conceal their sexuality, a policy with significant costs. Keeping one's sexual orientation a secret involves constant effort and vigilance. It requires the individual to lead a kind of double life and often interferes with normal social interaction, thereby reducing her or his opportunities for social support (Herek, 1996). Passing as heterosexual also utilizes cognitive resources, which may make the secret chronically salient and have a negative impact on well-being (Pachankis, 2007; Smart & Wegner, 2000; see also Lewis, Derlega, Clarke, & Kuang, 2006). These factors help to explain why concealment of one's gay identity has been linked to psychological distress and health problems whereas being out of the closet has been found to correlate with positive psychological and physical states (Cole, 2006; Morris, Waldo, & Rothblum, 2001; Strachan, Bennett, Russo, & Roy-Byrne, 2007; Ullrich, Lutgendorf, & Stapleton, 2003; but see Frable, Wortman, & Joseph, 1997). Thus, although concealing one's sexual orientation can protect an individual from experiencing enacted stigma, it also creates stress and may have deleterious effects on psychological and physical well-being.

For heterosexuals, sexual stigma tends not to be salient unless sexual orientation becomes personally relevant, as when they knowingly encounter a gay, lesbian, or bisexual person, or in situations where their own sexual orientation might be questioned. On those occasions, felt stigma can motivate them to ensure that their non-stigmatized status is readily evident to others, thereby avoiding the possibility that they will be inaccurately perceived as stigmatized (and hence become a target of enacted stigma).

Like sexual minority individuals, heterosexuals acquire the knowledge and expectations that constitute felt stigma during childhood and adolescence as they learn peer group attitudes toward homosexuality (Phoenix, Frosh, & Pattman, 2003; Poteat, Espelage, & Green, 2007). During this time, the negative consequences of being labeled a homosexual are often forcefully demonstrated to them (Poteat & Espelage, 2007; Smith, 1998). Self-presentation strategies become especially important for males, who are continually called upon to affirm their heterosexual masculinity (Herek, 1986). The pervasive threat of physical, social, and psychological punishment for transgressing sex and gender boundaries pressures men to monitor their own actions for tell-tale signs of effeminacy (Plummer, 2006), and can lead them to enact sexual stigma against others to prove to their peers that they are "real men" (Kimmel, 1997).

It can also have more subtle influences on behavior. For example, whereas American children frequently touch others of their same sex, adults are much more likely to touch different-sex adults than same-sex adults during public interactions (Major, Schmidlin, & Williams, 1990). Indeed, heterosexual men, especially those with strongly hostile attitudes toward homosexuality, tend not to touch their male friends in a manner more intimate than a handshake (Roese, Olson, Borenstein, Martin, & Shores, 1992), perhaps because such touching might cause one to be perceived as homosexual (Derlega, Lewis, Harrison, Winstead, & Costanza, 1989). Heterosexuals, especially men, may also be deterred from engaging in behaviors that could cause them to be labeled homosexual or gay, even when those behaviors might be psychologically beneficial (Bosson, Prewitt-Freilino, & Taylor, 2005; Bosson, Taylor, & Prewitt-Freilino, 2006).

Internalized Stigma

Internalization is the process whereby individuals adopt a social value, belief, regulation, or prescription for conduct as their own and experience it as a part of themselves (e.g., Kelman, 1961; Ryan & Connell, 1989). Thus, internalized stigma refers to an individual's personal acceptance of stigma as a part of her or his own value system and self-concept. When someone internalizes stigma, she or he embraces society's denigration and discrediting of the stigmatized group. Internalized stigma contrasts to felt stigma, which is all about one's awareness of social norms and expectations that stigma will be enacted but which does not necessarily reflect an individual's own attitudes.

The construct of internalized stigma has sometimes been subsumed under the definition of felt stigma. Writing about people with epilepsy, for example, Scambler and Hopkins (1986) proposed that "felt stigma refers principally to the fear of enacted stigma, but also encompasses a feeling of shame associated with being epileptic" (Scambler & Hopkins, 1986, p. 33). Such a "feeling of shame" is a manifestation of what is here labeled internalized stigma. Differentiating internalized from felt stigma is warranted for at least two reasons. First, the constructs are logically separable: An individual can recognize the imminent threat of an enactment of stigma in a particular situation without believing it is justified. Second, as explained later, internalized stigma can be usefully conceptualized as a phenomenon that is experienced by the nonstigmatized as well as the stigmatized. The social and psychological processes associated with the internalization of stigma differ between these two groups.

Self-Stigma

When a stigmatized individual's self-concept is congruent with the stigmatizing responses of society, the result is *self-stigma* (Corrigan & Watson, 2002; Jones et al., 1984). For sexual minorities, self-stigma involves accepting society's negative evaluation of homosexuality and consequently harboring negative attitudes toward oneself and one's own homosexual desires. Such attitudes may be manifested as a wish to renounce one's homosexuality and become heterosexual (e.g., Herek, Cogan, Gillis, & Glunt, 1998). Weinberg (1972) originally defined homophobia as encompassing self-stigma, which he labeled "internalized homophobia" (p. 83; see also Shidlo, 1994). According to Weinberg, "the person who from early life has loathed himself for homosexual urges arrives at this attitude by a process exactly like the one occurring in heterosexuals who hold the prejudice against homosexuals" (Weinberg, 1972, p. 74). This process, he explained, involves forming impressions about homosexuality in a cultural context that is "almost wholly derogatory" (p. 74).

Psychologists have often assumed that some degree of self-stigma is inevitable in members of socially marked groups. Writing about racial, ethnic, and religious minorities, for example, Allport (1954) observed that "since no one can be indifferent to the abuse and expectations of others we must anticipate that ego defensiveness will frequently be found among members of groups that are set off for ridicule, disparagement, and discrimination. It could not be otherwise" (Allport, p. 143; see also Major & Vick, 2005). Similarly, self-stigma has often been assumed to be virtually universal among sexual minorities, owing to the pervasiveness of sexual stigma. Writing about gay men, for example, Malyon (1981–1982) commented, "Since homophobic beliefs are a ubiquitous aspect of contemporary social mores and cultural attitudes, the socialization of the incipient homosexual individual nearly always involves an internalization of the mythology and opprobrium which characterize current social attitudes toward homosexuality" (Malyon, 1981–1982 p. 60, citation omitted).

Empirical research, however, indicates there is variability in the extent to which sexual minority individuals experience self-stigma related to their sexual orientation (e.g., Herek et al., 1998; Szymanski, Chung, & Balsam, 2001). Moreover, research on self-stigma among other minority groups suggests that it varies both among individuals and across situations (e.g., Crocker, 1999; Crocker & Major, 1989). Nevertheless, to the extent that it occurs in sexual minority individuals, sexual self-stigma – which has also been labeled *internalized heterosexism* (Szymanski & Chung, 2003a, b) and *internalized homonegativity* (Mayfield, 2001; Tozer & Hayes, 2004) – is generally considered maladaptive. It often has important negative consequences for one's physical and psychological well-being (Herek & Garnets, 2007; Meyer, 2003; Williamson, 2000).

Sexual Prejudice

As noted earlier, distinguishing between felt and internalized stigma permits consideration of the internalization of stigma by members of the nonstigmatized majority. Just as the internalization of societal stigma is manifested among the stigmatized as negative attitudes toward the self, so it is manifested among members of the nonstigmatized majority in the form of negative attitudes toward the stigmatized, that is, prejudice. Thus, *sexual prejudice* is internalized sexual stigma that results in the negative evaluation of sexual minorities.[4]

---

[4] Although sexual prejudice is typically manifested by heterosexuals, it is also possible for sexual minority individuals to hold negative attitudes toward other gay, lesbian, and bisexual people. As with prejudiced heterosexuals, these attitudes result from the internalization of sexual stigma. Such attitudes are often closely associated with self-stigma. In addition, some sexual minority individuals harbor negative attitudes toward heterosexuals. These attitudes can be appropriately labeled sexual prejudice but, because heterosexuality is not a stigmatized category in society, such prejudice does not reflect the internalization of societal stigma (for further discussion of this point, see Herek, 2007).

Sexual prejudice is conceptualized here as an *attitude*, that is, a category-based evaluative tendency to respond to individuals or groups according to their perceived sexual orientation (Albarracin, Zanna, Johnson, & Kumkale, 2005; Eagly & Chaiken, 1993). In contemporary social psychological theory, attitudes are understood as psychological entities based on information derived from behaviors, beliefs, and affect. Attitudes can both influence and be inferred from those three sources, but nevertheless are distinguishable from them (e.g., Albarracin et al.; Fabrigar, MacDonald, & Wegener, 2005; Haddock, Zanna, & Esses, 1993).

In practice, such distinctions can be difficult to make because expressions of particular beliefs, affects, and behaviors can themselves serve as symbolic expressions of attitudes. For example, negative *behaviors* toward sexual minority individuals (i.e., stigma enactments) are often motivated by prejudice (e.g., Bernat, Calhoun, Adams, & Zeichner, 2001; Parrott & Zeichner, 2005; San Miguel & Millham, 1976), but this is not always the case. Some heterosexuals who perpetrate antigay hate crimes nevertheless express favorable attitudes toward gay people as a group (Franklin, 1998), and most heterosexuals who hold negative attitudes toward sexual minorities never commit acts of antigay violence. As in other domains (Ajzen & Fishbein, 2005), patterns of antigay behavior are likely to be correlated with sexual prejudice, but only moderately so (Franklin, 2000; Patel, Long, McCammon, & Wuensch, 1995; Roderick, McCammon, Long, & Allred, 1998).[5]

Similarly, beliefs about sexual minorities are correlated with sexual prejudice but are distinct from it. Discussions of beliefs as the cognitive sources of attitudes usually focus on stereotypes. Broadly speaking, stereotypes result from normal processes of cognitive categorization and can be relatively benign. Malevolent stereotypes, however, such as the previously mentioned stereotype of gay men as child molesters, figure prominently in sexual prejudice (Simon, 1998). Belief in such stereotypes fuels sexual prejudice in some individuals while providing others with a means for justifying their preexisting antipathy toward sexual minorities. Prejudice impairs heterosexuals' ability to suppress stereotypical thoughts about sexual minorities (Monteith, Spicer, & Tooman, 1998). It can bias their perceptions of sexual minority individuals and influence their assimilation of new information about the group, which can perpetuate their stereotypical beliefs (e.g., Munro & Ditto, 1997; Sherman, Stroessner, Conrey, & Azam, 2005). Even when heterosexuals perceive intragroup variability among sexual

---

[5] Data from a heterosexual undergraduate student sample (described later and in the Appendix) illustrate this point. Respondents were asked to indicate how often they had engaged in each behavior on a list of 16 different acts. The list included 7 positive behaviors (e.g., "I started a conversation with a man whom I thought might be gay," "I confronted someone who was making negative comments or hostile jokes about lesbians") and 9 negative behaviors (e.g., "I damaged the property of a man I thought was gay," "I made unfriendly remarks or hostile jokes about lesbians"), which were summed separately to yield an index of Positive Behaviors Toward Gay Men (or Lesbians) and an index of Negative Behaviors Toward Gay Men (or Lesbians). Overall, moderate correlations were observed between the behavior scales and the Attitudes Toward Gay Men (ATG) and Attitudes Toward Lesbians (ATL) scales. For the ATG, $r(105) = -0.41$ with positive behaviors toward gay men and 0.41 for negative behaviors toward gay men. For the ATL, $r(120) = -.38$ for positive behaviors toward lesbians. The correlation between ATL scores and negative behaviors toward lesbians could not be interpreted because most respondents (57%) reported never having engaged in such behaviors.

minorities, they may assimilate it into stereotypical subgroups, e.g., groups that are cognitively organized in terms of their conformity to traditional gender roles, such as leathermen vs. drag queens (Clausell & Fiske, 2005). In addition to stereotypes, other beliefs about stigmatized groups also contribute to prejudice. For example, prejudiced heterosexuals may harbor the belief that sexual minorities endorse values that conflict with their own (Esses, Haddock, & Zanna, 1993; Haddock et al., 1993).

As with behaviors and beliefs, sexual prejudice is related to but distinct from negative affect toward sexual minorities (see generally Cottrell & Neuberg, 2005; Clore & Schnall, 2005; Mackie, Devos, & Smith, 2000). However, sexual prejudice and negative emotional reactions to sexual minorities are sometimes equated. Indeed, the presumption that sexual prejudice is rooted in the emotion of fear is inherent in the construct of homophobia (Weinberg, 1972) and some widely used measures of sexual prejudice are framed primarily in terms of affect (e.g., Ricketts & Hudson, 1998). Whereas attitudes have temporal stability and are focused on a specific object, however, emotions are ephemeral and need not be focused (Clore & Schnall, 2005). Moreover, heterosexuals' negative affect toward sexual minorities can have sources other than prejudice. For example, a heterosexual's discomfort about anticipated interactions with sexual minorities may reflect her or his anxiety about being in a novel social situation or fear of inadvertently behaving in a manner that is perceived as offensive (Hebl, Tickle, & Heatherton, 2000; Stephan & Stephan, 1985). Affective reactions to sexual minorities can form the basis for attitudes in some cases and may mediate the relationship between sexual prejudice and enactments of stigma (e.g., Parrott & Zeichner, 2005; Parrott, Zeichner, & Hoover, 2006) just as levels of sexual prejudice can moderate the affect that heterosexuals experience in response to interactions with sexual minorities (Blair, Park, & Bachelor, 2003).

Conceptualized as an attitude, sexual prejudice remains widespread in the United States. However, national survey data show that heterosexuals' attitudes toward homosexuality and toward lesbians and gay men have become less condemnatory and more accepting in recent years.[6] These trends are especially evident in patterns of responses to three questions that have been posed repeatedly in ongoing national surveys: the General Social Survey (GSS) question about homosexual behavior, the Gallup Poll question about homosexuality as an acceptable lifestyle, and the American National Election Studies (ANES) feeling thermometer question about "gays and lesbians."[7]

---

[6] My discussion in the present chapter focuses mainly on research that has employed explicit or direct measures of sexual prejudice. Some researchers have assessed heterosexuals' attitudes utilizing indirect measures, such as the Implicit Attitudes Test (e.g., Banse, Seise, & Zerbes, 2001; Dasgupta & Rivera, 2006; Gabriel, Banse, & Hug, 2007; Jellison et al., 2004; Rowatt et al., 2006; Steffens & Buchner, 2003). Although theoretical and methodological questions about such measures remain to be resolved (Arkes & Tetlock, 2004; Fazio & Olson, 2003), they hold promise for future research. A discussion of them, however, is beyond the scope of the present chapter.

[7] My discussion of polling data relies on my own examination of the data in publicly available archives (especially the Roper Center at the University of Connecticut), as well as the published sources cited here.

Since the early 1970s, GSS respondents have been asked whether sexual relations between two adults of the same sex are "always wrong, almost always wrong, wrong only sometimes, or not wrong at all." Between 1973 and 1993, they were considered "always wrong" by more than two-third of those surveyed. The proportion responding "never" or "only sometimes" wrong ranged around 20%. Beginning in 1993, however, the "always wrong" proportion began to decline, dropping to 54% in 1998 and remaining fairly stable since then (Loftus, 2001). Although a majority still regards homosexual behavior as wrong (57% in 2004), the trend clearly has been in the direction of less condemnation. This decline does not appear to be simply part of a general sexual permissiveness, as indicated by responses to two parallel GSS items that ask about premarital and extramarital sex. Condemnation of premarital sex has never been very strong and it remained fairly stable during the 1990s, ranging around 30%. And the proportion of respondents who considered extramarital relations always wrong remained high (close to 80%) even while condemnation of homosexual acts was declining. Thus, the decrease in moral condemnation for same-sex relations appears to reflect attitudes that are specific to homosexuality (Loftus, 2001).[8]

Gallup polls have assessed opinions about whether homosexuality should be considered an acceptable alternative lifestyle. Responses to this question between 1982 and 1992 indicated a roughly 3-to-2 ratio of "no" to "yes" responses. By a margin of 51–34%, respondents did not consider homosexuality an acceptable lifestyle in 1982. In 1992, the margin was 19 points (57–38%). During the late 1990s, however, the pattern began to reverse. In 1999, 50% considered homosexuality an acceptable lifestyle, compared to 46% who regarded it as unacceptable. By 2003, the acceptable-unacceptable gap had widened to 54–43%. Except for a brief reversal immediately after the US Supreme Court's 2003 *Lawrence v. Texas* ruling (when 49% of those surveyed felt that homosexuality was unacceptable, compared to 46% who felt it was acceptable), this pattern has held steady. In 2007, 57% of respondents considered homosexuality an acceptable lifestyle (Saad, 2007).

A third indicator of attitude trends comes from the ongoing ANES, whose participants rate political figures and social groups on "feeling thermometer" scales ranging from 0 (very cold or unfavorable feelings) to 100 (very warm or favorable feelings). In 1984, when the ANES first included a feeling thermometer referring to "gays and lesbians," the mean rating was 30. Thermometer scores have increased steadily since then, reaching an average of 39 in 1996, jumping to 48 in 2000 and remaining steady at 49 in 2004. Compared to the public's feelings toward other groups, "gays and lesbians" generally rank near the bottom of the list (Sherrill & Yang, 2000). In the 2004 ANES, for example, only illegal immigrants scored lower than gays and lesbians. Respondents felt warmer toward big business, unions, the

---

[8] The phrasing of the GSS question, which frames homosexual relations as wrong, might bias responses. In other surveys, however, responses to differently worded items about the morality of homosexual behavior have yielded similar findings. In Gallup polls between 2001 and 2007, for example, 49–55% of respondents believed that homosexual behavior is morally wrong, whereas 38–47% believed it is not morally wrong (Saad, 2007).

women's movement, and welfare recipients than they did toward gays and lesbians. It is also noteworthy that the number of respondents assigning gays and lesbians a zero – the coldest possible score – tends to be larger than for other groups. Most groups listed in the ANES receive zero ratings from no more than 1–2% of respondents. By contrast, about one-third of the 1984 and 1988 respondents gave gays and lesbians a zero (Sherrill & Yang, 2000). Since then, the proportion has dropped but it was still about 15% in 2004.

The ANES thermometer question asks simultaneously about respondents' feelings toward both gay men and lesbians, and it does not assess feelings toward bisexual men and women. In a 1999 national telephone survey, I asked participants to provide separate thermometer ratings for these four groups (Herek, 2002a). Consistent with the ANES data, overall ratings for the groups were in the mid- to high 40s, with ratings for bisexual men the lowest at 44. The aggregate ratings, however, obscure a gender difference in responses to the four groups. Heterosexual women rated bisexuals significantly less favorably than they rated homosexuals, regardless of gender, whereas heterosexual men rated sexual minority males less favorably than sexual minority females, regardless of whether the target was bisexual or homosexual. Thus, heterosexual men tended to respond to sexual minorities in terms of their gender, whereas heterosexual women tended to respond in terms of their orientation group, i.e., homosexual vs. bisexual (Herek, 2000b, 2002a). This pattern was also observed in the 2005 telephone survey data reported later.

In the national surveys described here, as well as in laboratory experiments and questionnaire studies with convenience samples, sexual prejudice has consistently been correlated with various demographic, psychological, and social variables. In contrast to heterosexuals with favorable attitudes toward gay people, those with high levels of sexual prejudice are more likely to be male, older, less educated, and residing in geographic regions where negative attitudes represent the norm (e.g., rural areas, the Midwestern or Southern United States). They are more likely to be highly religious, as indicated by their frequent attendance at religious services and the importance they attach to religion as a guide in their daily lives. Their religious beliefs are likely to be conservative or fundamentalist (e.g., as indicated by their belief in scriptural literalism). They are more likely to be a Republican than a Democrat or an Independent, and to describe themselves as politically conservative rather than liberal or moderate. They tend to display higher levels of psychological authoritarianism, less sexual permissiveness, and more traditional gender role attitudes. They are more likely to believe that a homosexual orientation is freely chosen and less likely to have close personal friends or family members who are openly lesbian or gay (for reviews, see Herek, 1984b, 1994; Loftus, 2001; Simon, 1998; Whitley & Lee, 2000). The limited data that are available suggest that heterosexuals' attitudes toward bisexual men and women manifest similar patterns of correlations (Herek, 2002b; Mohr & Rochlen, 1999).

A growing body of research addresses the situational and dispositional factors underlying sexual prejudice. A thorough review of this work is beyond the scope of the present chapter (for a more extensive discussion, see Herek, 2008), but it includes research examining the ways in which sexual prejudice is associated with religious and political values that are relevant to social identity (e.g., Batson, Floyd, Meyer, & Winner, 1999; Herek, 1987b; Jackson & Esses, 1997; Vescio & Biernat, 2003), adherence to gender roles and identity based on a heterosexual orientation (e.g., Jellison, McConnell, & Gabriel, 2004; Kilianski, 2003; Kite & Whitley, 1998), and perceived threats to self-esteem (e.g., Fein & Spencer, 1997; Meier, Robinson, Gaither, & Heinert, 2006).

One framework for understanding these sources of sexual prejudice is the functional theory of attitudes, which is based on the assumption that attitudes are formed and maintained because they serve one or more psychological needs for the individual (Katz, 1960; Maio & Olson, 2000; Smith, Bruner, & White, 1956). The function(s) served by an attitude can vary across situations and attitude objects, and among individuals. Thus, according to the functional approach, heterosexuals' attitudes toward lesbians and gay men are shaped by a combination of personal needs, situational factors, and perceptions of the cultural meanings attached to sexual minorities and to homosexuality. From a functional perspective, sexual prejudice provides a vehicle for some heterosexuals to affirm their self-concept as a religious and moral person, whereas it assists others by strengthening their bonds with valued groups, and still others in warding off threats to their self-esteem or in making sense of past experiences (e.g., Herek, 1987a, 2008).

Points of Connection: Intersections of Heterosexism and Sexual Prejudice

The foregoing conceptual framework is intended to facilitate the integration of sociocultural and individual perspectives in the study of phenomena related to sexual stigma. Using it as a foundation, in the remainder of the chapter I consider two points of intersection between sexual prejudice and cultural stigma. First, I explore how attitudes toward public policies related to sexual orientation can be understood as a domain in which sexual prejudice interacts with structural heterosexism. Then I consider how changes in sexual stigma and heterosexism during recent decades created conditions that have fostered reductions in sexual prejudice among key groups in society.

Public Policy Attitudes and Sexual Prejudice

Characterizing sexual prejudice as the internalization of sexual stigma might be misconstrued as implying that individuals are mere passive receptacles for cultural beliefs and norms concerning stigmatized conditions and groups. However, just as the stigmatized can accept or challenge their devalued status (Fine & Asch, 1988; Herek, 1996), so do the nonstigmatized play an active role in embracing or rejecting society's prescriptions for prejudice. In the social construction of stigma, meanings are attached to traits, characteristics, and group memberships not only by received tradition but also through ongoing social interaction.

The outcome of this process is perhaps most evident in individual attitudes toward stigmatized group members. But it can also be observed in majority group members' attitudes toward whether and how stigma should be embedded in society's institutions. Acting in concert, individuals can choose to reinforce and expand structural stigma, to abolish it entirely, or to allow it to persist unchanged. In the realm of law and public policy, such collective influence is strong in societies like the United States, where citizens can effect institutional change through both their elected representatives and mechanisms of direct democracy such as ballot initiatives and referenda.

Historically, when the public has directly participated in the policy process in the United States, as when gay rights legislation has been put to a popular vote, the outcome has usually been detrimental to sexual minorities (Haider-Markel, Querze, & Lindaman, 2007). For example, voters in many municipalities overturned antidiscrimination ordinances in the 1970s and 1980s, and Colorado voters enacted Amendment 2 in 1992, which banned such laws statewide (Donovan, Wenzel, & Bowler, 2000; Herman, 1997). More recently, individual voters' opposition to marriage equality has played a central role in fostering new forms of legislative heterosexism through the passage of state ballot initiatives prohibiting marriage between same-sex couples – and, in some cases, any legal recognition of same-sex relationships (e.g., Herek, 2006; Peterson, 2005). Nevertheless, an examination of recent opinion trends across a range of policy domains reveals a mix of pro- and antigay patterns, suggesting that the democratic process might also be used to restrict the scope of heterosexism in the law.[9]

In the realm of free speech, for example, the public has generally expressed a desire to respect basic civil liberties for sexual minorities. This is apparent in response trends for three GSS questions concerning willingness to grant basic rights to "a man who admits that he is a homosexual." Respondents are asked whether they would allow such a man to "make a speech in your community" or "teach in a college or university," and whether they would endorse the removal of "a book he wrote in favor of homosexuality" from the public library.[10] Even in 1973, responses to these items showed fairly strong support for First Amendment rights in connection with homosexuality. In that year, 61% would have allowed a homosexual man to speak, 47% would have allowed him to teach in a college, and 54% would have opposed censoring a book that he wrote in favor of homosexuality. By 2004, the proportions endorsing First Amendment rights regarding homosexuality had grown to 83% for speech, 79% for teaching, and 73% against library censorship.

Within the GSS, these three items are part of a series measuring general tolerance that also includes assessment of support for the free speech rights of groups

---

[9] Indeed, some antigay initiatives have been rejected by voters (e.g., Donovan et al., 2000).

[10] These questions are all framed in terms of granting civil liberties to a gay man. Because attitudes toward gay men often differ from attitudes toward lesbians (e.g., Herek, 2002a), it is conceivable that somewhat different patterns might emerge if the questions referred to a lesbian woman.

such as atheists, communists, and racists. When response patterns since the 1990s are compared, it is clear that tolerance has increased more rapidly for homosexuals than for the other target groups. By 2004, for example, when 83% would allow a homosexual man the right to give a speech, the proportions of respondents supporting a similar right for atheists, communists, and racists were 76%, 69%, and 62%, respectively. Analysis of trends indicates that the changes in attitudes toward civil liberties for a homosexual man are only partly explained by a general rise in public tolerance toward unpopular or stigmatized groups (Loftus, 2001).

By contrast, attitudes have fluctuated considerably in another domain of basic civil liberties – the right to private sexual conduct, as measured by responses to a Gallup poll item asking whether homosexual relations between consenting adults should or should not be legal (Saad, 2007). In 1977, respondents were evenly split, with 43% favoring legalization and 43% opposing it. By 1982, a plurality favored legalization (45–39%). During the mid-1980s, however, the trend sharply reversed. In 1986, for example, only 32% supported legalizing homosexual relations whereas 57% were opposed. During the 1990s, opinion fluctuated, with a plurality favoring legalization in 1992 (48–44%), but a similar plurality opposing it in 1996 (47–44%). In 1999, 50% favored legalization, compared to 43% who opposed it, and by the spring of 2003 the split had grown to 60% to 35%. In the immediate wake of the Supreme Court's 2003 *Lawrence v. Texas* ruling, responses indicated increased opposition to legalizing same-sex relations. But by May 2004, legalization was again favored by a majority (52%). In 2007, 59% said consenting homosexual relations should be legal, roughly the same proportion as immediately prior to the 2003 *Lawrence* ruling. Thus, a majority support sexual privacy rights although responses to this question have been volatile, especially during the early years of the AIDS epidemic in the 1980s and immediately after Supreme Court rulings on the constitutionality of sodomy laws (i.e., *Bowers v. Hardwick*, 1986; *Lawrence et al. v. Texas*, 2003).

Moving from the domain of basic civil liberties and freedoms to that of equal rights, general support for equality in job opportunities has increased steadily and dramatically. In Gallup polls, for example, the proportion endorsing equal employment rights has grown from 56% in 1977 to 89% in 2007 (Saad, 2007). Support for employment equality has been somewhat less enthusiastic when questions are asked about specific occupations (e.g., clergy, military personnel, doctors) but the trend nevertheless has been toward steadily increasing support, and clear majorities now support equal rights in all of these sectors. One remarkable change has been in the proportion of Americans who feel homosexuals should be hired as elementary school teachers, which grew from 27% in 1977 to 54% in 2005 (Saad, 2005). Consistent with this trend, polls by the Pew Research Center for the People and the Press show that the proportion of US adults who *disagreed* that school boards should be able to fire "teachers who are known homosexuals" rose from 42 to 62% between 1987 and 2003.

In contrast to its generally strong support for employment rights, the public has consistently opposed marriage equality for same-sex couples, although the opinion divide has narrowed during the 2000s. A 2007 Gallup poll found that 53% of respondents believed "marriages between same-sex couples" should not be "recognized by the law as valid, with the same rights as traditional marriages," whereas 46% believed such marriages should be valid. By comparison, marriage equality was opposed by a 62–35% majority in a 1999 Gallup poll (Saad, 2007). An August 2006 poll by the Pew Research Center found that 56% of respondents opposed "allowing gays and lesbians to marry legally," compared to 35% who supported marriage rights (Pew Research Center for the People and the Press, 2006).

Many individuals who oppose marriage equality are nevertheless supportive of civil unions and domestic partnerships, statuses that grant many of the same rights as marriage at the state government level. In most national surveys, when respondents who support full marriage equality are combined with those who support civil unions or their equivalent, the result is a majority of US adults supporting legal recognition of same-sex couples. In the 2004 November election exit polls, for example, 60% of voters supported some form of legal recognition for same-sex couples (Kohut, 2004). The August 2006 national survey of US adults by the Pew Center found that 54% favored allowing gay and lesbian couples to enter into legal agreements with each other that would give them many of the same rights as married couples (Pew Research Center for the People and the Press, 2006).

In summary, although sexual minorities have not usually benefited when popular opinion has been directly translated into public policy through the ballot box, the American public does not uniformly endorse the expression of sexual stigma through the law. The public strongly endorses basic civil liberties for sexual minorities, such as freedom of speech, and the principle of equal opportunity in employment has overwhelming support, although that support varies somewhat depending on the specific occupation in question. Opinion about the right to sexual privacy has fluctuated, but most of the public now opposes the criminalization of private consensual homosexual behavior. And whereas a majority of the public opposes marriage equality, most adults nevertheless favor some form of legal recognition for same-sex couples, e.g., through institutions such as civil unions.

Previous empirical research has often treated policy attitudes as direct expressions of an individual's level of sexual prejudice. Many attitude scales designed to measure sexual prejudice, for example, include questions about policies such as marriage laws, employment discrimination, or military personnel regulations. The high interitem correlations obtained in such scales confirm that policy attitudes and sexual prejudice are correlated. However, an argument can be made for distinguishing between attitudes toward sexual minorities as a group and attitudes toward policies affecting them.

For example, the GSS data show that much of the public condemns homosexual behavior as immoral while simultaneously endorsing civil liberties for homosexual men (see Loftus, 2001), suggesting that policy attitudes are independent of attitudes toward homosexuality to at least some extent. This distinction is inherent in the origins of the GSS questions about free speech rights. They were first conceptualized as measures of *tolerance* which, by definition, can be extended to members of a disliked group. Indeed, the true test of tolerance is whether one is willing to protect the civil liberties of groups whose conduct or ideas one dislikes (McClosky & Brill, 1983; Stouffer, 1955).

Further support for a distinction between prejudice and policy attitudes can be found in empirical research showing that heterosexuals' attitudes toward gay men and lesbians do not fully account for the variation in their attitudes toward policies implicating sexual minorities. Analyses of national survey data assessing attitudes toward various policy attitudes, for example, have shown that factors such as humanitarian values, concern about "big government," political ideology, and religiosity are important predictors of public opinion, independent of respondents' affective reactions to gay men and lesbians (Strand, 1998; see also Wood & Bartkowski, 2004). Thus, distinguishing empirically between heterosexuals' attitudes toward sexual minorities and their policy attitudes concerning sexual orientation has potential value for yielding a greater understanding of sexual prejudice and, perhaps, of the ways it affects heterosexism.

To explore this idea, I collected data to assess the strength of the association between sexual prejudice and policy attitudes, and to examine whether this relationship might vary depending on how sexual prejudice is measured. Furthermore, I investigated whether other relevant variables might explain variations in policy attitudes, after controlling for sexual prejudice. I analyzed data from two different samples: (a) a convenience sample of UC Davis undergraduates ($N=244$) and (b) a national probability sample of English-speaking US citizens at least 18 years old who participated in a 2005 telephone survey ($N=2,214$). (Methodological details and scale items are reported in the Appendix.)

Respondents completed three measures of sexual prejudice, including my own Attitudes Toward Lesbians and Gay Men (ATLG) scale which consists of the Attitudes Toward Lesbians (ATL) and Attitudes Toward Gay Men (ATG) subscales (Herek, 1994, 1998). The ATLG presents respondents with evaluative statements about lesbians and gay men, to which they indicate their agreement or disagreement using a Likert-type response scale. The ATLG's reliability and validity in both self-administered and interviewer-administered formats have been well established in numerous questionnaire and survey studies whose participants ranged from convenience samples of college students to national probability samples of adults (Herek, 1988, 2002a; Herek & Capitanio, 1999b; Herek & Gonzalez-Rivera, 2006). Although the original subscales consisted of only ten different items each, still shorter 3-item parallel versions have proved to be adequate for most purposes. In addition to their brevity, the parallel versions have the advantage of permitting direct comparison of each respondent's attitudes toward gay men and toward lesbians. They were used in the present study.[11]

---

[11] The items in the short form of the ATLG (as worded for the ATL subscale) are: (1) "Sex between two women is just plain wrong." (2) "I think female homosexuals (lesbians) are disgusting." (3) "Female homosexuality is a natural expression of sexuality in women."

The ATLG was developed on the basis of a series of factor analytic studies of responses to a large pool of attitude statements that included items from existing scales as well as newly constructed items (Herek, 1984a). Across multiple convenience samples, a single factor consistently accounted for a large portion of the variance in attitudes toward both lesbians and gay men for male and female respondents alike. This factor, labeled *Condemnation-Tolerance*, comprised statements characterizing homosexuality as unnatural, disgusting, perverse, sinful, a danger to society, and warranting negative social sanctions (Herek, 1984a). As suggested by the Condemnation-Tolerance label, the ATLG's operationalization of sexual prejudice fits squarely with the present chapter's definition of attitudes as an evaluative stance. Indeed, the items in the short versions of the ATL and ATG – which assess respondents' evaluation of homosexuality as wrong, unnatural, and disgusting – map onto key dimensions of a worldview hypothesized by Lakoff (2002) to underlie contemporary political attitudes in the United States.[12]

In addition to administering the ATLG, I collected information about the affective bases of respondents' attitudes using two different types of measures: feeling thermometers (with separate thermometers for lesbians and for gay men) and a measure of respondents' personal comfort or discomfort in social interactions with lesbians and with gay men. In the student sample, the latter construct was measured with a 10-item Social Discomfort Questionnaire (SDQ), with separate versions targeting situations involving lesbians (SDQ-L) and gay men (SDQ-G). In the national telephone survey, costs and time constraints prohibited administration of the full SDQs. Instead, single-item measures of discomfort about social contact with gay men or lesbians were administered to all respondents.

In the student sample, respondents were randomly assigned to complete either the gay male or lesbian version of all questionnaires. For each version, the sexual prejudice measures proved to be highly intercorrelated (for all coefficients, $p < 0.001$). For gay male targets ($n = 120$ respondents with complete data on all scales), the zero-order correlation between ATG scores and the gay male feeling thermometer was $r = -0.70$; between ATG scores and the SDQ-G, $r = 0.73$; between the gay male feeling thermometer and the SDQ-G, $r = -0.63$. For the measures targeting lesbians ($n = 123$ respondents with complete data for all scales), the correlations were $r = -0.64$ (ATL with thermometer), $r = 0.77$ (ATL with SDQ-L), and $r = -0.63$ (thermometer with SDQ-L).

---

[12] Although the ATLG scale predates Lakoff's analysis, the scale items coincide with key constructs in what Lakoff labeled "strict father morality," a moral system that invokes a mythic model of the family and underlies modern conservative politics (Lakoff, 2002, p. 65). According to his analysis, this system of moral thought is based on multiple metaphors, including moral order (which posits a dominance hierarchy of God over people, adults over children, and men over women), moral boundaries (which delineate permissible and impermissible ranges of behavior), and moral purity (which designates violations of morality as impure and thus tainted and corrupting). According to Lakoff, challenges to the moral order are understood as wrong, transgressions of moral boundaries are regarded as unnatural, and moral impurities are viewed as disgusting.

Table 1 Zero-order correlations among measures of reactions to lesbians and gay men (national sample)

	ATG	ATL	Gay male thermometer	Lesbian thermometer	Discomfort: Gay men
ATL	.80				
Gay Male Thermometer	−.59	−.54			
Lesbian Thermometer	−.54	−.58	.89		
Discomfort around gay men	.60	.53	−.57	−.51	
Discomfort around lesbians	.46	.55	−.43	−.49	.60

Note: $N \geq 1{,}835$ for all paired variables. For ATG and ATL scores, high scores = more prejudice. For thermometers, high scores = warmer, more favorable feelings. For discomfort variables, higher scores = greater discomfort. All coefficients are significant at $p < .001$

In the telephone sample, all respondents completed the sexual prejudice measures for both gay male and lesbian targets. As shown in Table 1, the correlations between different types of measures (e.g., ATG vs. thermometers) tended to be of lower magnitude than among the students, ranging from $r=0.43$ to $r=0.60$.

In addition to completing the sexual prejudice measures, respondents reported their attitudes toward different policies related to sexual orientation. The students completed three policy scales which assessed their support for or opposition to marriage equality for same-sex couples, allowing openly gay or lesbian personnel to serve in the military, and allowing sexual minorities to teach and care for children. For each student, the target of the policy attitude scales (lesbians or gay men) matched the target of the sexual prejudice measures they completed. Higher scores indicated greater opposition to sexual minority rights in each policy area. Respondents in the national sample were asked their opinions about passing a federal law to ensure that gay men and lesbians have equal rights in employment and allowing or forbidding marriage between two people of the same sex.

To examine the relationship between policy attitudes and sexual prejudice, I computed a series of ordinary least squares regression equations. For the student sample, Table 2 reports the unstandardized regression coefficients (which permit comparisons of each independent variable's contribution across policy issues and targets) and proportion of unique variance explained by each variable (which permits comparisons among variables within each policy issue and target), as well as the total variance explained by the sexual prejudice measures and by all variables included in the equations. To facilitate interpretation of the OLS regression results, the ATG and ATL scores, thermometer scores, and SDQ scores were all recoded to range from 0 to 1.

In combination, the sexual prejudice measures explained substantial portions of variation in each policy domain, ranging from 17.4% for military service by lesbians, to 65.7% for marriage equality for gay men. Examination of the unique variance associated with each aspect of sexual prejudice reveals that the measures were differentially related to the various policy attitudes in this sample. As shown in the first three rows of Table 2, ATG scores accounted for substantial portions of

Table 2 OLS regression analyses: sexual prejudice and value variables as predictors of policy attitudes (student sample)

Independent variable	Marriage equality (ME)		Military personnel policy (MPP)		Childcare and peaching policy (CTP)	
	Gay men	Lesbians	Gay men	Lesbians	Gay men	Lesbians
ATG/ATL	3.97^c (.096)	3.57^c (.048)	2.08^a (.036)	0.40 (.001)	1.68^b (.035)	1.04 (.007)
SDQ	1.87^b (.019)	1.74 (.009)	0.74 (.004)	2.34 (.021)	1.85^b (.038)	4.20^c (.091)
Thermometer	0.02 (.000)	−1.27 (.007)	−1.10 (.012)	−0.63 (.002)	−1.09^a (.017)	0.06 (.000)
Total R^2 (all sexual prejudice variables)	.657^c	.619^c	.301^c	.174^c	.540^c	.530^c
Protestant Ethic	0.44 (.008)	0.43 (.006)	−0.20 (.002)	−0.63 (.017)	−0.25 (.005)	0.48 (.013)
Humanitarianism	−0.18 (.001)	−0.63^a (.016)	0.05 (.000)	−0.91^a (.040)	−0.71^b (.040)	−0.42 (.012)
Political Ideology (High = conservative)	0.29^b (.021)	0.32^a (.015)	0.05 (.001)	0.27 (.015)	−0.06 (.002)	0.13 (.004)
Religiosity (High = more religious)	0.40^c (.031)	0.22 (.008)	0.36^a (.034)	−0.21 (.010)	0.25^a (.024)	0.01 (.000)
Total R^2 (all variables)	.746^c	.708^c	.340^c	.287^c	.599^c	.577^c

For each independent variable, the table reports the unstandardized regression coefficient and, in parentheses, the unique R^2 associated with that variable. Higher scores on the ME, MPP, and CTP scales reflect attitudes opposing pro-gay or pro-lesbian policies. Scores for the feeling thermometers, ATG/ATL, and SDQ measures were all transformed to a 0–1 scale. For feeling thermometers, high scores indicate warmer, more favorable feelings. For the ATG/ATL and SDQ measures, higher scores indicate more prejudice or greater discomfort.

[a] $p < .05$; [b] $p < .01$; [c] $p < .001$.

unique variance in all three policy realms, whereas ATL scores were significant only in predicting marriage equality attitudes. Social discomfort played an important role in predicting attitudes toward gay male and lesbian teachers, whereas feeling thermometer scores accounted for at least 1% of unique variance for attitudes toward gay male military personnel and teachers.

Do factors other than sexual prejudice account for heterosexuals' policy attitudes? As shown in the remaining rows of Table 2, humanitarianism scores, self-rated political ideology, and religiosity (i.e., self-rated importance of religion as a guide in daily life) all contributed independently to policy attitudes, even when the effects of sexual prejudice were statistically controlled.

Similar patterns were observed in the national sample. Table 3 shows that, as in the student sample, the measures of sexual prejudice explained substantial proportions of the variance in policy attitudes: 14.3% for employment laws and 51.9% for marriage equality. Although they shared a considerable amount of variance, the sexual prejudice measures once again had differential predictive power. Attitudes toward marriage equality were predicted by both ATG and ATL scores, whereas employment nondiscrimination attitudes were predicted mainly by discomfort associated with gay men. Finally, as in the student sample, policy attitudes were not based solely on sexual prejudice. With reactions to sexual minorities statistically controlled, antigay policy attitudes were predicted significantly by nonegalitarianism, moral traditionalism, and political conservatism.

Table 3 OLS regression analyses: sexual prejudice and value variables as predictors of policy attitudes (national sample)

Independent variable	Employment nondiscrimination	Marriage equality
ATG	−0.19 (.001)	1.90ᶜ (.022)
ATL	0.29 (.003)	1.75ᶜ (.018)
Discomfort: Gay Men	0.44ᶜ (.012)	0.30 (.001)
Discomfort: Lesbians	0.22 (.003)	0.05 (.000)
Thermometer: Gay Male	−0.22 (.001)	−0.66 (.001)
Thermometer: Lesbian	0.13 (.000)	0.42 (.001)
Total R^2 (all sexual prejudice variables)	.143ᶜ	.519ᶜ
Egalitarianism/Nonegalitarianism (High = nonegalitarian)	0.36ᶜ (.017)	0.45ᵃ (.005)
Moral Traditionalism/Relativism (High = relativist)	−0.34ᶜ (.015)	−0.65ᶜ (.010)
Political Ideology (High = Conservative)	0.24ᵃ (.005)	0.65ᶜ (.007)
Religiosity	−0.05 (.000)	0.33 (.002)
Age	−0.00 (.000)	0.01ᵇ (.006)
Total R^2 (all variables)	.194ᶜ	.565ᶜ

For each independent variable, the table reports the unstandardized regression coefficient and, in parentheses, the proportion of unique R^2 explained by that variable. Higher scores indicate greater opposition to employment nondiscrimination laws and marriage equality. Scores for all independent variables except age were transformed to a 0-1 scale.
ᵃ$p < .05$; ᵇ$p < .01$; ᶜ$p < .001$.

The results indicate that although policy attitudes are highly correlated with sexual prejudice, they are distinct entities that are differentially associated with different aspects of sexual prejudice. Moreover, whereas sexual prejudice is an important predictor of policy attitudes, the latter are also shaped by political and moral attitudes and values.

These findings highlight the value of distinguishing between attitudes toward sexual minorities and attitudes toward policies that affect them. Whereas the former can be understood as the internalization of sexual stigma, the latter have other psychological roots as well, including political and religious values. In terms of the conceptual framework discussed in the present chapter, the data highlight the need for empirical research on how sexual prejudice influences heterosexism through public opinion, voting behavior, political advocacy, and other means.

In practical terms, the findings confirm the intuition that changes in sexual prejudice are likely to lead to changes in attitudes toward policies affecting sexual minorities. To the extent that policy attitudes have additional social psychological sources as well, however, they might be influenced by factors other than sexual prejudice. On the one hand, this suggests that eradicating sexual prejudice will not necessarily lead to an immediate end to heterosexism insofar as the latter is perpetuated by the collective actions of individuals. On the other hand, some aspects of heterosexism (e.g., laws concerning employment discrimination) could be amenable to change even in the absence of a significant reduction in the heterosexual public's sexual prejudice. If these structural manifestations of stigma are perceived as intolerant, for example, public support for them might erode independent of changes in individual heterosexuals' prejudice.

Cultural Change and Reductions in Sexual Prejudice

In addition to asking how sexual prejudice might influence policy attitudes, it is also important to consider how events in society affect sexual prejudice. This final section of the chapter discusses how societal changes have created conditions that fostered a diminution of sexual prejudice in the United States in recent decades, with the trend toward greater tolerance and less hostility accelerating in the early 1990s.

Cultural Factors in Reducing Sexual Stigma

Using the vocabulary articulated earlier, trends in sexual prejudice over the past three decades are understood as a reflection of diminishing sexual stigma and an attendant weakening of structural heterosexism. Cultural shifts in stigma have facilitated individual attitude change, including reduced sexual prejudice among elites and opinion leaders, which, in turn, has fostered further erosion of heterosexism. These changes have come to be reflected in socialization processes, with the consequence that younger generations have different expectations, beliefs, and experiences about sexual orientation and sexual minorities, compared to their elders. Moreover, societal changes have created new linkages between sexual prejudice and social identities. For example, expressing antigay prejudice has come to play a central role in the identities of many religious conservatives whereas tolerance for sexual minorities has become part of the identities of many liberals, libertarians, and feminists. In this section, I briefly describe some of these changes and consider their implications for individual attitudes. Recognizing that change has not been uniform throughout society, my overall focus is on the ways in which sexual stigma has diminished and sexual prejudice has abated.

To begin, three societal trends since World War II created a context for reductions in sexual stigma (Page & Shapiro, 1992). First, Americans' average level of education rose steadily after World War II. Whereas fewer than 5% of adults older than 25 had completed 4 years of college in 1940, Census data show that the figure was more than 25% by 2000. There is a well-documented association between education and many varieties of tolerance (e.g., Bobo & Licari, 1989), including heterosexuals' attitudes toward sexual minorities (e.g., Herek, 1994; Loftus, 2001; Strand, 1998). Second, the civil rights movements of the 1950s and 1960s brought about dramatic changes in White Americans' attitudes toward racial and ethnic minority groups and in institutional expressions of racism. They also created a new consciousness about the negative consequences of prejudice and discrimination for minority groups in general. Third, during the 1960s and 1970s, the feminist movement fostered changes in public attitudes toward gender roles, while the development of new contraceptive technologies led to an increased freedom to engage in heterosexual sex without fear of pregnancy. During that era, Americans' belief in a basic right to sexual privacy was reinforced by a series of US Supreme Court decisions that established constitutional rights to use contraception (*Griswold et al. v. Connecticut*, 1965; *Eisenstadt v. Baird*, 1972) and to possess erotica for private use (*Stanley v. Georgia*, 1969), as well as a qualified right to terminate a pregnancy (*Roe et al. v. Wade*, 1973). Sexual expression was increasingly recognized as a legitimate concern and sexuality became an acceptable topic in public discourse.

The gay and lesbian movement arose against this backdrop. The emergence of visible homosexual communities in large urban centers after World War II made possible the rise of a gay culture and a nascent gay political movement in the 1950s, which exploded into the national gay liberation movement after the 1969 Stonewall riots (Adam, 1995; D'Emilio, 1983). Gay people increasingly came to be regarded as a quasiethnic minority group, rather than an aggregation of deviants, criminals, or psychopaths (Epstein, 1999). To the extent that gay and lesbian (and, eventually, bisexual) people were framed as a minority group, the heterosexual public was able to accommodate their critique of discrimination and demands for rights into a preexisting set of categories and values that had been shaped by earlier movements for civil rights for racial and ethnic minorities.

The removal of homosexuality from the American Psychiatric Association's *Diagnostic and Statistical Manual of Mental Disorders* in 1973 was a signal event for the new movement (Bayer, 1987; Minton, 2002). Until then, heterosexism rested on homosexuality's tripartite condemnation as a sin, a crime, and a sickness. When mental health professionals and behavioral scientists concluded that homosexuality is not a mental illness, a principal institutional support for legitimizing sexual stigma vanished. This turnabout has had important consequences for shaping public opinion about homosexuality (Zaller, 1992).

Nevertheless, gay rights were still widely regarded as a "fringe" issue in the 1970s. However, a conservative antigay backlash – signaled by the success of Anita Bryant's 1977 "Save Our Children" campaign in overturning a Dade County (FL) gay rights law – had the ironic effect of convincing many heterosexuals that gay people needed support because they were being persecuted by religious and political conservatives. Gay rights increasingly came to be seen as a legitimate political concern by liberals, civil libertarians, feminists, and other critics of the newly influential Christian Right. In 1980, as conservative Christian influences were coming to dominate the Republican Party, the Democrats included a gay rights plank in their party platform (Adam, 1995; Epstein, 1999).

In 1981, the first cases of what would eventually be called Acquired Immunodeficiency Syndrome were reported among young gay men. The US AIDS epidemic was initially centered in the gay community, and AIDS provided a symbolic hook on which many opponents of gay rights hung their longstanding hostility toward nonheterosexuals (Herek & Capitanio, 1999a). The gay and lesbian community responded to AIDS by creating an extensive network of formal and informal caregiving groups and institutions, and by organizing to demand an effective government response to the health crisis while staving off the growing threats to its civil liberties. Many gay people came out to their heterosexual relatives and friends because of AIDS, either as a result of their own illness or as a political and existential response to the epidemic. Meanwhile, media coverage of the epidemic gave the gay community a more human face. It documented the rich and varied lives led by gay men with AIDS and depicted the devoted care they were receiving from their same-sex partners and their extended gay and lesbian families, often as their biological relatives rejected them because of their homosexuality. Thus, the epidemic forced many heterosexuals to think about gay men and lesbians in new ways that extended beyond sexuality: as members of their immediate family and friendship circles, coworkers, contributors to society, partners in relationships, and members of a besieged community. This more nuanced, individuated, and humanized way of perceiving gay people most likely played an important role in reducing heterosexuals' prejudice against them (Herek, 1997; see generally Levine, Nardi, & Gagnon, 1997).

These and related events had important consequences. They increased the overall visibility of gay men and lesbians and afforded them opportunities to publicly articulate an account of homosexuality that challenged previous religious, legal, and psychiatric discourses. Consequently, heterosexuals became newly aware of the presence of sexual minorities in many sectors of society and were exposed to new information that called into question the tenets of heterosexism. In addition, historical events created new opportunities for gay and bisexual people to organize politically and to form coalitions with other interest groups. As a result, sexual minority concerns came to be integrated into value systems such as liberalism, feminism, and civil libertarianism. Sexual tolerance and the renunciation of sexual stigma became hallmarks of the social identities associated with those value systems. Moreover, heterosexuals experienced new opportunities to have personal contact with openly gay men and lesbians.

The trend toward increased tolerance accelerated in the early 1990s, and at least three general factors probably spurred key groups of heterosexuals to change their attitudes and publicly declare their tolerance for sexual minorities around this time. First, events during the early 1990s increased the extent to which gay Americans were perceived as being under attack and thereby fostered greater sympathy for them. For example, many political moderates were disturbed by the escalating antigay discourse associated with the so-called culture wars in the 1992 Presidential campaign, as exemplified by speeches vilifying sexual minorities at the Republican national convention. State antigay ballot campaigns (e.g., in Oregon and Colorado) further identified nonheterosexuals as a persecuted minority and ultimately led to the US Supreme Court's 1996 *Romer v. Evans* decision, which marked a significant departure from the Court's previous hostility to the gay community as articulated in its 1986 *Bowers v. Hardwick* ruling (Herman, 1997; Keen & Goldberg, 1998). More generally, the increasing linkage of antigay politics to the Christian Right further solidified coalitions between gay people and pro-choice and feminist voters, civil libertarians, liberals, and like-minded others. The widespread visibility and concern afforded to antigay hate crimes further increased public sympathy for sexual minorities.

Second, the early 1990s saw an increase in public discussion of homosexuality as an inborn characteristic, spurred by several widely publicized scientific reports claiming to have found biological correlates of male sexual orientation (e.g., Hamer, Hu, Magnuson, Hu, & Pattatucci, 1993; LeVay, 1991). Among heterosexuals, the belief that homosexuality is innate is correlated with more favorable attitudes toward gay people and greater support for gay rights, whereas the belief that it is chosen is associated with sexual prejudice and opposition to gay rights (Haider-Markel & Joslyn, 2005; Herek & Capitanio, 1995; Whitley, 1990; Wood & Bartkowski, 2004). The psychological sources of this correlation are debatable (Hegarty, 2002; Hegarty & Golden, 2008), but attributions about the origin of sexual orientation clearly play an important role in justifying many heterosexuals' attitudes.

Third, major opinion leaders emerged as proponents of gay rights. Perhaps the most notable such figure in the early 1990s was President Bill Clinton. Although his term in office included enactment of legislation hostile to gay people – most notably the military's "Don't Ask, Don't Tell" policy and the Defense of Marriage Act – he was the first US President to align himself with the gay community and articulate a progay civil rights message.

The events described here signaled a significant erosion in sexual stigma's previously monolithic façade. They fostered a sea change in heterosexuals' perceptions of gay men and lesbians – and in the gay community's perceptions of itself – from the once prevalent view that homosexuals comprised a small, dysfunctional aggregation of isolated, mentally ill individuals to the widespread perception that gay people constitute a quasiethnic minority group whose members are valuable, contributing members of society. Changes in sexual prejudice at the individual level should be understood against this backdrop.

As a result of this shift in the cultural contours of sexual stigma, social norms have changed in many segments of society. Liberals, civil libertarians, feminists, and many who simply consider themselves fair-minded now perceive that sexual prejudice is incompatible with their personal value systems. Such individuals are likely to experience discomfort if they feel that their reactions to sexual minorities are inconsistent with their personal standards of being unprejudiced (Devine, Monteith, Zuwerink, & Elliot, 1991).

Social psychological research suggests that deeply rooted prejudices do not disappear simply because they are accompanied by inner conflicts and guilt (Devine, 2005). The mere experience of compunction in relation to prejudice is not always sufficient to overcome the entrenched habits of thinking that underlie it, and even heterosexuals who eschew prejudice against sexual minorities may have difficulty changing their negative attitudes (e.g., Devine, 1989; Monteith, Sherman, & Devine, 1998). This is because well-learned aspects of internalized stigma are manifested as immediate, reflexive responses to the stigmatized group (e.g., Pryor, Reeder, Yeadon, & Hesson-McInnis, 2004). These responses are largely automatic, although they can be subsequently overridden by more reflective, purposeful thought processes which enable the individual to refrain from applying stereotypes that have been activated (Devine, 1998; Kunda & Spencer, 2003). Over time, people can learn to suppress the activation of those stereotypes in the first place, especially if they have a strong intrinsic motivation to inhibit their ingrained prejudiced responses to outgroups (Dunton & Fazio, 1997; Plant & Devine, 1998; Ratcliff, Lassiter, Markman, & Snyder, 2006). Thus, individuals can learn how to be unprejudiced, provided they have sufficient motivation to do so.

What might motivate heterosexuals to disavow their sexual prejudice? In this regard, it is instructive to consider the experiences of many sexual minority individuals in overcoming their own internalization of sexual stigma. Because most children are raised with the expectation that they will be heterosexual, sexual stigma is internalized by many boys and girls who will eventually grow up to be gay, lesbian, or bisexual. Unlike heterosexuals, however, they experience a conflict between their negative view of homosexuality and their own sexual and romantic feelings. Successfully resolving this conflict requires that individuals reconcile their attitudes toward homosexuality with their experience of their own sexuality. Although this is fairly unproblematic for some, it is a challenging, slow, and painful process for many. They are motivated to get through it by their need for a positive and integrated sense of self (see generally Bieschke, Perez, & DeBord, 2006; Herek & Garnets, 2007).

Heterosexuals are unlikely to experience comparable conflicts about their sexuality as a result of sexual stigma. As noted earlier, however, they may be motivated to confront their own sexual prejudice if they experience it as inconsistent with their self concept. Such ego-dystonic prejudice may arise simply from an individual's perceived inconsistencies between her or his self-concept and attitudes. However, it seems especially likely among heterosexuals with a strong, positive emotional bond with a sexual minority person, especially a gay, lesbian, or bisexual close friend or family member. Because of the societal changes noted earlier, heterosexuals' opportunities for having such a relationship have expanded significantly. The implications of this development are considered next.

Personal Contact and Prejudice Reduction

Heterosexuals who personally know gay men or lesbians have been consistently found to express more accepting attitudes toward gay people as a group, compared to their counterparts lacking such contact (Herek & Capitanio, 1996; Lewis, 2006). In part, this association reflects gay people's selective disclosure to heterosexuals whom they expect to be supportive. However, gay people often do not have control over who knows about their sexual orientation. In the 1990s, for example, only about one-third of heterosexuals who personally knew a gay man or lesbian were told about the latter's sexual orientation directly by the sexual minority individual; most learned about it from a third party or simply guessed (Herek & Capitanio, 1996). This pattern held in the 2005 telephone survey described earlier: About 41% of respondents said they first learned about a friend or relative's sexual orientation directly from the gay or lesbian individual, whereas the majority learned about it from a third party (32%) or said they had guessed or "always knew" (27%).

There are empirical grounds for believing that a causal relationship exists between knowing a gay person and the diminution of sexual prejudice. Longitudinal data indicate that heterosexuals' contact experiences predict their subsequent prejudice reduction to a greater extent than initially low levels of prejudice predict having subsequent contact experiences (Herek & Capitanio, 1996). In addition, when heterosexuals are matched on other relevant characteristics, those reporting personal contact have significantly lower levels of sexual prejudice and are more supportive of policies benefiting sexual minorities than are those without contact (Lewis, 2007).

Moreover, there are strong theoretical reasons for expecting heterosexuals' personal experiences with gay men and lesbians to result in lower levels of prejudice. As formulated by Allport (1954), the contact hypothesis predicts that prejudice will be reduced by contact between majority and minority group members in the pursuit of common goals. Allport noted that contact's beneficial effects are enhanced to the extent that it is "sanctioned by institutional supports" and "leads to the perception of common interests and common humanity between members of the two groups" (Allport, p. 281). A large body of empirical research supports the contact hypothesis and indicates that, although the four conditions specified by Allport (equal group status, common goals, intergroup cooperation, institutional support) are not essential for contact to decrease intergroup hostility, their presence typically leads to even greater prejudice reduction (Pettigrew & Tropp, 2006).

Pettigrew (1998) has suggested that contact situations fostering the development of friendship between group members are the most likely to reduce prejudice, in part because intergroup friendship potentially invokes all four of the facilitative factors identified by Allport (Pettigrew, 1998). Moreover, such contact is likely to increase heterosexuals' knowledge about sexual minorities, foster a capacity for greater empathy for them, and reduce anxieties about interacting with them, all of which are likely to be associated with decreases in prejudice (Pettigrew, 1998; Stephan & Finlay, 1999; Stephan & Stephan, 1985). To the extent that heterosexuals have multiple lesbian or gay friends, these beneficial effects of contact should increase. In addition, knowing multiple members of a stigmatized group is more likely to foster recognition of that group's variability than is knowing only one group member (Wilder, 1978) and may reduce the likelihood that nonstereotypical behavior is discounted as atypical (Rothbart & John, 1985).

When group membership is readily evident, as is often the case with race or ethnicity, any situation that brings different groups into contact is likely to make the participants' respective category memberships immediately salient. By contrast, because sexual orientation is usually concealable, heterosexuals often have contact with sexual minority individuals without being aware of it. Such contact even includes longstanding friendships and family relationships. Indeed, because most gay, lesbian, and bisexual adults do not recognize their sexual orientation until adolescence or adulthood, their circle of family and friends typically includes people who knew them before they themselves were aware of their minority status. Thus, although initial categorization according to readily apparent characteristics plays an important role in the impression formation process (e.g., Fiske, Lin, & Neuberg, 1999), nonvisible characteristics such as sexual orientation often are not part of that process. Hence, many relationships between heterosexuals and sexual minority individuals become established before the former knows about the latter's sexual orientation.

This fact is important for analyzing the social and psychological processes whereby heterosexuals' contact experiences with specific lesbians and gay men may lead to reduced prejudice toward sexual minorities as a group. In trying to understand the factors that affect whether the beneficial effects of specific contact experiences generalize to reduce prejudice against the group as a whole, social psychologists have focused on the salience of group categories during contact situations. Brewer and Miller (1984) proposed that contact is optimal in reducing prejudice when the salience of intergroup boundaries is minimized, a situation that fosters differentiation and personalization of outgroup individuals. Rather than perceiving outgroup members as a homogeneous group, the ingroup member learns that they have distinctive characteristics and comes to respond to them in terms of relationships to the self rather than their category membership (Brewer & Miller, 1984). A competing perspective notes that if outgroup members are perceived entirely as individuals, the positive effects of contact are unlikely to generalize to the outgroup as a whole. Thus, maintaining the salience of category membership is necessary for the contact experience to translate into a reduction in prejudice (Brown & Hewstone, 2005). A third perspective, the Common Group Identity Model, proposes that the effects of contact will be best generalized when the categories of ingroup and outgroup are transcended by a superordinate category that includes both (Gaertner & Dovidio, 2005b).

These three perspectives have not proved to be as incompatible as they might first appear (Brown & Hewstone, 2005; Dovidio, Gaertner, & Kawakami, 2003; Miller, 2002). For present purposes, it is relevant to recall that much of the research on which they are based involved racial and ethnic prejudice. Contact between heterosexuals and sexual minorities, as noted earlier, often has quite different dynamics. Instead of involving strangers whose respective group memberships constitute some of the first information available, contact between heterosexual people and sexual minority individuals often involves revelation of the latter's status within the context of an already established relationship. When heterosexuals learn about a friend or relative's homosexuality or bisexuality, an intergroup relationship is imposed on the preexisting interpersonal relationship. To the extent that the qualities of that personal relationship – including positive affect, individuation, and personalization – are carried over to the new intergroup relationship, it is likely that the heterosexual individual will be able to generalize from her or his feelings toward the sexual minority individual to a more positive attitude toward lesbians and gay men as a group.

This dynamic is perhaps most likely to occur in the case of close friendships (Pettigrew, 1998). Having a lesbian or gay close friend may lead a heterosexual person to reconceptualize her or his most important group affiliations, such that she or he feels a common group membership with sexual minorities (e.g., Gaertner & Dovidio, 2005a). In this process of recategorization, the ingroup may become more broadly defined so that it now includes nonheterosexuals. What is necessary is for the relationship to survive the revelation of the new information about the friend's sexual orientation. It is important, for example, that the heterosexual person not perceive the new information about her or his friend's sexual orientation as calling into question all of her or his prior knowledge about and impressions of the friend, which could lead to a negative recategorization of the individual (e.g., Fiske et al., 1999) rather than the outgroup. This outcome is less likely to occur when the heterosexual and the sexual minority person openly discuss the latter's experiences.

Data from the previously described 2005 telephone survey support the hypotheses that contact is most likely to reduce sexual prejudice when heterosexuals know multiple sexual minority individuals, when those contacts include emotionally close relationships, and when the relationships include open discussion of what it means to be a sexual minority. Table 4 reports mean ATL and ATG, feeling thermometer, and discomfort scores for respondents who reported having no gay or lesbian friends or relatives vs. those who reported any such contact.[13] The latter

---

[13] Respondents were asked "How many friends, relatives, or close acquaintances have you ever had who were gay, lesbian, or homosexual?" A total of 80% reported having at least one such contact. When asked about their sole or closest relationship, 30% characterized the gay or lesbian person as a close friend, 44% as an acquaintance or distant friend, 10% as an immediate family member, and 16% as a relative outside the immediate family. In addition to the 41% who first learned about the gay or lesbian person's sexual orientation through the latter's self-disclosure, another 10% said they had talked with her or him about being lesbian or gay.

Table 4 Mean feeling thermometers scores, ATL and ATG scores, and discomfort levels by contact variables (national sample)

Contact variable	ATLG		Thermometer		Discomfort	
	ATG	ATL	Gay Male	Lesbian	Gay Men	Lesbians
No G/L friend, acquaintance, or relative	3.27 (3.13–3.40)	3.07 (2.92–3.21)	23.6 (19.88–27.25)	28.7 (24.3–33.1)	3.04 (2.87–3.21)	2.70 (2.54–2.86)
G/L friend, acquaintance, or relative	2.60 (2.54–2.67)	2.41 (2.34–2.48)	53.1 (51.0–55.1)	54.8 (52.8–56.9)	1.97 (1.90–2.04)	1.92 (1.85–1.98)
Lesbian/gay close friend	2.33 (2.20–2.45)	2.09 (1.98–2.21)	61.10 (57.52–64.69)	61.81 (58.34–65.29)	1.65 (1.54–1.76)	1.69 (1.58–1.80)
Contact without discussion	2.83 (2.74–2.92)	2.61 (2.52–2.71)	47.45 (44.40–50.49)	49.28 (46.31–52.26)	2.19 (2.09–2.29)	2.11 (2.01–2.20)
Contact with discussion	2.36 (2.26–2.46)	2.20 (2.10–2.29)	59.09 (56.42–61.77)	60.44 (57.78–63.11)	1.73 (1.64–1.82)	1.73 (1.64–1.81)

For each contact variable, the table reports the mean score and, in parentheses, the 95% CI. ATG and ATL scores can range from 1 (low prejudice) to 4 (high prejudice). Thermometer scores can range from 0 (least favorable) to 100 (most favorable). Discomfort scores can range from 1 ("very comfortable") to 4 ("very uncomfortable").

group is further divided according to whether the respondent's reported contact was described as a close friend (vs. a relative or acquaintance), and whether or not the respondent reported ever having discussed that person's sexual orientation with her or him. For ease of comparison, 95% confidence intervals (CIs) are reported for each parameter estimate. Nonoverlapping CIs can be interpreted as indicating reliable differences between groups.

Comparing rows 1 and 2 in Table 4, it is clear that heterosexuals with contact experiences have substantially more positive reactions to sexual minorities as a group, compared to heterosexuals without such experiences. Moreover, those reactions are even more positive when the gay or lesbian individual is a close friend (row 3) and when he or she has talked with the heterosexual person about what it is like to be lesbian or gay (row 4 vs. row 5).

To assess the relative importance of the different features of contact in predicting sexual prejudice, Table 5 reports the results of a series of OLS regression analyses. Scores on the various sexual prejudice measures were predicted simultaneously by the respondent's number of relationships with gay men and with lesbians, whether or not the respondent reported having a gay or lesbian close friend, and whether or not the respondent reported having discussed the friend or relative's sexual orientation with her or him. As the table shows, the number of contacts reported by respondents consistently accounts for the greatest proportion of unique variance, with the number of lesbian contacts playing an especially important role in predicting responses to lesbians. By contrast, reactions to gay men tend to be explained by both gay male and lesbian contacts. In addition, consistent with the research cited earlier, defining the relationship as a friendship and having openly discussed the friend or relative's sexual orientation also account for additional variance.

Table 5 OLS regression equations with contact variables as predictors of sexual prejudice scores

Independent variable	ATLG		Thermometer		Discomfort	
	ATG	ATL	Gay male	Lesbian	Gay men	Lesbians
Number of gay male contacts	-0.05^c (.017)	-0.02^a (.004)	1.60^c (.015)	1.04^c (.007)	-0.08^c (.035)	-0.02^a (.003)
Number of lesbian contacts	-0.05^c (.017)	-0.07^c (.025)	1.90^c (.020)	2.33^c (.030)	-0.05^c (.011)	-0.08^c (.038)
Closest relationship is close friend?	-0.22^b (.008)	-0.31^c (.015)	7.90^c (.009)	6.16^b (.006)	-0.31^c (.012)	-0.19^b (.005)
Any conversation about being gay/lesbian?	-0.33^c (.022)	-0.30^c (.018)	11.08^c (.023)	9.80^c (.018)	-0.41^c (.028)	-0.30^c (.017)
Total R^2	$.178^c$	$.158^c$	$.182^c$	$.158^c$	$.227^c$	$.157^c$

For each independent variable, the table reports the unstandardized regression coefficient and, in parentheses, the independent R^2 associated with that variable. ATG and ATL scores can range from 1 (low prejudice) to 4 (high prejudice). Thermometer scores can range from 0 (least favorable) to 100 (most favorable). Discomfort scores can range from 1 ("very comfortable") to 4 ("very uncomfortable").
$^a p < .05$; $^b p < .01$; $^c p < .001$.

Thus, two factors that account for reductions in sexual prejudice at the individual level are an increase in heterosexuals' personal contact with openly gay and lesbian people and a redefinition of heterosexuals' personal identities such that rejecting sexual prejudice is integral to them. These developments have been made possible by a confluence of cultural changes since World War II.

Conclusion

In the present chapter, I have proposed a general framework for thinking about sexual prejudice in its cultural context. Moving beyond "homophobia," this framework begins with the construct of stigma and distinguishes between its structural and individual manifestations, with the latter further differentiated into enacted, felt, and internalized stigma. This conceptual road map offers insights into heterosexuals' and sexual minorities' experiences of stigma; the connections between societal stigma and individual heterosexuals' attitudes toward gay, lesbian, and bisexual people; and between sexual prejudice and social policy. Perhaps most importantly, it can provide a vocabulary and directions for future research that will better describe and explain sexual stigma and prejudice, and ultimately will offer insights into how they can be eradicated.

Appendix: Questionnaire and Survey Studies Methodology

Student Questionnaire Study

The data reported here were collected during a single academic quarter as part of an ongoing study of attitudes conducted with students at the University of California at Davis. One goal of the study was to assess the continuing utility of the ATLG as a measure of sexual prejudice and to construct brief measures of related constructs.

A large pool of items was assembled using the ATLG (Herek, 1994) and other measures of heterosexuals' responses to gay men and lesbians (Altemeyer, 1996; Kite & Deaux, 1986; Larsen, Reed, & Hoffman, 1980; Ricketts & Hudson, 1998; Wright, Adams, & Bernat, 1999) as sources. Duplicate items and items with substantially overlapping meaning were eliminated, and some new items were constructed. Two parallel versions of this lengthy questionnaire were administered, one in which all of the statements applied to lesbians and female homosexuality, another in which they targeted gay men and male homosexuality. Respondents were randomly assigned to receive either the lesbian (n=122) or gay male (n=120) questionnaire. In addition, all questionnaires included the 3-item versions of both the ATL and ATG, separate feeling thermometers for *gay men* and for *lesbians*, the Protestant Ethic and Humanitarian scales (Katz & Hass, 1988), measures of religiosity and political ideology, and demographic questions.

The items concerning sexual minorities were organized into three main sections relevant to the present chapter (a) attitudes toward gay men, lesbians, or homosexuality (including the ATLG items); (b) affective responses to actual and hypothetical interactions with a gay man or lesbian; and (c) attitudes toward policies related to sexual minorities and sexual orientation.

Attitudes Toward Lesbians and Gay Men

Responses to the items assessing attitudes toward gay men and lesbian were submitted to a principal components analysis with oblique rotation. The results were consistent with the original ATLG Condemnation-Tolerance factor. Although three factors emerged for the gay male items and two factors emerged for the lesbian items, they were conceptually similar and highly intercorrelated ($0.23 < |r| < 0.71$). Thus, it seemed warranted to consider them all facets of the same construct that is measured by the ATLG. This hypothesis was tested with the 30 items that loaded highly on at least one factor. The three items comprising the short ATL/ATG were removed and the remaining 27 items were combined into single scales of attitudes toward gay men and attitudes toward lesbians, with item scoring reversed as appropriate. As expected, both scales displayed a high level of internal consistency ($\alpha = 0.97$ for each). Total scores on each 27-item scale were highly correlated with the respective 3-item ATLG counterpart (between the gay male scale and the ATG, $r = 0.82$; between the lesbian scale and the ATL, $r = 0.85$). Given these high correlations and the ATLG's well-documented reliability and validity with national probability samples (Herek, 2002a; Herek & Capitanio, 1996, 1999b), the short versions of the ATL and ATG were used in the present study as measures of sexual prejudice.

Affective Responses to Lesbians and Gay Men

Brief measures were created to assess respondents' affective response to the prospect of interactions with gay men and with lesbians. They were based on items from the Index of Attitudes Toward Homosexuals, or IAH (Ricketts & Hudson, 1998) — a revised version of the Index of Homophobia (Hudson & Ricketts, 1980) — which ascertains respondents' anticipated affective response in 25 hypothetical situations. Building on the fact that nearly two-thirds of the IAH items assess anticipated comfort or discomfort or related feelings ("at ease," "nervous," "bothered"), a more homogeneous scale was constructed by rephrasing the remaining items so that all of them focused on comfort or discomfort. Items from other sexual prejudice measures that assessed levels of comfort in hypothetical social situations were also included.

Based on principal components analyses of these items, a 10-item Social Discomfort Questionnaire (SDQ) was constructed to assess respondents' discomfort in social situations with gay men (SDQ-G, $\alpha = 0.96$) and lesbians (SDQ-L,

$\alpha = 0.95$). For each version of the scale, respondents were asked "How comfortable would you feel in each of the following situations?" Response options were *very comfortable, fairly comfortable, somewhat comfortable, somewhat uncomfortable, fairly uncomfortable, very uncomfortable*. The items for the SDQ-L are (1) Working closely with a lesbian; (2) Learning that I will have a lesbian as my work supervisor; (3) Learning that a neighbor is a lesbian; (4) Learning that my daughter's teacher is a lesbian; (5) Learning that a longtime friend is a lesbian; (6) Learning that a family member is a lesbian; (7) Attending a social function where lesbians are present; (8) Being in a group of lesbians; (9) Talking with a lesbian at a party; and (10) Seeing two women holding hands in public.

Policy Attitudes

Based on a principal components analysis with oblique rotation, gay male and lesbian versions of three scales assessing policy attitudes were constructed, each employing a 7-point Likert-type response format ranging from *very strongly agree* to *very strongly disagree*. They included a 4-item Marriage Equality (ME) scale ($\alpha = 0.94$ for the gay male version [ME-G], $\alpha = 0.95$ for the lesbian version [ME-L]), a 2-item Military Personnel Policy (MPP) scale ($\alpha = 0.79$ for the MPP-G and 0.82 for the MPP-L), and a 3-item Childcare and Teaching Policy (CTP) scale ($\alpha = 0.92$ for the CTP-G and 0.94 for the CTP-L). High scores on each scale indicate an antigay or antilesbian policy stance.

The ME-L items are (1) Lesbian couples should be allowed to marry legally, the same as heterosexual couples; (2) Allowing women to marry other women would hurt the institution of marriage (Reverse-scored); (3) Allowing marriage between two women would be a good thing for society; and (4) The idea of lesbian marriages seems ridiculous to me (Reverse-scored).

The MPP-L items are (1) Openly lesbian women should be allowed to join the military and (2) Whether or not a woman is lesbian should have no bearing on her ability to join the Armed Services.

The CTP-L items are (1) Lesbians should be barred from teaching school; (2) Elementary schools should be able to fire a female teacher for being lesbian; and (3) I think lesbians should be prohibited from working with children. All items on the CTP scale are reverse-scored.

National Telephone Survey

The data for these analyses were collected between August 1 and October 27, 2005, from a national probability sample of English-speaking US adults (≥ 18 years) who were eligible to vote.[14] The total sample comprised 2,114 respondents and

[14] Data collection was conducted by The Henne Group and funded by the Gill Foundation. I express my sincere appreciation to Jeff Henne, Ethan Geto, and Murray Edelman for their assistance and support in this project.

included partially overlapping oversamples of African Americans ($n=444$), Latinos ($n=461$), and California residents ($n=560$). However, not all modules of the survey were administered to all respondents, and some respondents declined to answer specific questions. For the analyses presented here, the minimum sample size was $n=1,311$ for the analyses of marriage policy attitudes, $n=1,332$ for the analyses of employment policy attitudes, and $n=1,906$ for the analyses of contact variables.

All interviews were conducted using computer-assisted telephone interviewing, with each respondent selected at random from adults residing in the household. Up to 12 calls were attempted for each telephone number in the sample. The data were weighted by the number of adults residing in the household and the number of telephone lines, and were poststratified by gender, race and ethnicity, age, geographic region, and education, based on data from the most recent Current Population Survey (CPS) conducted by the US Census Bureau for the population of adults 18 and older. Because the use of weighted data necessitates special analytic techniques to correct standard errors (Lee & Forthofer, 2006), analyses were conducted using STATA and SPSS Complex Samples, which permit such correction.

Three measures of sexual prejudice were included: (a) the 3-item versions of the ATL and ATG with four response alternatives (*strongly agree*, *agree somewhat*, *disagree somewhat*, and *strongly disagree* — these four response alternatives were also used with other items described later), (b) feeling thermometers assessing reactions to gay men and to lesbians, and (c) single-item assessments of personal discomfort with gay men and with lesbians (e.g., "In general, how comfortable do you feel around men who are gay or homosexual — very comfortable, somewhat comfortable, somewhat uncomfortable, or very uncomfortable?"). Respondents' attitudes toward passing a federal law to ensure that gay men and lesbians have equal rights in employment and toward allowing or forbidding marriage between two people of the same sex were assessed.[15]

Along with demographic variables, the survey also included questions about political ideology, religiosity, and the extent to which respondents reported having had close personal contact with lesbians and gay men. In addition, to assess general values that might affect policy attitudes independent of sexual prejudice, two items were included that have been shown to predict policy attitudes related to sexual orientation (Brewer, 2003). One item measures general nonegalitarian values ("We have gone too far in pushing equal rights in this country") and the other measures moral traditionalism vs. relativism ("The world is changing, and we should adjust our view of moral behavior to those changes"). Both items used the same four response alternatives as the ATLG items. To facilitate interpretation of the regression analyses reported in Table 3, all independent variables except age were recoded as dummy variables (categorical variables) or as 0–1 (scales and ordinal variables).

---

[15] The survey included experimental manipulations of the wording of the policy items. However, these manipulations did not significantly affect the response patterns and are not considered here.

References

Adam, B. D. (1995). *The rise of a gay and lesbian movement* (Rev. ed..). New York, NY: Twayne.

Ajzen, I., & Fishbein, M. (2005). The influence of attitudes on behavior. In D. Albarracin, B.T. Johnson, & M.P. Zanna (Eds.), *The handbook of attitudes* (pp. 173–221). Mahwah, NJ: Erlbaum.

Albarracin, D., Zanna, M. P., Johnson, B. T., & Kumkale, G. T. (2005). Attitudes: Introduction and scope. In D. Albarracin, B.T. Johnson, & M.P. Zanna (Eds.), *The handbook of attitudes* (pp. 3–19). Mahwah, NJ: Erlbaum.

Allport, G. W. (1954). *The nature of prejudice*. Garden City, NY: Doubleday.

Altemeyer, B. (1996). *The authoritarian specter*. Cambridge, MA: Harvard University Press.

Arkes, H. R., & Tetlock, P. E. (2004). Attributions of implicit prejudice, or "Would Jesse Jackson 'fail' the Implicit Association Test?". *Psychological Inquiry, 15*, 257–278.

Banse, R., Seise, J., & Zerbes, N. (2001). Implicit attitudes towards homosexuality: Reliability, validity, and controllability of the IAT. *Zeitschrift Fuer Experimentelle Psychologie, 48*(2), 145–160.

Batson, C. D., Floyd, R. B., Meyer, J. M., & Winner, A. L. (1999). "And who is my neighbor? ": Intrinsic religion as a source of universal compassion. *Journal for the Scientific Study of Religion, 38*, 445–457.

Bayer, R. (1987). *Homosexuality and American psychiatry: The politics of diagnosis* (Rev. ed.). Princeton, NJ: Princeton University Press.

Bernat, J. A., Calhoun, K. S., Adams, H. E., & Zeichner, A. (2001). Homophobia and physical aggression toward homosexual and heterosexual individuals. *Journal of Abnormal Psychology, 110*, 179–187.

Berrill, K. T. (1992). Antigay violence and victimization in the United States: An overview. In G.M. Herek & K.T. Berrill (Eds.), *Hate crimes: Confronting violence against lesbians and gay men* (pp. 19–45). Thousand Oaks, CA: Sage.

Bieschke, K. J., Perez, R. M., & DeBord, K. A. (Eds.). (2006). *Handbook of counseling and psychotherapy with lesbian, gay, bisexual, and transgender clients* (2nd ed.). Washington, DC: American Psychological Association.

Blair, I. V., Park, B., & Bachelor, J. (2003). Understanding intergroup anxiety: Are some people more anxious than others? *Group Processes and Intergroup Relations, 6*, 151–169.

Bobo, L., & Licari, F. C. (1989). Education and political tolerance: Testing the effects of cognitive sophistication and target group affect. *Public Opinion Quarterly, 53*, 285–308.

Bosson, J. K., Haymovitz, E. L., & Pinel, E. C. (2004). When saying and doing diverge: The effects of stereotype threat on self-reported versus non-verbal anxiety. *Journal of Experimental Social Psychology, 40*, 247–255.

Bosson, J. K., Prewitt-Freilino, J. L., & Taylor, J. N. (2005). Role rigidity: A problem of identity misclassification? *Journal of Personality and Social Psychology, 89*, 552–565.

Bosson, J. K., Taylor, J. N., & Prewitt-Freilino, J. L. (2006). Gender role violations and identity misclassification: The roles of audience and actor variables. *Sex Roles, 55*, 13–24.

Bowers v. Hardwick, 478 U.S. 186 (1986).

Brewer, M. B., & Miller, N. (1984). Beyond the contact hypothesis: Theoretical perspectives on desegregation. In N. Miller & M.B. Brewer (Eds.), *Groups in contact: The psychology of desegregation* (pp. 281–302). Orlando, FL: Academic.

Brewer, P. R. (2003). The shifting foundations of public opinion about gay rights. *The Journal of Politics, 65*, 1208–1220.

Brown, R., & Hewstone, M. (2005). An integrative theory of intergroup contact. In M.P. Zanna (Ed.), *Advances in experimental social psychology Vol. 37*, (pp. 255–343). San Diego, CA: Elsevier.

Carmichael, S., & Hamilton, C. V. (1967). *Black power: The politics of liberation in America*. New York, NY: Vintage.

Chauncey, G., Jr. (1993). The postwar sex crime panic. In W. Graebner (Ed.), *True stories from the American past* (pp. 160–178). New York, NY: McGraw-Hill.

Clausell, E., & Fiske, S. T. (2005). When do subgroup parts add up to the stereotypic whole? Mixed stereotype content for gay male subgroups explains overall ratings. *Social Cognition, 23,* 161–181.

Clore, G. L., & Schnall, S. (2005). The influence of affect on attitude. In D. Albarracin, B.T. Johnson, & M.P. Zanna (Eds), *The handbook of attitudes* (pp. 437–489). Mahwah, NJ: Erlbaum.

Cole, S. W. (2006). Social threat, personal identity, and physical health in closeted gay men. In A.M. Omoto & H.S. Kurtzman (Eds.), *Sexual orientation and mental health: Examining identity and development in lesbian, gay, and bisexual people* (pp. 245–267). Washington, DC: American Psychological Association.

Conger, J. J. (1975). Proceedings of the American Psychological Association, Incorporated, for the year 1974: Minutes of the annual meeting of the Council of Representatives. *American Psychologist, 30,* 620–651.

Corrigan, P. W., & Watson, A. C. (2002). The paradox of self-stigma and mental illness. *Clinical Psychology: Science and Practice, 9,* 35–53.

Corrigan, P. W., Watson, A. C., Heyrman, M. L., Warpinski, A., Gracia, G., Slopen, N., Hall, L.L. (2005). Structural stigma in state legislation. *Psychiatric Services, 56,* 557–563.

Cottrell, C. A., & Neuberg, S. L. (2005). Different emotional reactions to different groups: A sociofunctional threat-based approach to "prejudice". *Journal of Personality and Social Psychology, 88,* 770–789.

Crocker, J. (1999). Social stigma and self-esteem: Situational construction of self-worth. *Journal of Experimental Social Psychology, 35,* 89–107.

Crocker, J., & Major, B. (1989). Social stigma and self-esteem: The self-protective properties of stigma. *Psychological Review, 96,* 608–630.

Crocker, J., Major, B., & Steele, C. (1998). Social stigma. In D.T. Gilbert, S.T. Fiske, & G. Lindzey (Eds.), *The handbook of social psychology, Vol. 2* (4th ed.) (pp. 504–553). Boston, MA: McGraw-Hill.

D'Augelli, A. R., & Grossman, A. H. (2001). Disclosure of sexual orientation, victimization, and mental health among lesbian, gay, and bisexual older adults. *Journal of Interpersonal Violence, 16,* 1008–1027.

D'Augelli, A. R., Grossman, A. H., & Starks, M. T. (2006). Childhood gender atypicality, victimization, and PTSD among lesbian, gay, and bisexual youth. *Journal of Interpersonal Violence, 21,* 1462–1482.

D'Emilio, J. (1983). *Sexual politics, sexual communities: The making of a homosexual minority in the United States 1940–1970.* Chicago, IL: University of Chicago Press.

Dasgupta, N., & Rivera, L. M. (2006). From automatic antigay prejudice to behavior: The moderating role of conscious beliefs about gender and behavioral control. *Journal of Personality and Social Psychology, 91,* 268–280.

Derlega, V. J., Lewis, R. J., Harrison, S., Winstead, B. A., & Costanza, R. (1989). Gender differences in the initiation and attribution of tactile intimacy. *Journal of Nonverbal Behavior, 13,* 83–96.

Devine, P. G. (1989). Stereotypes and prejudice: Their automatic and controlled components. *Journal of Personality and Social Psychology, 56,* 5–18.

Devine, P. G. (2005). Breaking the prejudice habit: Allport's "inner conflict" revisited. In J. Dovidio, P. Glick, & L. Rudman (Eds.), *On the nature of prejudice: Fifty years after Allport* (pp. 327–342). Malden, MA: Blackwell.

Devine, P. G., Monteith, M. J., Zuwerink, J. R., & Elliot, A. J. (1991). Prejudice with and without compunction. *Journal of Personality and Social Psychology, 60,* 817–830.

Donovan, T., Wenzel, J., & Bowler, S. (2000). Direct democracy and gay rights initiatives after Romer. In C.A. Rimmerman, K.D. Wald, & C. Wilcox (Eds.), *The politics of gay rights* (pp. 161–190). Chicago, IL: University of Chicago Press.

Dovidio, J. F., Gaertner, S. L., & Kawakami, K. (2003). Intergroup contact: The past, present, and the future. *Group Processes and Intergroup Relations, 6,* 5–20.

Dunton, B. C., & Fazio, R. H. (1997). An individual difference measure of motivation to control prejudiced reactions. *Personality and Social Psychology Bulletin, 23*, 316–326.

Eagly, A. H., & Chaiken, S. (1993). *The psychology of attitudes*. Ft Worth, TX: Harcourt Brace Jovanovich.

Eisenstadt v. Baird, 405 U.S. 438 (1972).

Epstein, S. (1999). Gay and lesbian movements in the United States: Dilemmas of identity, diversity, and political strategy. In B.D. Adam, J.W. Duyvendak, & A. Krouwel (Eds.), *The global emergence of gay and lesbian politics: National imprints of a worldwide movement* (pp. 30–90). Philadelphia, PA: Temple University Press.

Esses, V. M., Haddock, G., & Zanna, M. P. (1993). Values, stereotypes, and emotions as determinants of intergroup attitudes. In D.M. Mackie & D.L. Hamilton (Eds.), *Affect, cognition and stereotyping: Interactive processes in intergroup perception communication* (pp. 137–166). San Diego, CA: Academic.

Fabrigar, L. R., MacDonald, T. K., & Wegener, D. T. (2005). The structure of attitudes. In D. Albarracin, B.T. Johnson, & M.P. Zanna (Eds), *The handbook of attitudes* (pp. 79–125). Mahwah, NJ: Erlbaum.

Family Research Institute. (2006). Getting the facts: Same-sex marriage. Retrieved May 7, 2007, from http://familyresearchinst.org/

Fazio, R. H., & Olson, M. A. (2003). Implicit measures in social cognition research: Their meaning and uses. *Annual Review of Psychology, 54*, 297–327.

Fein, S., & Spencer, S. J. (1997). Prejudice as self-image maintenance: Affirming the self through derogating others. *Journal of Personality and Social Psychology, 73*, 31–44.

Fine, M., & Asch, A. (1988). Disability beyond stigma: Social interaction, discrimination, and activism. *Journal of Social Issues, 44*, 3–21.

Fiske, S. T., Lin, M., & Neuberg, S. L. (1999). The continuum model: Ten years later. In S. Chaiken & Y. Trope (Eds.), *Dual-process theories in social psychology* (pp. 231–254). New York, NY: Guilford.

Frable, D. E. S., Wortman, C., & Joseph, J. (1997). Predicting self-esteem, well-being, and distress in a cohort of gay men: The importance of cultural stigma, personal visibility, community networks, and positive identity. *Journal of Personality, 65*, 599–624.

Franklin, K. (1998). Unassuming motivations: Contextualizing the narratives of antigay assailants. In G.M. Herek (Ed.), *Stigma and sexual orientation: Understanding prejudice against lesbians, gay men, and bisexuals* (pp. 1–23). Thousand Oaks, CA: Sage.

Franklin, K. (2000). Antigay behaviors among young adults: Prevalence, patterns and motivators in a noncriminal population. *Journal of Interpersonal Violence, 15*, 339–362.

Freedman, E. (1989). "Uncontrolled desires": The response to the sexual psychopath, 1920–1960. In K. Peiss & C. Simmons (Eds.), *Passion and power: Sexuality in history*. Philadelphia: Temple University Press.

Gabriel, U., Banse, R., & Hug, F. (2007). Predicting private and public helping behaviour by implicit attitudes and the motivation to control prejudiced reactions. *British Journal of Social Psychology, 46*, 365–382.

Gaertner, S. L., & Dovidio, J. F. (2005a). Categorization, recategorization, and intergroup bias. In J. Dovidio, P. Glick, & L. Rudman (Eds.), *On the nature of prejudice: Fifty years after Allport* (pp. 71–88). Malden, MA: Blackwell.

Gaertner, S. L., & Dovidio, J. F. (2005b). Understanding and addressing contemporary racism: From aversive racism to the Common Ingroup Identity model. *Journal of Social Issues, 61*, 615–639.

Goffman, E. (1963). *Stigma: Notes on the management of spoiled identity*. Englewood Cliffs, NJ: Prentice-Hall.

Griswold et al. v. Connecticut, 381 U.S. 479 (1965).

Haddock, G., Zanna, M. P., & Esses, V. M. (1993). Assessing the structure of prejudicial attitudes: The case of attitudes toward homosexuals. *Journal of Personality and Social Psychology, 65*, 1105–1118.

Haider-Markel, D. P., & Joslyn, M. R. (2005). Attributions and the regulation of marriage: Considering the parallels between race and homosexuality. *PS: Political Science and Politics, 38(2)*, 233–239.

Haider-Markel, D. P., Querze, A., & Lindaman, K. (2007). Lose, win, or draw? A reexamination of direct democracy and minority rights. *Political Research Quarterly, 60*, 304–314.

Hamer, D. H., Hu, S., Magnuson, V. L., Hu, N., & Pattatucci, A. M. (1993). A linkage between DNA markers on the X chromosome and male sexual orientation. *Science, 261*, 321–327.

Harlow, C.W. (2005). Hate crime reported by victims and police. Washington, DC: U.S. Department of Justice. Retrieved. July 4, 2006, from http://www.ojp.usdoj.gov/bjs/pub/pdf/hcrvp.pdf

Hebl, M. R., Tickle, J., & Heatherton, T. F. (2000). Awkward moments in interactions between nonstigmatized and stigmatized individuals. In T.F. Heatherton, R.E. Kleck, M.R. Hebl, & J.G. Hull (Eds.), *The social psychology of stigma.* (pp. 275–306). New York, NY: Guilford.

Hegarty, P. (2002). 'It's not a choice, it's the way we're built': Symbolic beliefs about sexual orientation in the US and Britain. *Journal of Community and Applied Social Psychology, 12*, 153–166.

Hegarty, P., & Golden, A. M. (2008). Attributional beliefs about the controllability of stigmatized traits: Antecedents or justifications of prejudice? *Journal of Applied Social Psychology, 38(4)*, 1023–1044.

Hegarty, P., & Pratto, F. (2004). The differences that norms make: Empiricism, social constructionism, and the interpretation of group differences. *Sex Roles, 50*, 445–453.

Herek, G. M. (1984a). Attitudes toward lesbians and gay men: A factor analytic study. *Journal of Homosexuality, 10(1–2)*, 39–51.

Herek, G. M. (1984b). Beyond "homophobia": A social psychological perspective on attitudes toward lesbians and gay men. *Journal of Homosexuality, 10(1–2)*, 1–21.

Herek, G. M. (1986). On heterosexual masculinity: Some psychical consequences of the social construction of gender and sexuality. *American Behavioral Scientist, 29*, 563–577.

Herek, G. M. (1987a). Can functions be measured? A new perspective on the functional approach to attitudes. *Social Psychology Quarterly, 50*, 285–303.

Herek, G. M. (1987b). Religious orientation and prejudice: A comparison of racial and sexual attitudes. *Personality and Social Psychology Bulletin, 13*, 34–44.

Herek, G. M. (1988). Heterosexuals' attitudes toward lesbians and gay men: Correlates and gender differences. *Journal of Sex Research, 25*, 451–477.

Herek, G. M. (1989). Hate crimes against lesbians and gay men: Issues for research and policy. *American Psychologist, 44*, 948–955.

Herek, G. M. (1994). Assessing heterosexuals' attitudes toward lesbians and gay men: A review of empirical research with the ATLG scale. In B. Greene & G.M. Herek (Eds.), *Lesbian and gay psychology: Theory, research, and clinical applications* (pp. 206–228). Thousand Oaks, CA: Sage.

Herek, G. M. (1996). Why tell if you're not asked? Self-disclosure, intergroup contact, and heterosexuals' attitudes toward lesbians and gay men. In G.M. Herek, J. Jobe, & R. Carney (Eds.), *Out in force: Sexual orientation and the military* (pp. 197–225). Chicago, IL: University of Chicago Press.

Herek, G. M. (1997). The HIV epidemic and public attitudes toward lesbians and gay men. In M.P. Levine, P. Nardi, & J. Gagnon (Eds.), *In changing times: Gay men and lesbians encounter HIV/AIDS* (pp. 191–218). Chicago, IL: University of Chicago Press.

Herek, G. M. (1998). The Attitudes Toward Lesbians and Gay Men scale. In C.M. Davis, W.L. Yarber, R. Bauserman, G. Schreer, & S.L. Davis (Eds.), *Handbook of sexuality-related measures* (pp. 392–394). Thousand Oaks, CA: Sage.

Herek, G. M. (2000a). The psychology of sexual prejudice. *Current Directions in Psychological Science, 9*, 19–22.

Herek, G. M. (2000b). Sexual prejudice and gender: Do heterosexuals' attitudes toward lesbians and gay men differ? *Journal of Social Issues, 56*, 251–266.

Herek, G. M. (2002a). Gender gaps in public opinion about lesbians and gay men. *Public Opinion Quarterly, 66*, 40–66.

Herek, G. M. (2002b). Heterosexuals' attitudes toward bisexual men and women in the United States. *Journal of Sex Research, 39*, 264–274.

Herek, G. M. (2004). Beyond "homophobia": Thinking about sexual stigma and prejudice in the twenty-first century. *Sexuality Research and Social Policy, 1(2)*, 6–24.

Herek, G. M. (2006). Legal recognition of same-sex relationships in the United States: A social science perspective. *American Psychologist, 61*, 607–621.

Herek, G. M. (2007). Confronting sexual stigma and prejudice: Theory and practice. *Journal of Social Issues, 63*, 905–925.

Herek, G. M. (2008). Sexual prejudice. In T. Nelson (Ed.), *Handbook of prejudice, stereotyping and discriminatic*. Mahwah, NJ: Erlbaum.

Herek, G. M. (in press). Hate crimes and stigma-related experiences among sexual minority adults in the United States: Prevalence estimates from a national probability sample. *Journal of Interpersonal Violence*.

Herek, G. M., & Berrill, K. T. (Eds.). (1992). *Hate crimes: Confronting violence against lesbians and gay men*. Newbury Park, CA: Sage.

Herek, G. M., & Capitanio, J. P. (1995). Black heterosexuals' attitudes toward lesbians and gay men in the United States. *Journal of Sex Research, 32*, 95–105.

Herek, G. M., & Capitanio, J. P. (1996). "Some of my best friends": Intergroup contact, concealable stigma, and heterosexuals' attitudes toward gay men and lesbians. *Personality and Social Psychology Bulletin, 22*, 412–424.

Herek, G. M., & Capitanio, J. P. (1999a). AIDS stigma and sexual prejudice. *American Behavioral Scientist, 42*, 1130–1147.

Herek, G. M., & Capitanio, J. P. (1999b). Sex differences in how heterosexuals think about lesbians and gay men: Evidence from survey context effects. *Journal of Sex Research, 36*, 348–360.

Herek, G. M., Chopp, R., & Strohl, D. (2007). Sexual stigma: Putting sexual minority health issues in context. In I. Meyer & M. Northridge (Eds.), *The health of sexual minorities: Public health perspectives on lesbian, gay, bisexual, and transgender populations* (pp. 171–208). New York, NY: Springer.

Herek, G. M., Cogan, J. C., & Gillis, J. R. (2002). Victim experiences in hate crimes based on sexual orientation. *Journal of Social Issues, 58*, 319–339.

Herek, G. M., Cogan, J. C., Gillis, J. R., & Glunt, E. K. (1998). Correlates of internalized homophobia in a community sample of lesbians and gay men. *Journal of the Gay and Lesbian Medical Association, 2*, 17–25.

Herek, G. M., & Garnets, L. D. (2007). Sexual orientation and mental health. *Annual Review of Clinical Psychology, 3*, 353–375.

Herek, G. M., Gillis, J. R., & Cogan, J. C. (1999). Psychological sequelae of hate-crime victimization among lesbian, gay, and bisexual adults. *Journal of Consulting and Clinical Psychology, 67*, 945–951.

Herek, G. M., & Gonzalez-Rivera, M. (2006). Attitudes toward homosexuality among U.S. residents of Mexican descent. *Journal of Sex Research, 43*, 122–135.

Herek, G. M., & Sims, C. (2008). Sexual orientation and violent victimization: Hate crimes and intimate partner violence among gay and bisexual males in the United States. In R.J. Wolitski, R. Stall, & R.O. Valdiserri (Eds.), *Unequal opportunity: Health disparities among gay and bisexual men in the United States* (pp. 35–71). New York, NY: Oxford University Press.

Herman, D. (1997). *The antigay agenda: Orthodox vision and the Christian Right*. Chicago, IL: University of Chicago Press.

Hudson, W. W., & Ricketts, W. A. (1980). A strategy for the measurement of homophobia. *Journal of Homosexuality, 5(4)*, 357–372.

Huebner, D. M., Rebchook, G. M., & Kegeles, S. M. (2004). Experiences of harassment, discrimination, and physical violence among young gay and bisexual men. *American Journal of Public Health, 94*, 1200–1203.

Jackson, L. M., & Esses, V. M. (1997). Of scripture and ascription: The relation between religious fundamentalism and intergroup helping. *Personality and Social Psychology Bulletin, 23*, 893–906.

Jellison, W. A., McConnell, A. R., & Gabriel, S. (2004). Implicit and explicit measures of sexual orientation attitudes: Ingroup preferences and related behaviors and beliefs among gay and straight men. *Personality and Social Psychology Bulletin, 30,* 629–642.

Jenness, V., & Grattet, R. (2001). *Making hate a crime: From social movement to law enforcement.* New York, NY: Russell Sage.

Jones, E. E., Farina, A., Hastorf, A. H., Markus, H., Miller, D. T., & Scott, R. A. (1984). *Social stigma: The psychology of marked relationships.* New York, NY: Freeman.

Katz, D. (1960). The functional approach to the study of attitudes. *Public Opinion Quarterly, 24,* 163–204.

Katz, I., & Hass, R. G. (1988). Racial ambivalence and American value conflict: Correlational and priming studies of dual cognitive structures. *Journal of Personality and Social Psychology, 55,* 893–905.

Keen, L., & Goldberg, S. B. (1998). *Strangers to the law: Gay people on trial.* Ann Arbor, MI: University of Michigan Press.

Kelman, H. C. (1961). Processes of opinion change. *Public Opinion Quarterly, 25,* 57–78.

Kilianski, S. E. (2003). Explaining heterosexual men's attitudes toward women and gay men: The theory of exclusively masculine identity. *Psychology of Men and Masculinity, 4,* 37–56.

Kimmel, M. S. (1997). Masculinity as homophobia: Fear, shame and silence in the construction of gender identity. In M.M. Gergen & S.N. Davis (Eds.), *Toward a new psychology of gender* (pp. 223–242). New York, NY: Routledge.

Kite, M. E., & Deaux, K. (1986). Attitudes toward homosexuality: Assessment and behavioral consequences. *Basic and Applied Social Psychology, 7,* 137–162.

Kite, M. E., & Whitley, B. E., Jr. (1998). Do heterosexual women and men differ in their attitudes toward homosexuality? A conceptual and methodological analysis. In G.M. Herek (Ed.), *Stigma and sexual orientation: Understanding prejudice against lesbians, gay men, and bisexuals* (pp. 39–61). Thousand Oaks, CA: Sage.

Kohut, A. (2004). Voters liked campaign 2004, but too much "mud-slinging". Pew Research Center for the People and the Press. Retrieved November 12, 2004, from http://people-press.org/reports/pdf/233.pdf

Kunda, Z., & Spencer, S. J. (2003). When do stereotypes come to mind and when do they color judgment? A goal-based theoretical framework for stereotype activation and application. *Psychological Bulletin, 129,* 522–544.

Lakoff, G. (2002). *Moral politics: How liberals and conservatives think* (2nd ed.). Chicago, IL: University of Chicago Press.

Larsen, K. S., Reed, M., & Hoffman, S. (1980). Attitudes of heterosexuals toward homosexuality: A Likert-type scale and construct validity. *Journal of Sex Research, 16,* 245–257.

Lawrence et al. v. Texas, 539 U.S. 558 (2003).

Lazarus, R. S., & Folkman, S. (1984). *Stress, appraisal, and coping.* New York, NY: Springer.

Lee, E. S., & Forthofer, R. N. (2006). *Analyzing complex survey data* (2nd ed.). Thousand Oaks, CA: Sage.

LeVay, S. (1991). A difference in hypothalamic structure between heterosexual and homosexual men. *Science, 253,* 1034–1037.

Levin, J., & McDevitt, J. (1993). *Hate crimes: The rising tide of bigotry and bloodshed.* New York, NY: Plenum.

Levine, M. P., Nardi, P. M., & Gagnon, J. H. (Eds.). (1997). *In changing times: Gay men and lesbians encounter HIV/AIDS.* Chicago, IL: University of Chicago Press.

Lewis, G. B. (2006, September 2). *Personal relationships and support for gay rights.* Paper presented at the meeting of the American Political Science Association, Philadelphia, PA.

Lewis, G. B. (2007, August). *The friends and family plan: Knowing LGBs and supporting gay rights.* Paper presented at the meeting of the American Psychological Association, San Francisco, CA.

Lewis, R. J., Derlega, V. J., Clarke, E. G., & Kuang, J. C. (2006). Stigma consciousness, social constraints, and lesbian well-being. *Journal of Counseling Psychology, 53,* 48–56.

Lewis, R. J., Derlega, V. J., Griffin, J. L., & Krowinski, A. C. (2003). Stressors for gay men and lesbians: Life stress, gay-related stress, stigma consciousness, and depressive symptoms. *Journal of Social and Clinical Psychology, 22*, 716–729.

Link, B. G., & Phelan, J. C. (2001). Conceptualizing stigma. *Annual Review of Sociology, 27*, 363–385.

Loftus, J. (2001). America's liberalization in attitudes toward homosexuality. *American Sociological Review, 66*, 762–782.

Mackie, D. M., Devos, T., & Smith, E. R. (2000). Intergroup emotions: Explaining offensive action tendencies in an intergroup context. *Journal of Personality and Social Psychology, 79*, 602–616.

Maio, G. R., & Olson, J. M. (Eds.). (2000). *Why we evaluate: Functions of attitudes*. Mahwah, NJ: Erlbaum.

Major, B., Schmidlin, A. M., & Williams, L. (1990). Gender patterns in social touch: The impact of setting and age. *Journal of Personality and Social Psychology, 58*, 634–643.

Major, B., & Vick, S. B. (2005). The psychological impact of prejudice. In J. Dovidio, P. Glick, & L. Rudman (Eds.), *On the nature of prejudice: Fifty years after Allport* (pp. 139–154). Malden, MA: Blackwell.

Malyon, A. K. (1981–1982). Psychotherapeutic implications of internalized homophobia in gay men. *Journal of Homosexuality, 7*(2–3), 59–69.

Mayfield, W. (2001). The development of an Internalized Homonegativity Inventory for gay men. *Journal of Homosexuality, 41*(2), 53–76.

McClosky, H., & Brill, A. (1983). *Dimensions of tolerance: What Americans believe about civil liberties*. New York, NY: Russell Sage.

Meier, B. P., Robinson, M. D., Gaither, G. A., & Heinert, N. J. (2006). A secret attraction or defensive loathing? Homophobia, defense, and implicit cognition. *Journal of Research in Personality, 40*, 377–394.

Meyer, I. H. (2003). Prejudice, social stress, and mental health in lesbian, gay, and bisexual populations: Conceptual issues and research evidence. *Psychological Bulletin, 129*, 674–697.

Micheler, S. (2002). Homophobic propaganda and the denunciation of same-sex-desiring men under National Socialism. *Journal of the History of Sexuality, 11*(1–2), 95–130.

Miller, C. T., & Major, B. (2000). Coping with stigma and prejudice. In T.F. Heatherton, R.E. Kleck, M.R. Hebl, & J.G. Hull (Eds.), *The social psychology of stigma* (pp. 243–272). New York, NY: Guilford.

Miller, N. (2002). Personalization and the promise of contact theory. *Journal of Social Issues, 58*, 387–410.

Mills, T. C., Paul, J., Stall, R., Pollack, L., Canchola, J., Chang, Y. J., Moskowitz, J.T., & Catania, J.A. (2004). Distress and depression in men who have sex with men: The Urban Men's Health Study. *American Journal of Psychiatry, 161*, 278–285.

Minton, H. L. (2002). *Departing from deviance: A history of homosexual rights and emancipatory science in America*. Chicago, IL: University of Chicago Press.

Mohr, J. J., & Rochlen, A. B. (1999). Measuring attitudes regarding bisexuality in lesbian, gay male, and heterosexual populations. *Journal of Counseling Psychology, 46*, 353–369.

Monteith, M. J., Sherman, J. W., & Devine, P. G. (1998). Suppression as a stereotype control strategy. *Personality and Social Psychology Review, 2*, 63–82.

Monteith, M. J., Spicer, C. V., & Tooman, G. D. (1998). Consequences of stereotype suppression: Stereotypes on AND not on the rebound. *Journal of Experimental Social Psychology, 34*, 355–377.

Morris, J. F., Waldo, C. R., & Rothblum, E. D. (2001). A model of predictors and outcomes of outness among lesbian and bisexual women. *American Journal of Orthopsychiatry, 71*, 61–71.

Munro, G. D., & Ditto, P. H. (1997). Biased assimilation, attitude polarization, and affect in reactions to stereotyped-relevant scientific information. *Personality and Social Psychology Bulletin, 23*, 636–653.

Neuberg, S. L., Smith, D. M., Hoffman, J. C., & Russell, F. J. (1994). When we observe stigmatized and "normal" individuals interacting: Stigma by association. *Personality and Social Psychology Bulletin, 20*, 196–209.

Pachankis, J. E. (2007). The psychological implications of concealing a stigma: A cognitive-affective-behavioral model. *Psychological Bulletin, 133*, 328–345.

Page, B. I., & Shapiro, R. Y. (1992). *The rational public: Fifty years of trends in Americans' policy preferences.* Chicago, IL: University of Chicago Press.

Parrott, D. J., & Zeichner, A. (2005). Effects of sexual prejudice and anger on physical aggression toward gay and heterosexual men. *Psychology of Men and Masculinity, 6*, 3–17.

Parrott, D. J., Zeichner, A., & Hoover, R. (2006). Sexual prejudice and anger network activation: Mediating role of negative affect. *Aggressive Behavior, 32*, 7–16.

Patel, S., Long, T. E., McCammon, S. L., & Wuensch, K. L. (1995). Personality and emotional correlates of self-reported antigay behaviors. *Journal of Interpersonal Violence, 10*, 354–366.

Peterson, K. (2005, February 9). 50-state rundown on gay marriage laws. Retrieved June 5, 2007, from http://www.stateline.org/

Pettigrew, T. F. (1998). Intergroup contact theory. *Annual Review of Psychology, 49*, 65–85.

Pettigrew, T. F., & Tropp, L. R. (2006). A meta-analytic test of intergroup contact theory. *Journal of Personality and Social Psychology, 90*, 751–783.

Pew Research Center for the People and the Press. (2006, August 3). Pragmatic Americans liberal and conservative on social issues. Retrieved August 8, 2006, from http://people-press.org/reports/pdf/283.pdf

Phoenix, A., Frosh, S., & Pattman, R. (2003). Producing contradictory masculine subject positions: Narratives of threat, homophobia and bullying in 11–14 year old boys. *Journal of Social Issues, 59(1)*, 179–195.

Pilkington, N. W., & D'Augelli, A. R. (1995). Victimization of lesbian, gay, and bisexual youth in community settings. *Journal of Community Psychology, 23*, 34–56.

Pinel, E. C. (1999). Stigma consciousness: The psychological legacy of social stereotypes. *Journal of Personality and Social Psychology, 76*, 114–128.

Plant, E. A., & Devine, P. G. (1998). Internal and external motivation to respond without prejudice. *Journal of Personality and Social Psychology, 75*, 811–832.

Plummer, D. C. (2006). Sportophobia: Why do some men avoid sport? *Journal of Sport and Social Issues, 30*, 122–137.

Poteat, V. P., & Espelage, D. L. (2007). Predicting psychosocial consequences of homophobic victimization in middle school students. *Journal of Early Adolescence, 27*, 175–191.

Poteat, V. P., Espelage, D. L., & Green, H. D., Jr. (2007). The socialization of dominance: Peer group contextual effects on homophobic and dominance attitudes. *Journal of Personality and Social Psychology, 92*, 1040–1050.

Pryor, J. B., Reeder, G. D., Yeadon, C., & Hesson-McInnis, M. (2004). A dual-process model of reactions to perceived stigma. *Journal of Personality and Social Psychology, 87*, 436–452.

Ratcliff, J. J., Lassiter, G. D., Markman, K. D., & Snyder, C. J. (2006). Gender differences in attitudes toward gay men and lesbians: The role of motivation to respond without prejudice. *Personality and Social Psychology Bulletin, 32*, 1325–1338.

Ricketts, W. A., & Hudson, W. W. (1998). Index of Homophobia (Index of Attitudes Toward Homosexuals). In C.M. Davis, W.L. Yarber, R. Bauserman, G. Schreer, & S.L. Davis (Eds.), *Handbook of sexuality-related measures* (pp. 367–368). Thousand Oaks, CA: Sage.

Roderick, T., McCammon, S. L., Long, T. E., & Allred, L. J. (1998). Behavioral aspects of homonegativity. *Journal of Homosexuality, 36(1)*, 79–88.

Roe et al. v. Wade, 410 U.S. 113 (1973).

Roese, N. J., Olson, J. M., Borenstein, M. N., Martin, A., & Shores, A. L. (1992). Same-sex touching behavior: The moderating role of homophobic attitudes. *Journal of Nonverbal Behavior, 16*, 249–259.

Rothbart, M., & John, O. P. (1985). Social categorization and behavioral episodes: A cognitive analysis of the effects of intergroup contact. *Journal of Social Issues, 41(3)*, 81–104.

Rowatt, W. C., Tsang, J.-A., Kelly, J., LaMartina, B., McCullers, M., & McKinley, A. (2006). Associations between religious personality dimensions and implicit homosexual prejudice. *Journal for the Scientific Study of Religion, 45*(3), 397–406.

Ryan, R. M., & Connell, J. P. (1989). Perceived locus of causality and internalization: Examining reasons for acting in two domains. *Journal of Personality and Social Psychology, 57,* 749–761.

Saad, L. (2005). Gay rights attitudes a mixed bag. Gallup Poll News Service. Retrieved May 20, 2005, from http://www.gallup.com

Saad, L. (2007). Tolerance for gay rights at high ebb. Gallup Poll News Service. Retrieved May 29, 2007, from http://www.gallup.com

San Miguel, C. L., & Millham, J. (1976). The role of cognitive and situational variables in aggression toward homosexuals. *Journal of Homosexuality, 2*(1), 11–27.

Scambler, G. (1989). *Epilepsy.* London: Routledge.

Scambler, G., & Hopkins, A. (1986). Being epileptic: Coming to terms with stigma. *Sociology of Health and Illness, 8,* 26–43.

Sherman, J. W., Stroessner, S. J., Conrey, F. R., & Azam, O. A. (2005). Prejudice and stereotype maintenance processes: Attention, attribution, and individuation. *Journal of Personality and Social Psychology, 89,* 607–622.

Sherrill, K., & Yang, A. (2000). From outlaws to in-laws: Anti-gay attitudes thaw. *The Public Perspective, 11*(1), 20–23.

Shidlo, A. (1994). Internalized homophobia: Conceptual and empirical issues in measurement. In B. Greene & G.M. Herek (Eds.), *Lesbian and gay psychology: Theory, research, and clinical applications* (pp. 176–205). Thousand Oaks, CA: Sage.

Sigelman, C. K., Howell, J. L., Cornell, D. P., Cutright, J. D., & Dewey, J. C. (1991). Courtesy stigma: The social implications of associating with a gay person. *Journal of Social Psychology, 131,* 45–56.

Simon, A. (1998). The relationship between stereotypes of and attitudes toward lesbians and gays. In G.M. Herek (Ed.), *Stigma and sexual orientation: Understanding prejudice against lesbians, gay men, and bisexuals* (pp. 62–81). Thousand Oaks, CA: Sage.

Smart, L., & Wegner, D. M. (2000). The hidden costs of hidden stigma. In T.F. Heatherton, R.E. Kleck, M.R. Hebl, & J.G. Hull (Eds.), *The social psychology of stigma* (pp. 220–242). New York, NY: Guilford.

Smith, G. W. (1998). The ideology of "fag": The school experience of gay students. *Sociology Quarterly, 39,* 309–335.

Smith, M. B., Bruner, J. S., & White, R. W. (1956). *Opinions and personality.* New York, NY: Wiley.

Stanley v. Georgia, 394 U.S. 557 (1969).

Steele, C. M., & Aronson, J. (1995). Stereotype threat and the intellectual test performance of African Americans. *Journal of Personality and Social Psychology, 69,* 797–811.

Steffens, M. C., & Buchner, A. (2003). Implicit Association Test: Separating transsituationally stable and variable components of attitudes toward gay men. *Experimental Psychology, 50*(1), 33–48.

Stephan, W. G., & Finlay, K. (1999). The role of empathy in improving intergroup relations. *Journal of Social Issues, 55,* 729–743.

Stephan, W. G., & Stephan, C. W. (1985). Intergroup anxiety. *Journal of Social Issues, 41*(3), 157–175.

Stouffer, S. A. (1955). *Communism, conformity, and civil liberties: A cross-section of the nation speaks its mind.* Garden City, NY: Doubleday.

Strachan, E. D., Bennett, W. R. M., Russo, J., & Roy-Byrne, P. P. (2007). Disclosure of HIV status and sexual orientation independently predicts increased absolute CD4 cell counts over time for psychiatric patients. *Psychosomatic Medicine, 69,* 74–80.

Strand, D. A. (1998). Civil liberties, civil rights, and stigma: Voter attitudes and behavior in the politics of homosexuality. In G.M. Herek (Ed.), *Stigma and sexual orientation: Understanding prejudice against lesbians, gay men, and bisexuals* (pp. 108–137). Thousand Oaks, CA: Sage.

Szymanski, D. M. (2005). Heterosexism and sexism as correlates of psychological distress in lesbians. *Journal of Counseling and Development, 83*, 355–360.

Szymanski, D. M., & Chung, Y. B. (2003a). Feminist attitudes and coping resources as correlates of lesbian internalized heterosexism. *Feminism and Psychology, 13*, 369–389.

Szymanski, D. M., & Chung, Y. B. (2003b). Internalized homophobia in lesbians. *Journal of Lesbian Studies, 7*(1), 115–125.

Szymanski, D. M., Chung, Y. B., & Balsam, K. F. (2001). Psychosocial correlates of internalized homophobia in lesbians. *Measurement and Evaluation in Counseling and Development, 34*, 27–38.

Tozer, E. E., & Hayes, J. A. (2004). Why do individuals seek conversion therapy? The role of religiosity, internalized homonegativity, and identity development. *Counseling Psychologist, 32*, 716–740.

Ullrich, P. M., Lutgendorf, S. K., & Stapleton, J. T. (2003). Concealment of homosexual identity, social support and CD4 cell count among HIV-seropositive gay men. *Journal of Psychosomatic Research, 54*, 205–212.

Vescio, T. K., & Biernat, M. (2003). Family values and antipathy toward gay men. *Journal of Applied Social Psychology, 33*, 833–847.

Weinberg, G. (1972). *Society and the healthy homosexual.* New York, NY: St. Martin's.

Whitley, B. E., Jr. (1990). The relationship of heterosexuals' attributions for the causes of homosexuality to attitudes toward lesbians and gay men. *Personality and Social Psychology Bulletin, 16*, 369–377.

Whitley, B. E., Jr., & Lee, S. E. (2000). The relationship of authoritarianism and related constructs to attitudes toward homosexuality. *Journal of Applied Social Psychology, 30*, 144–170.

Wilder, D. A. (1978). Reduction of intergroup discrimination through individuation of the outgroup. *Journal of Personality and Social Psychology, 36*, 1361–1374.

Williamson, I. R. (2000). Internalized homophobia and health issues affecting lesbians and gay men. *Health Education Research, 15*, 97–107.

Wood, P. B., & Bartkowski, J. P. (2004). Attribution style and public policy attitudes toward gay rights. *Social Science Quarterly, 85*, 58–74.

Wright, L. W. Jr., Adams, H. E., & Bernat, J. (1999). Development and validation of the Homophobia Scale. *Journal of Psychopathology and Behavioral Assessment, 21*, 337–347.

Zaller, J. R. (1992). *The nature and origins of mass opinion.* New York, NY: Cambridge University Press.

An Overview of Same-Sex Couples in Relation Ships: A Research Area Still at Sea

Esther D. Rothblum

"Sometime during the day that Susan and I decided to have a relationship, we heard a knock at the door. Rushing from different places in the house to answer it, we opened the door together. To our amazed delight, there on our doorstep rode a magnificent ship. No ordinary ocean-going vessel this but a luxury liner tiered with staterooms, looking for all the world like a great floating wedding cake. 'Our relation Ship!' we cried joyously in union" (Johnson, 1991, p. 1).

Heterosexuals are not the only ones who are socialized to value romantic love, sexual relationships, marriage, and "living happily ever after" with a partner. Not only is the research on same-sex couples sparse compared to the enormous literature on heterosexual married couples, but there are some intriguing methodological issues that will also be the focus of this chapter. Who, for example, is lesbian, gay, bisexual, or heterosexual? In the absence of legal marriage, what constitutes a "couple"? What are the criteria that researchers have used to define same-sex couples in their studies, and what kinds of heterosexual couples have been used for comparison purposes? What about lesbians, gay men, and bisexuals (LGBs) who were previously married to heterosexuals, or those who are still in heterosexual marriages? And how has all this changed over time?

Same-sex couples researchers have investigated many of the same issues that interest heterosexual couples researchers, including demographic factors, relationship satisfaction, division of labor, the role of children, conflict, and relationship terminations. This literature will be reviewed, with the exception of the role of children in the lives of same-sex couples. That topic will be covered by Charlotte Patterson in this volume.

In addition, there are many unique factors that same-sex couples face, and some of these have been the focus of research. Does it matter if the two partners are different in level of outness? How does the presence of two women or two men in a relationship affect sexual activity, including monogamy? What is lesbian "merger" and gay male "disengagement"? How do same-sex couples relate to their families of origin? Where do same-sex couples turn for social support? What is the role of ex-lovers in the LGB communities?

This chapter will also review the status of same-sex marriage and other forms of legalized same-sex relationships. There has been little research on same-sex couples in legalized relationships anywhere in the world. How does legal status affect

D.A. Hope (ed.), *Contemporary Perspectives on Lesbian, Gay, and Bisexual Identities,*
DOI: 10.1007/978-0-387-09556-1, © Springer Science+Business Media, LLC 2009

same-sex couples, compared with marriage for heterosexual couples? What about same-sex couples who do not want marriage? This is a new area, with little data so far.

Most of the research on same-sex couples has had mostly white participants. Using data from the 2000 US Census, Rosenfeld and Kim (2005) found that same-sex couples are more likely to be inter-racial than are heterosexual couples. Yet little is known about lesbians and gay men of color in relationships, including interracial and interethnic couples. A notable exception has been the research of Mays and Cochran (see Peplau, Cochran, & Mays, 1997, for a review) that surveyed 1,400 African American lesbians and gay men, and this research will be reviewed later. There is still little published about LGBs in relationships who are Latina/o, Native American, or Asian American, as well as those who are immigrants or political refugees.

Finally, the whole concept of focusing on the psychological aspects of the individuals in romantic relationships is a western concept. Dion and Dion (1993, pp. 53–54) state: "They met, fell in love, decided to marry (or cohabit), and hoped to live happily ever after." To many North Americans, this depiction of the development of an intimate relationship between a woman and a man has been an enduring prototype, and its features seem very familiar and self-evident. This depiction, however, reflects several assumptions about the nature of intimate, opposite-sex relationships that are culturally based. These assumptions are by no means universally shared, particularly in non-Western societies; even in Western societies, this view of love, intimacy, and marriage has not always prevailed." This review will focus on same-sex couples who mostly reside in the United States and other Western nations. Consequently, the focus of research studies on such concepts as romantic love, personal autonomy, and intimacy that are typical of individualistic societies would not be typical of more collectivistic societies such as Taiwan, Pakistan, Japan, and China (Dion & Dion).

What is Same-Sex Sexual Orientation?

Most of the psychological studies of LGBs have recruited survey participants by placing announcements in lesbian or gay newsletters, distributing surveys at gay/ lesbian organizations or events, or leaving questionnaires at gay bars, feminist bookstores, gay or lesbian churches, or gay restaurants (see Rothblum, 1994, for a review of methodology). The assumption underlying such recruitment methods has been that women and men who fill out surveys asking about LGB issues are lesbian, gay, or bisexual. In fact, there are a number of dimensions of sexual orientation that are not highly intercorrelated.

Laumann, Gagnon, Michael, and Michaels (1994) interviewed close to 3,500 individuals using representative sampling. They examined various dimensions of sexual orientation including behavior (sexual activity with a same-sex partner), desire (same-sex sexual attraction), and identity (self-identity as LGB). Only 24 women and 49 men in this large sample identified as gay, lesbian, bisexual, or "other."

Among women in the total sample, 150 (8.6%) reported some same-sex behavior, desire or identity, but only 23 women reported all three dimensions. Among men, 143 (10.1%) reported some same-sex behavior, desire or identity, but only 34 reported all three dimensions.

Morris and Rothblum (1999) examined the degree to which 2,393 women who answered a "Lesbian Wellness Survey" were distributed on five aspects of lesbian sexuality and the coming out process. The five aspects were (a) Sexual Orientation (numerical rating of sexual identity from exclusively lesbian/gay to exclusively heterosexual); (b) Years Out (length of time of self-identity as lesbian/gay/bisexual); (c) Outness/disclosure (amount of disclosure of sexual orientation to others); (d) Sexual Experience (proportion of sexual relationships with women); and (e) Lesbian Activities (extent of participation in lesbian community events). The correlations found among these dimensions were significant but modest, indicating that being lesbian is not a homogeneous experience. Closer examination by the demographic characteristics of race/ethnicity and age revealed a diversity of experience. African American, Native American, and Latina respondents had moderate correlations among the aspects of the lesbian experience, whereas those of European American and Asian American respondents tended to be mild or nonsignificant. The results indicate that researchers who are studying one aspect of sexual orientation (e.g., sexual activity) should not infer such behavior from another dimension (e.g., self-identity as lesbian).

Given this heterogeneity of sexual orientation, there has been little research on how these dimensions interact when two individuals become partnered in a same-sex relationship. How do these dimensions affect how same-sex couples meet each other, what makes them attractive to each other, and what makes them decide to enter into a relationship? Do women and men who have had exclusively same-sex relationships become partnered with similar others, or with partners who have been heterosexually married? Do bisexuals become involved with partners who also identify as bisexual? What if one partner identifies as gay and the other as "I'm not gay, I just love Eric"? Do these dimensions change over time, perhaps resulting in conflict within couples? How do these similarities and differences affect satisfaction in the relationship? This is an area badly in need of research, with potentially complex and interesting interactions.

Who is Bisexual?

Although this chapter (and many other reviews) refers to LGBs, the truth is that very little research has focused on bisexual women and men. Some studies recruit same-sex couples, but do not ask about sexual identity. This issue is further complicated by the fact that bisexuals are less likely than lesbians and gay men to use labels in identifying their own sexual orientation (Rust, 1995).

How many participants in same-sex couples research identify as bisexual? Schreurs and Buunk (1996) report that 9% of their participants in female same-sex relationships in the Netherlands identified as bisexual, 11% refused to label themselves, and 80% identified as lesbian. About 10% of the 1,400 African American respondents in Mays and Cochran's sample identified as bisexual (Peplau et al., 1997).

Bisexual women and men are an interesting group for further research, since they have often been in sequential relationships with women and men. There has been relatively little research on bisexuals' gender roles, but it would be interesting to see whether bisexuals assume more traditional gender roles when in relationships with different-sex than when with same-sex partners. If that were the case, then childhood socialization and modeling may have less to do with partners' roles in relationships (e.g., adult gendered division of labor) than gender of current partner.

Who are the Heterosexual "Controls"?

It is not easy to find LGBs and heterosexuals using the same sources. Researchers who recruit participants via subscribers to LGB periodicals and members of LGB organizations will find few heterosexuals; those who recruit participants via "mainstream" sources will find few LGBs. Consequently, heterosexual comparison groups are often far from ideal.

Green, Bettinger, and Zacks (1996) compared 52 lesbian couples and 50 gay male couples recruited via convenience samples with 1,140 heterosexual married couples from a national study and 218 heterosexual married couples from another study. Gottman et al. (2003) compared 22 gay male and 18 lesbian couples recruited in Berkeley, California, around 2000 with a sample of married heterosexual couples recruited in Bloomington, Indiana, in 1983. Heterosexual married couples were selected for comparison purposes if they matched the relationship satisfaction and length of relationship of the same-sex couples. Although this is the only study to match heterosexual and same-sex couples on length of relationship, the large difference in geographical region and decade in which the study was conducted leaves a lot to be desired. In his longitudinal study, Kurdek (2003) recruited lesbian and gay male couples without children via LGB periodicals and snowball sampling. The heterosexual comparison group was recruited from newlywed announcements in the Dayton, Ohio, newspaper. Thus, over time, many of the heterosexual samples had children whereas the same-sex sample did not.

What further complicates the difficulty in finding appropriate heterosexual comparison groups for LGBs is that studies of LGBs find them to be demographically very different from heterosexuals in the general population. For example, gay men tend to live in large cities, lesbians are highly educated, and both lesbians and gay men are not very religious. This could be due to actual differences between LGBs and heterosexuals, or to the very different recruiting sources that have been used.

I have argued in the past (see Rothblum, Balsam, Solomon, & Factor, 2005, for a review) that a useful comparison group for LGB would be their heterosexual siblings. Siblings are generally the same race, ethnicity, and age cohort, and grew up with the same religion and parental socioeconomic status. My research on LGBs and their siblings (Rothblum & Factor, 2001; Rothblum, Balsam, & Mickey, 2004; Rothblum et al.) has shown that lesbians are more highly educated, have occupations with greater status, are less religious, and more geographically mobile than heterosexual women. Heterosexual women are more similar to census data in terms of marriage, children, religion, and homemaker status. Gay men have moved to large cities and are more highly educated than heterosexual men. In general, bisexual women are more comparable demographically to lesbians whereas bisexual men are more similar to heterosexual men.

Our research on same-sex couples who had civil unions in Vermont during the first year of that legislation (Solomon, Rothblum, & Balsam, 2004, 2005; Rothblum et al., 2005) also compared them with married heterosexual siblings and spouses. This ensured that the couples were similar on age, race, ethnicity, and religion in childhood. Once again there were numerous demographic differences in adulthood. Lesbians in civil unions were more highly educated, less likely to belong to a formal religion, less likely to attend religious services, and less likely to have children than heterosexual married women. Gay men in civil unions were more likely to live in large cities, less likely to belong to a formal religion, rate religion as less important, and less likely to have children than heterosexual married men.

These results demonstrate that siblings are a feasible comparison group for LGBs, including same-sex couples. It is not possible to tell whether the demographic differences may be the cause or consequence of sexual orientation. Nevertheless, these results indicate that same-sex couples differ from heterosexual married couples on a number of factors, not just sexual orientation.

In the Absence of Legal Marriage, What is a Couple?

The vast majority of the heterosexual couple literature has focused on married couples. When cohabiting heterosexual couples are included in research, they are usually considered a more nontraditional type of relationship and compared with married couples (e.g., Blumstein & Schwartz, 1983). In the absence of legal marriage, who is included in studies of same-sex couples?

Researchers who have studied same-sex couples have used various criteria. Some have included anyone who was in a same-sex relationship, no matter how recently. For example, Caron and Ulin (1997) did not place a limit on length of relationship; their sample of lesbians had been together from 2 months to 25.5 years, with a mean of 4.5 years. In contrast, Schreurs and Buunk (1996) included only lesbian couples who had been together a minimum of 3 years. Gottman et al. (2003) stipulated that same-sex couples had to be living together for at least 2 years. In their qualitative study of 50 same-sex couples from Massachusetts who had either been married or not, Porche, Purvin, and Waddell (2005) stipulated that couples had to have been together for at least 1 year. Elizur and Mintzer's study of

121 gay men in Israel stipulated that the men had to have been in their relationship for at least 5 years.

Thus it is difficult to know how the results of each study were influenced by the criteria they used for couple inclusion. For example, Kurdek's (1989) research has found that relationship satisfaction was higher in lesbian and gay male couples who had been together longer. Sexual frequency among gay male couples declines with length of the relationship (see Peplau, Fingerhut, & Beals, 2004, for a review).

In one of the only studies to focus on long-term couples, Mackey, Diemer, and O'Brien (2004) recruited 108 same-sex couples who had been together for at least 15 years; their sample of lesbian, gay male, and heterosexual couples had been together a mean of 30 years. These authors found that the best predictors of relationship satisfaction among all three types of long-term couples were psychologically intimate communication and minimal conflict. Variables such as conflict management styles, couple decision making, expressing physical affection, equity, quality of sexual relations, and the importance of sex were not predictors of relationship satisfaction.

For same-sex couples not in legalized relationships, it may be difficult to define the relationship. As Green and Mitchell (2002, p. 552) describe the possibly varieties of relationships, "Is it a best friendship, a social acquaintanceship, a romantic involvement, a lifelong primary commitment, a temporary dating relationship, a mainly sexual encounter, a commercial exchange, a temporary separation, a mentoring arrangement, an ongoing affair secondary to a primary relationship, or a former-lovers-now-friends bond?" Furthermore, one member of the couple may have a very different interpretation of the relationship than the other, given that same-sex couples may not have a formal period of dating or being "engaged," a wedding, involvement of their families of origin in decisions about the relationship, or children (Green & Mitchell).

Same-Sex Couples who are Married or in Legalized Relationships

There are few places in the world where same-sex couples can legalize their relationship. In 1989, Denmark became the first nation in the world to have gay and lesbian registered partnerships (Soland, 1998). Currently only Belgium, Canada, the Netherlands, and Spain have legalized marriage for same-sex couples at the federal level. Countries with registered same-sex cohabitants or civil unions at the federal level include Australia, Brazil, Croatia, Denmark, Finland, France, Germany, Great Britain, Greenland, Hungary, Iceland, Israel, New Zealand, Norway, Portugal, South Africa, Sweden, and Switzerland (see Wintemute & Anderaes, 2001, for a review). Other countries may have legalized same-sex relationships in some cities or counties but not in the whole nation (e.g., Buenos Aires, Argentina) and the United States falls into this category. Currently only Massachusetts has legalized marriage for same-sex couples (only for those who reside in the state); Connecticut, Vermont,

New Hampshire, and New Jersey have civil unions; and California, Hawaii, Maine, Washington, Oregon, and the District of Columbia have domestic partnerships.

The list of countries and regions offering legalized same-sex relationships can be misleading. For example, same-sex couples in Belgium can get legally married, but this does not include legal coparenting status. Denmark has had registered partnerships for same-sex couples since 1989, but these partners could not adopt each other's children until 1999 (Lund-Andersen, 2001). In contrast, a number of US states and the District of Columbia currently permit a child to have two legal mothers or two fathers (Eskridge, 2001).

The majority of US states have introduced legislation prohibiting recognition of same-sex marriage from other states. Because the US Constitution stipulates that the laws of one state, including marriage, should be recognized by other states, the Defense of Marriage Act was signed into law in 1996, which states that no US state is required to honor same-sex marriages from other states. Furthermore, opponents of same-sex marriage are currently advocating for a constitutional amendment banning same-sex marriage at the national level in the US.

Not all LGBs Want Same-Sex Marriage

Based on the media focus on same-sex marriage, one could conclude that all same-sex couples would marry given the chance. In fact, this topic is not without controversy in the LGB communities (see Rothblum, 2004, for a review). Yep, Lovaas, and Elia (2003) have presented a model of two competing sexual ideologies in the US. The *assimilationist* position argues that all people have the right to get married, and that marriage results in stable relationships. In contrast, the *radical* position asserts that marriage is an oppressive institution, and that same-sex relationships should be unique and freely chosen, not mimicking heterosexual norms.

Heterosexuals who do not believe in marriage are likely to discuss this with potential partners at an early stage of the relationship. LGBs did not grow up in societies where same-sex marriage was a possibility. Now that some couples can get married or legally partnered, this may cause conflict within the relationship when one partner wants the legality and the other one does not. There has been very little research on same-sex couples in legalized relationship in any nation, including comparisons between same-sex couples who do and do not choose to legalize their relationship.

Due to the very nature of their definition as "same-sex" legal relationships, national registries keep data of the number of female vs. male couples. Thus, one of the few facts known about legal same-sex partnerships is the ratio of men to women. Waaldijk (2001) has provided the numbers of same-sex partnerships in Denmark, Norway, Sweden, Iceland, and the Netherlands for each year since the legislation began. In all these countries men predominated, usually in a ratio of 3:1. In Canada too, slightly more male than female couples have married (http://www. gaydemographics.org). In contrast, in the United States where same-sex partnerships are only legal in a few states, more women than men have entered into these legal-ized relationships. In Vermont, twice as many women as men have had civil unions (Solomon et al., 2004). In Massachusetts in 2004, the first year of that legislation, 65% of same-sex marriages were female (Belge, 2005). And in San Francisco, where same-sex marriages were performed for about a month in early 2004, women predominated.

What could account for this difference in gender ratios between Europe and the US? Although it is impossible to know the actual number of lesbians and gay men in any society, most studies (e.g., Laumann et al., 1994) have more gay male than lesbian respondents. Thus, one could argue that the ratio of gay men to lesbians who have legalized relationships in European countries more accurately reflects the gender ratio. Secondly, Soland (1998) theorized that fewer lesbians than gay men took advantage of the Danish registered partnership legislation because until recently same-sex partners could not adopt children, including children of their partner. A third argument is that two men in a couple on average would have higher incomes than two women. Thus, gay men may benefit more from the financial aspects of legalized relationships, such as inheritance (all the European countries with same-sex legalized relationships have national health care coverage, so this is not an issue). Finally, Soland suggests that more lesbians questioned the notion of marriage as socially conservative. It is possible that radical politics among lesbians are more prevalent in Scandinavian and northern European nations than in North America as a whole.

In the United States, legalized relationships are only at the statewide level. Thus, in contrast to Europe and Canada, same-sex legalized relationships in the US are primarily a symbolic act, and it is possible that women are socialized to value the symbolism of marriage more so than men. Most benefits of marriage are at the federal level (e.g., inheritance, retirement, social security, sponsoring a partner from another country for US immigration, filing joint income tax; Cahill, Ellen, & Tobias, 2002) and so men, whose higher incomes may have more to gain from legal marriage, may not be interested.

There has been surprisingly little research about same-sex marriage other than the gender ratio. We do not know, for example, what motivates couples to get married (or have civil unions, domestic partnerships, or informal commitment ceremonies) when they do.

Attitudes by the General Public About Same-Sex Couples

In the past few years the US media has focused on the issue of same-sex marriage. Politicians, religious leaders, educators, and members of the general public discuss whether same-sex marriage is feasible on legal or moral grounds, whether it is good for children, and whether it will impact heterosexual marriage. It is not uncommon to read in the media that lesbians and gay men do not form lasting relationships, that they are promiscuous, that they expose young children to sex, or that same-sex marriage will cause the end of traditional marriage. Herek's (1994) research with random-digit dialing telephone surveys found that only one in three people reported knowing someone lesbian or gay. Those that do have lesbian or gay male acquaintances, friends, or family members have more positive attitudes about lesbians and gay men. As Peplau, Veniegas, and Campbell (1996, p. 250) stated: "Many Americans do not view lesbians and gay men as real people, but rather as abstract symbols who challenge conventional roles for women and men and who threaten traditional religious and family values....and a common belief is that same-sex couples have transient and troubled relationships."

When it comes to marriage, the public opposes legalizing same-sex marriage by a strong margin. A July 2003 opinion survey indicated that 59% of Americans opposed allowing gays and lesbians to marry compared with 32% who were in favor (Lochhead, 2003). When asked about support of "legal agreements giving many of the same rights as marriage," 51% were opposed and 41% in favor (Lochhead). A multitude of factors accounts for this opposition. Yep et al. (2003) state that the debate in the mainstream media has consisted of "historical, philosophical, religious, moral, political, legal, personal, and emotional grounds" (p. 46).

Most LGBs grew up in families and now live in neighborhoods and work with people who hold such attitudes. As a result, LGBs may internalize these negative attitudes about themselves. They may delay coming out to their families and friends or joining LGB communities in order to avoid negative stereotypes. Their own partnered relationships may be affected by these cultural views of the behavior of lesbians and gay men.

Testa, Kinder, and Ironson (1987) asked 380 college students to read hypothetical profiles of lesbian, gay male, or heterosexual couples. The profile of each couple had a high, medium, or low description of how much the couple was "in love." College students were asked to complete a modified version of the Dyadic Adjustment Scale about the couple's degree of relationship satisfaction and also the quality of love present in the relationship. Lesbian and gay male couples were perceived as being less satisfied with their relationship and less in love than heterosexual couples, despite the fact that the profiles were written so as to be identical except for the gender of the partners.

Lesbians and Gay Men who were Previously Married to Heterosexuals

The general heterosexual public may not know much about same-sex couples, but LGBs know a great deal about heterosexual marriage. Fairy tales in childhood end with couples getting married and living "happily ever after." Most official documents ask about marital status. There are other constant reminders about the importance of marriage. Popular songs, television shows, magazines, books, and advertised products focus on marriage themes.

And, in fact, many LGBs have been previously heterosexually married. An early survey by Bell and Weinberg (1978) found 13% of African American gay men, 20% of

European American gay men, 47% of African American lesbians, and 35% of European American lesbians had been married. Although these data indicate that lesbians were more likely to have been previously married then gay men, gay men had been in their former marriages for longer periods than lesbians. In a study of same-sex registered partnerships in Norway and Sweden (Andersson, Noack, Seierstad, & Weedon-Fekjaer, 2004), one-quarter of lesbians had been previously heterosexually married, which was also the case for prior marriages of their heterosexual counterparts.

Wyers (1987) interviewed 74 lesbian and gay male participants who were separated or divorced from heterosexual marriages. Former marriages of lesbians lasted 8.6 years on average, compared with 11 years for former marriages of gay men. Additionally, gay men were about twice as likely to rate their former marriage satisfying than were lesbians. Only 26.5% of female participants were aware of their lesbianism when they got married, compared with 68.8% of men who were aware that they were gay. Few participants had disclosed their sexual orientation to their former spouse before marriage. Among the gay men, 81% found the coming out process during marriage to be difficult, compared with 53% of lesbians.

LGBs Currently Married to Heterosexuals

This review has not begun to discuss the ways in which self-identified LGBs differ from women and men in heterosexual marriages who covertly have sexual relationships with same-sex individuals. In many cases, the spouses, the children, and/or society at large, are unaware of the same-sex relationship. Three books on this phenomenon are *And Then I Met This Woman: Previously Married Women's Journeys Into Lesbian Relationships* (Cassingham & O'Neil, 1993), *Married Women Who Love Women* (Strock, 2000), and *When Husbands Come Out of the Closet* (Gochros, 1989), but there has been little systematic research on such families.

Such closeted couples surely differ from "out" same-sex couples in myriads of ways, but finding samples for research would be challenging. For example, Wyers (1987) set out to study lesbian and gay male parents who were heterosexually married, separated, or divorced. The study was widely publicized in the Portland, Oregon area, but only two out of 74 people who agreed to participate were currently married. Yet one could speculate that, even today, LGBs who are heterosexually married yet partnered with same-sex lovers may be a very large subgroup.

Changes in Same-Sex Relationships over Time

Are same-sex relationships today similar to those of 30 years ago? The late 1970s were the beginning of research of same-sex couples, most notably by Anne Peplau and her colleagues and by Blumstein and Schwartz. This was the height of the second wave of the feminist movement, and, not surprisingly, feminism played a role in lesbians' lives. Peplau and her collaborators (Peplau, Cochran, Rook, & Padesky, 1978) asked lesbians to rate the importance to them of various statements about romantic/sexual relationships. A factor analysis yielded two factors: one on dyadic attachment (having a close, monogamous and permanent relationship with shared activities) and the other on personal autonomy (having an independent and equal relationship). About half the sample belonged to current feminist organizations. Feminism was positively associated with personal autonomy and negatively with dyadic attachment. It is possible that feminism would be less important for younger lesbians today.

Both Diamond (2005) and Savin-Williams (2005) have conducted longitudinal research with sexual minority youth. Although their research does not focus on couples, it is apparent that concepts of sexual orientation have changed drastically in the past decade. Sexual orientation and self-identity are more fluid and flexible, more resistant to easy categorization, and may be independent of sexual behavior. As this age cohort enters long-term partnered same-sex relationships, they may appear markedly different from older generations. Much of the research reviewed later may be inapplicable to this younger generation as they enter adulthood.

Given all These Methodological Issues, What does the Research Say About Same-Sex Couples?

All of the issues discussed are potential methodological problems when conducting research about same-sex couples. We do not know much about how the complexity of dimensions of sexual orientation affects the two members of the couple, and their relationship. If studies included more bisexual women and men, how would this change the results? What if the heterosexual comparison groups were more similar in recruitment method, or demographics? Would it be possible to study LGBs who are currently heterosexually married? And how will increased legality of same-sex marriage affect same-sex couples? The following review describes what is known about same-sex couples, including factors that are similar to married heterosexual couples and those that are unique to same-sex couples. Despite the challenges involved in studying LGB couples over time, it is impressive that a number of researchers have managed to obtain the consent of following couples as they live their lives.

Demographic Similarity Within Couples

A large literature on married heterosexual couples indicates that demographic similarity ("assortative mating") is a predictor of relationship satisfaction (e.g., Adams, 1979). Laumann et al. (1994) describe how assortative mating among heterosexuals is the norm, given how schools, colleges, neighborhoods, and the military are stratified by such factors as age, social class, race, ethnicity, and religion. They speculate that LGBs might meet partners in settings (e.g., gay bars, LGB pride marches) that are less demographically stratified. Rosenfeld and Kim (2005) argue that both inter-racial couples and same-sex couples are more geographically mobile and more likely to live in urban settings. This frees them from parental control and makes them more likely to meet similar others.

So far, little research has explored assortative mating in lesbian and gay couples, and the results have been mixed. Peplau et al. (1997) found that African American lesbians and gay men were generally similar to their partners in age, educational level, and employment status. However, over one-third of African Americans were in inter-racial relationships (30% of lesbians and 42% of gay men). This is in marked contrast to US census data on heterosexuals, where only 2.1% of African women and 4.6% of African American men marry spouses who are not African American (in Peplau et al.).

Peplau, Padesky, and Hamilton (1982) proposed that demographic similarity between lesbian partners would predict greater satisfaction. Contrary to expectations, the results showed that relationship satisfaction was not significantly related to similarity on age, number of previous lesbian relationships, level of education, and/or the degree of religiousness. Kurdek and Schmitt (1987a) explored the relationship of partner homogamy on demographic factors and relationship satisfaction among 44 heterosexual married, 35 heterosexual cohabiting, 56 lesbian, and 50 gay male couples. Even though gay male couples showed greater discrepancies between partners in age, income, and education than the other three types of couples, no significant correlation was found between similarity on demographic factors and relationship quality. Todosijevic, Rothblum, and Solomon (2005) examined partner similarity among 199 lesbian couples and 114 gay male couples who had civil unions in Vermont. Couple similarity on income and education was not related to relationship satisfaction. However, similarity in age was related to relationship satisfaction among gay men, whereas a greater age difference was related to relationship satisfaction among lesbians.

Outness to Others

Given the mixed results on demographic similarity and relationship satisfaction among same-sex couples, it is possible that couple similarity in level of outness may be more important for relationship satisfaction than couple similarity on demographic variables. For example, similarity on actual age (a demographic variable) may be less important than developmental stage in the coming out process (including level of disclosure to others). Couples who are discrepant on outness may have conflict around such issues as where to live (e.g., in an obvious gay neighborhood), whether to bring a partner to work-related social events, and how to introduce their partner to family members. Jordan and Deluty (2000) investigated the correlation between outness and relationship quality in 305 lesbians in committed relationships. Their results indicated that the degree of openness regarding sexual orientation was positively correlated with relationship satisfaction and that discrepancy in outness between partners was negatively correlated with relationship satisfaction. Caron and Ulin (1997) surveyed 124 lesbians in coupled relationships via convenience sampling in Maine. There was a significant correlation between self and partner's degree of openness to others.

In contrast, using data from 784 lesbian couples surveyed in 1979 for the American Couples Study by Blumstein and Schwartz (1983), Beals and Peplau (2001) found that discrepancy in outness among partners was not predictive of relationship quality. Todosijevic et al. (2005) assessed similarity in level out outness among 199 lesbian and 114 gay male couples who had civil unions in Vermont. There was no significant correlation between relationship satisfaction and similarity in level of outness.

Sexual Activity

Prior researchers have reported that gay men have sex more frequently, and lesbians less frequently, than heterosexual married couples (Blumstein & Schwartz, 1983; Peplau et al., 2004). Solomon et al. (2005) found that lesbian couples (those who had had civil unions in Vermont and those not in civil unions) had sex less frequently than did married heterosexual women. Heterosexual married women were more likely to report that their partner initiated sex, and that they themselves were more likely to refuse sex, than were women in lesbian couples.

When couples consist of two women, they lack someone socialized to be the sexual initiator (Blumstein & Schwartz, 1983; Peplau et al., 2004; Rothblum & Brehony, 1993). Lesbian couples, being female, may spend more time on romance than on genital sex, but it is also true that in Western societies "real" sex consists of genital activity (c.f., McCormick, 1994; Rothblum & Brehony). This is a domain where lack of traditional roles may reduce relationship satisfaction among lesbians. In contrast, gay men report having sex more often than do heterosexuals and lesbians (e.g., Blumstein & Schwarz).

Monogamy

Whereas monogamy is highly valued among lesbian and heterosexual couples, non-monogamy is often an accepted part of gay male culture (Blumstein & Schwartz, 1983; Peplau et al., 2004). For example, Blumstein and Schwartz emphasized the importance of impersonal sex with strangers ("tricking") as follows (p. 295): "But the trick mentality allows many men to have sex without emotional involvement. This is why gay male couples can tolerate very high rates of non-monogamy."

Researchers in the United Kingdom found that the majority of gay male couples had a specific agreement about sex outside their relationship (Hickson et al., 1992).

Peplau et al. (1997) found African American gay men to be more non-monogamous than African American lesbians. Similarly, Solomon et al. (2005) found that gay men were less monogamous than married heterosexual men. Whereas few lesbians, heterosexual women, or heterosexual men had had sex outside their current relationship, non-monogamy was reported by over one-half of gay men. Furthermore, non-monogamy was an accepted part of gay men's relationships in that over 40% of gay men in civil unions and those not in civil unions had an agreement that sex outside their relationship was permissible in some circumstances, whereas 5% or fewer of lesbian and heterosexual couples had such an agreement.

Kurdek (1988b) recruited 74 gay male and 47 lesbian couples via ads in LGB periodicals and snowball sampling. All lesbian couples were monogamous whereas about half the gay male couples were not. There were no demographic differences between monogamous and non-monogamous gay male couples except that the non-monogamous couples had lived together longer. Blasband and Peplau (1985) surveyed 17 monogamous and 23 non-monogamous gay male couples. The couples did not differ on any variable, including relationship satisfaction. However, Peplau et al. (1997) did find that non-monogamy was correlated with relationship dissatisfaction among both African American lesbians and gay men.

Although non-monogamy is much less common among lesbians than among gay men, there has been little focus on "polyamory" or non-monogamy among lesbians (see Munson & Stelboum, 1999, for an anthology on this topic). What factors correlate with non-monogamy for lesbians, and how do non-monogamous lesbians negotiate their relationships in a culture of monogamy? For example, is there a difference between sex outside the primary relationship (non-monogamy) without emotional attachment vs. a relationship consisting of three people involved with and committed to each other (polyamory)? There has been virtually no research on this phenomenon.

Overinvolvement vs. Autonomy

The notion that lesbians in couples are at risk for becoming "merged" or overinvolved stems from theoretical articles by lesbian therapists and mental health professionals in the early 1980s (e.g., Kaufman, Harrison, & Hyde, 1984; Krestan & Bepko, 1980; McCandlish, 1982; Roth, 1985). According to this concept, women are socialized to be relational, and thus two women in a relationship may become overinvolved with each other. In contrast, gay male couples are theorized to be overly autonomous and disengaged. However, there has been little empirical research about this concept.

Solomon et al. (2004) found that lesbian couples (those in civil unions and those not in civil unions) did more leisure activities as a couple, attended more social events with their partner, and had more mutual friends, than did heterosexual women. In contrast, gay men did not differ from heterosexual men on the first two of these variables, though they did have more mutual friends than did heterosexual men.

Schreurs and Buunk (1996) surveyed 119 lesbian couples in the Netherlands who had been together for at least 3 years. They included various measures about closeness, including emotional dependency, intimacy, autonomy, equity, and social support from others, and participation in the lesbian community. Autonomy and intimacy were not correlated, indicating that these are independent measures. However, autonomy was negatively correlated with emotional dependency, and positively correlated with equity in the relationship and greater participation in the lesbian community. In a regression equation of factors contributing to relationship satisfaction, 36% of the variance was accounted for by intimacy, emotional dependency, equity, and autonomy. This study was important in pointing out two issues: that intimacy in lesbian relationships is not related to lack of autonomy, and that both emotional dependency and autonomy are associated with relationship satisfaction.

Green et al. (1996) compared 52 lesbian couples and 50 gay male couples recruited via convenience samples with 1,140 heterosexual married couples from a national survey. Couples completed measures of cohesion (emotional closeness), flexibility (adaptability), and relationship satisfaction. Lesbian couples scored highest on the measure of cohesion, but gay men scored higher on this measure than did heterosexual married couples. Lesbian couples scored highest on the measure of flexibility, and both lesbian and gay male couples had higher scores on this measure than did heterosexual couples. Both cohesion and flexibility were positively correlated with relationship satisfaction. Thus, the concepts of lesbian merger and gay male disengagement do not show much empirical evidence.

Division of Household Tasks

As Green et al. (1996) have pointed out, the general public often believes that lesbians and gay men play "male" and "female" roles in relationships. They state (p. 219): "Yet this same public remains largely unconscious...about its own problematic conformity to the socially constructed 'butch/femme' roles in heterosexual relationships."

Kurdek (1993) studied the allocation of household tasks in lesbian, gay male, and heterosexual married couples. Lesbian couples tended to share tasks, and both lesbian and gay male couples divided tasks so that each partner performed an equal number of tasks. In married heterosexual couples, women did the majority of household tasks.

Solomon et al. (2005) examined the division of household tasks and finances among same-sex couples who had civil unions in Vermont, their coupled same-sex friends who had not had civil unions, and married heterosexual siblings and spouses. Compared with lesbian and gay male couples (whether or not they were in civil unions), married heterosexuals had a more traditional, gendered division of household tasks and finances (women did the housework and men paid for more items). Money and housework are not unrelated concepts; Blumstein and Schwartz (1983) noted the relationship between money and power. Those who earn a higher income (men) do less housework than those who earn a lower income (women). In this regard, same-sex couples are a model for ways of equalizing the division of housework.

One of the problems in studying division of labor among heterosexual couples is that gender is confounded with income. Because most men earn higher incomes than most women, it is hard to know whether women do more of the housework because of gender role socialization, or because they have less power due to earning less money than their male partners. Analysis of division of household labor among same-sex couples in the Solomon et al. (2005) study allowed examination of income difference without the confound of gender. Sexual orientation was a stronger predictor of the division of household tasks than was income difference within couples. For both women and men, only sexual orientation made a unique contribution to the model that predicted division of household labor. Thus, being in a same-sex relationship is more important in equalizing housework than is having similar incomes.

What is interesting about the results by Solomon et al. (2005) is that the married couples in this study are not typical heterosexuals, because each heterosexual respondent was the sibling or in-law of a lesbian or gay man. In order to participate in this study, same-sex couples had to be "out" to the sibling and in-law who were sent questionnaires. This raises questions about how women and men are socialized to assume gendered roles in adult relationships, because heterosexuals grew up in the same households as some of the lesbians and gay men in this study.

Nevertheless, some researchers have criticized the equal division of labor among same-sex couples as exaggerated. Part of the problem is that when a couple consists of two women or two men, it is difficult to conduct between-partner comparisons across a large number of participants (see for example, Oerton, 1998, for a discussion). Carrington (1999) dealt with this problem by interviewing 52 same-sex couples in the San Francisco Bay Area and also accompanying and observing eight couples for a week as they went about household duties. He found a large variety of patterns of domestic labor among same-sex couples.

Heterosexual women are also unique among other groups in that they alone typically identify as homemakers if they are not employed outside the home. This identity is rarely assumed by lesbians or gay men in couples when one partner is not employed. Dunne (1997, 1998) interviewed 60 nonheterosexual women in the United Kingdom. What was striking to these women as they came out as sexual minorities was a realization that they could not rely on men for an income. Dunne states (1998, p. 3): "It could be seen, for example, that a lesbian lifestyle both *necessitates* and *facilitates* financial self-reliance." Consequently, a number of women obtained higher education or changed to higher-paying jobs (often blue-collar and more nontraditional for women).

Power

Blumstein and Schwartz surveyed 12,000 couples in the 1970s. What was unique about this study was the inclusion of 788 lesbian and 969 gay male couples as well as heterosexual married and heterosexual cohabiting couples. Much of the focus of their book *American Couples* is the issue of power in couples. For example, they found that the partner who earns a higher income has more power relative to their partner, except in lesbian couples, where relative income does not affect power. Among lesbian, gay male, and heterosexual cohabiting couples, the partner with a higher income has more control over the couple's recreational activities. The more powerful partner in all types of relationships is more likely to refuse sex.

Reilly and Lynch (1990) asked lesbian couples about power sharing (e.g., who has more say in the relationship, who initiated sexual activity, who had final say about what they did together). Their sample consisted of 70 lesbian couples from New England who had lived together for at least 1 year (median length of relationship was 2.9 years). Couples were divided into those in which both partners reported that the relationship was equal, those in which both partners agreed that one partner had more power, and those in which the partners disagreed about power sharing. Power sharing could not be attributed to age, income, education, or asset difference between partners.

Conflict

Kurdek (1994) examined self-reported conflict in his sample of lesbian, gay male, and heterosexual married couples without children. Twenty areas of conflict were factor analyzed into six factors: power (e.g., being critical), social issues (e.g., politics and social issues), personal flaws (e.g., drinking alcohol and smoking), distrust (e.g., distrust or lying), intimacy (e.g., sex), and personal distance (e.g., job commitment). Issues around intimacy and power were areas of conflict for all three types of couples. Heterosexual couples had more conflict around social issues than did lesbian and gay male couples. Kurdek explains this by the fact that lesbian and gay male couples, as members of stigmatized groups, may have greater similarity on political and social issues than do heterosexual couples. Lesbian and gay male couples argued more over issues of distrust, which might be due to the presence of ex-lovers in the LGB communities and friendship circles. Conflict was related to relationship dissatisfaction in all three types of couples.

Gottman has conducted extensive physiological and behavioral observations of married heterosexual couples to examine correlates of conflict and relationship duration (see Gottman, 1979, 1994, for a review). There was extensive media coverage of his first behavioral study of same-sex couples (Gottman et al., 2003) in which he compared 22 gay male couples (12 happy and 10 unhappy) and 18 lesbian couples (10 happy and 8 unhappy) recruited via convenience samples in Berkeley,

California, with heterosexual married couples recruited in Bloomington, Indiana, in 1983. Forty heterosexual married couples from that data set were selected as a comparison group because they matched the same-sex couples in relationship satisfaction and length of relationship.

The results indicated that same-sex couples showed less negative affect belligerence, whining, and fear/tension, and greater affection, humor, and joy/excitement than the heterosexual married couples. The authors interpret these findings in light of equity in same-sex couples as follows (Gottman et al., 2003, p. 88): "It is well known that the status hierarchy in heterosexual relationships breeds hostility, particularly from women, who tend to have less power than men, and who also typically bring up most of the relationship issues. Because there are fewer barriers to leaving homosexual compared to heterosexual relationships, homosexual couples may be more careful in the way they accept influence from one another. Thus, we suggest that the process variables by which they resolve conflicts may be the very glue that keeps these relationships stable."

Contact with Family of Origin

Parents and relatives of heterosexuals are generally aware when their son or daughter gets married and usually stay involved with the couple. In contrast, lesbians and gay men may not be out to their family of origin, and even if they are, feel some disapproval or lack of acceptance of the relationship. What is the effect of contact with family of origin on same-sex couples?

First, research with LGBs and their siblings indicates that heterosexual siblings are geographically closer to their family of origin. Lesbians live further away from their mother and father than do their heterosexual sisters (Rothblum & Factor, 2001) and lesbians attended a college that was further from home than the one that heterosexual women attended (Rothblum et al., 2004). As mentioned earlier, gay men tend to live in large cities (Rothblum et al.).

Murphy (1989) surveyed 20 European American, middle-class lesbians, all of whom were in partnered relationships, had no children, and were "out" to their parents. Participants reported that being out to their parents decreased their sense of isolation, made it easier to come out to other family members, and enabled them to live their lives without compartmentalizing themselves. Nevertheless, participants reported that their parents often ignored their partner, and also tended to like their daughter's partner more when they thought she was a friend, before the daughter came out to them.

Caron and Ulin (1997) surveyed 124 lesbians in coupled relationships via convenience sampling in Maine. Openness to immediate and extended family was correlated with relationship satisfaction, whereas openness to coworkers was not. In contrast, Green et al. (1996) did not find a correlation between outness to mothers, fathers, or siblings and relationship satisfaction.

In the study of same-sex couples who had civil unions in Vermont and their heterosexual married siblings and spouses, Solomon et al. (2004) asked a number of questions about contact with family of origin. Heterosexual married women had more contact with their mother than did lesbians in civil unions, and also initiated more contact with their partner's mother and father. Heterosexual married men initiated more contact with their partner's father, and also reported that their father makes them feel "part of the family," compared with gay men in civil unions. These results mesh with the findings that LGBs have moved further away from their parents. Parents may be less supportive of their LGB children so that LGBs have less reason to visit or contact their parents. LGBs may not be "out" to their parents and thus would not want to introduce their partner to their parents, or meet their partner's parents. Finally, LGBs may have less in common with their family of origin (e.g., values, politics, lifestyle, etc.) and thus spend less time with them.

Mays, Cochran, and Rhue (1993) interviewed eight African American lesbians, all currently partnered with African American lovers. The participants reported that the African American community tended to welcome them. Most of the women referred to their lover as a "friend," although they acknowledged that their families knew that these were lover relationships. However, when the participants had been involved with lovers who were not African American in the past, there was less acceptance by their family of origin and the African American community. Some of the participants had also felt marginalized when involved with white women and had consciously chosen an African American lover.

Social Supports and Communities

Kurdek and Schmidt (1987b) examined sources of perceived social support for lesbian, gay male, and heterosexual couples. Heterosexual married couples perceived more support from family than did lesbian or gay male couples. Lesbian and gay male couples perceived more social support from friends, and social support from friends was related to lower psychological distress. Kurdek (1988a) found that for lesbian and gay male couples, the most common sources of support were, in order, friends, partners, family, and coworkers. High social support was related to positive psychological adjustment, and discrepancies between partners in social support were related to lower relationship quality. Eleven years after Kurdek began his longitudinal couples study (2004), he concluded that lack of social support from family was the only domain in which same-sex couples were deficient relative to heterosexual married couples.

Solomon et al. (2004) asked couples in same-sex civil unions and married heterosexual siblings and spouses about perceived social support from family and friends. Heterosexual married women perceived more support from family of origin than did lesbians in civil unions (gay men did not differ from heterosexual men on this measure). However, gay men perceived more support from friends than did heterosexual married men (lesbians did not differ from heterosexual women on this measure).

These results fit with the results described that lesbians attended a college that was further away and also live further from their parents in adulthood. Thus, lesbians may leave home because there is less to lose, or else lesbians may drift apart emotionally from their families of origin because they live further away. Gay men may also move to large cities to find friends, or else have more friends because they live in a large city. Traditional male gender roles may not allow heterosexual men to have close friendships, whereas male friendships are highly valued in gay male communities. These geographic moves may enable lesbians and gay men to be more out (for example to friends and coworkers) without the knowledge of their family.

Kurdek's (2003) 7-year longitudinal study comparing heterosexual married couples recruited from Dayton, Ohio, and lesbian/gay male couples recruited from LGB periodicals included a measure of satisfaction with social support. Heterosexual couples had higher satisfaction with social support from own family and partner's family than did lesbian and gay male couples. Lesbian couples had higher satisfaction with friends and partner's friends than did heterosexual couples. Kurdek (1988b) also found that for lesbian and gay male couples, high satisfaction with social support was related to greater relationship satisfaction.

Elizur and Mintzer (2003) included social support from friends and friends' acceptance of their relationship in a path analysis of relationship satisfaction and relationship durability among 121 gay men in Israel who had been in a relationship for at least 5 years. Both social support from friends and perceived acceptance of the relationship from friends were related to relationship satisfaction. In contrast, social support from family and family support of their relationship were not correlated with relationship satisfaction.

May, Chatters, Cochran, and Mackness (1998, p. 74) describe how the families of choice created by LGBs are similar to the concept of "fictive kin" (i.e., nonbiological networks) among African Americans. Beals and Peplau (2001) reanalyzed the lesbian data set of the American Couples Study (Blumstein & Schwarz, 1983) to look at lesbians' social involvement in their communities. They found a curvilinear relationship between involvement in lesbian community activities and relationship satisfaction – those couples who were moderately involved were most satisfied with their relationship.

Relationship Terminations

Green et al. (1996) compared heterosexual, lesbian, and gay male couples who had been partnered for at least 6 months. Heterosexual couples had been in their current relationship for a longer time period than same-sex couples, and the authors speculated on a number of reasons for this. Married heterosexual couples receive more support from family of origin and society to stay together, and may also stay together for religious or traditional values, even if unhappy in their relationship. Furthermore, heterosexual married couples are more likely to have children than are same-sex couples, and divorce has more legal and economic obstacles than terminations for couples who are not legally married.

In Kurdek's 11-year follow-up of his longitudinal study (2004), he found that same-sex couples terminated their relationship sooner, on average, than heterosexual married couples, especially heterosexual married couples with children. Using a wide variety of relationship measures, including psychological adjustment, personality traits, relationship styles, conflict resolution, and social support, he concluded that same-sex couples fare better than heterosexual married couples on 76% of all variables. Thus, it is likely that same-sex couples terminate relationships sooner than married heterosexual because there is an absence of formal barriers (such as legal divorce, child custody, etc.).

What happens when same-sex couples break up? When lesbian and gay male couples are closeted, there may be little support from others, including friends, coworkers, and family members. Family members who might be supportive when heterosexuals divorce may express hope that their lesbian or gay relative will now find a partner of the opposite sex. Morton (1998) reviewed some issues following "lesbian divorce," including lack of legal and economic protections. When lesbian or gay male couples were coparenting children, a relationship termination may offer one partner no access to the child that is not legally theirs.

Green et al. (1996) followed their sample of 52 lesbian couples over 2 years. At that second assessment period, 48 couples could be contacted and 14 of them had terminated the relationship. These couples had lower scores on cohesion and flexibility at Time 1 than did couples who were still together. There was no relationship between outness to family of origin and termination.

In Kurdek's longitudinal study (1992), 10 out of 80 gay male couples had separated (12%) compared with 12 out of 53 lesbian couples (22%). These were compared with similar intact couples at each assessment period. Couples who separated were younger, reported more negative affectivity, lower relationship satisfaction, and more independence (e.g., lived together for a shorter time period, were less likely to pool finances). Later on, Kurdek (1998) compared relationship dissolution for lesbian, gay male, and heterosexual couples after Year Five. Couples who terminated their relationship were more likely at Year One to have low levels of intimacy, low levels of equality, nonconstructive problem solving, and fewer barriers to leaving the relationship. Autonomy at Year One was not related to relationship termination.

What about terminations of legal same-sex relationships, including marriage? Despite the fact that gay men are more likely to enter into registered partnerships than are lesbians, the divorce rate in Denmark is higher for lesbians (16.2%) than for gay men (11.4%; Wockner, 1997). Noack, Seierstad, and Weedon-Fekjaer (2005) found a divorce rate of 8% after 4 years and 16% after 6 years among same-sex couples who had registered partnerships in Norway. After 6 years lesbians had a divorce rate of 21% compared with 13% among gay men in Norway. Other risk factors for divorce in Norway for same-sex couples were being younger, having a greater age difference between partners, and having a partner who was not from Norway.

The Importance of Ex-Lovers

Lesbians and gay men tend to remain friends with their ex-lovers. Given the small size of the LGB community, it is not surprising that there is pressure for ex-lovers to remain friends, so that it will not divide the community. Yet there has been little research on this phenomenon unique to same-sex ex-lovers. Solomon et al. (2004) found that lesbian and gay male couples were much more likely to report that ex-lovers were still friends, compared with heterosexuals. Similarly, Harkless and Fowers (2005) studied contact with ex-lovers and found that lesbians and gay men had more contact with ex-lovers than did heterosexuals, including telephone contact, in person contact, desire to see the person, contact at social gatherings, and having a current friendship. Weinstock (2004) referred to the phenomenon as "FLEX" (friends and family connections among ex-lovers). She points to a number of avenues for future research about the blurred boundaries between friends and lovers, especially when they are found from "the same-sex pool" (p. 215).

Conclusion: Relation Ships Still at Sea

What do we know about same-sex couples at this time? More specifically, what does the ideal LGB "relation Ship" (Johnson, 1991) look like? First, it does not appear as though LGBs need to find same-sex partners who are demographically similar to them, or even similar in level of outness, since those factors are generally not related to level of relationship satisfaction. Gay men are likely to have sex more often than other types of couples, though over time sex with their partner decreases and sex outside the relationship increases. In contrast, lesbian communities are encouraged to redefine what sex means between two women (or else lesbians should be socialized to initiate genital sex more often).

Despite the popular belief that lesbian couples are "merged" and gay male couples are disengaged, the research does not generally support this notion. Furthermore, same-sex couples could serve as role models for heterosexuals on how to divide up household tasks and finances. The behavioral research of Gottman et al. (2003) also implies that same-sex couples are good models for heterosexuals on how to discuss areas of conflict.

On the other hand, same-sex couples have less contact with families of origin – LGBs move away and lose contact or else lose contact and have more freedom to move away. This may permit lesbians and bisexual women to pursue higher levels of education than their heterosexual sisters, and may be the reason that gay men gravitate toward large cities. Similarly, LGBs perceive less social support from families of origin, which may again be a cause or consequence of lack of contact with families or the greater geographical distance from them. Instead, LGBs seek out their "families of friends" in the LGB communities, including ex-lovers. It will be interesting to see if same-sex couples have increased contact with families of origin if heterosexism decreases in society and/or same-sex relationships become more legitimate.

Same-sex couples do not stay together as long as married heterosexuals, and this may be the result of lack of legal marriage, less likelihood of having children, greater autonomy, or less stigma attached to being single than among heterosexuals. They do not stay together as long as heterosexuals because there is less social support (by families of origin or society in general) for same-sex couples to be together and less social resistance to breaking up.

A number of changes in the coming decades will soon render much of these researches obsolete. If more countries legalize same-sex marriage, then researchers are likely to focus on married same-sex couples and compare them with married heterosexual couples. LGB youth may grow up to view sexual orientation as more fluid and flexible than same-sex couples today, so that sexual orientation may become a continuous rather than a categorical dimension for studying relationship satisfaction and longevity. Some of the methodological problems described at the beginning of this chapter may be improved, so that LGB samples include more bisexuals and more people of color, and use better heterosexual comparison groups (such as siblings). In sum, same-sex relation Ships may consist of a whole new armada – a sea change, so to speak.

Acknowledgment I would like to thank Nanette Gartrell, Marcia Hill, and Anne Peplau for their helpful comments on an earlier draft of this chapter.

References

Adams, B. (1979). Mate selection in the United States: A theoretical summarization. In W. Burr, R. Hill, F. Nie, & I. Reiss (Eds.), *Contemporary theories about the family* (Vol. 1, pp. 259–267). New York: Free.

Andersson, G., Noack, T., Seierstad, A., & Weedon-Fekjaer, H. (April 2004).*Divorce-risk patterns in same-sex "marriages" in Norway and Sweden.* Paper presented at the annual convention of the Population Association of America, Boston, MA.

Beals, K., & Peplau, L. A. (2001). Social involvement, disclosure of sexual orientation, and the quality of lesbian relationships.*Psychology of Women Quarterly, 25,* 10–19.

Belge, K. (2005).*Gay marriages in Massachusetts: One year later, May 2005.* http://lesbianlife. about.com/od/wedding/a/MassOneYear.htm.

Bell, A. P., & Weinberg, M. S. (1978).*Homosexualities: A study of diversities among men and women.* New York, NY: Simon & Schuster.

Blasband, D., & Peplau, L. A. (1985). Sexual exclusivity versus openness in gay male couples.*Archives of Sexual Behavior, 14*(5), 395–412.

Blumstein, P., & Schwartz, P. (1983).*American couples: Money, work, sex.* New York, NY: William Morrow.

Cahill, S., Ellen, M., & Tobias, S. (2002).*Family policy: Issues affecting gay, lesbian, bisexual and transgender families.* The National Gay and Lesbian Task Force Policy Institute.

Caron, S. L., & Ulin, B. M. (1997). Closeting and the quality of lesbian relationships.*Families in Society: The Journal of Contemporary Human Services, 78*(4), 413–419.

Carrington, C. (1999).*No place like home: Relationships and family life among lesbians and gay men.* Chicago, IL: University of Chicago Press.

Cassingham, B. J., & O'Neil, S. M. (1993).*And Then I Met This Woman: Previously Married Women's Journeys Into Lesbian Relationships.* Racine, WII: Mother Courage Press.

Diamond, L. M. (2005). A new view of lesbian subtypes: Stable versus fluid identity trajectories over an 8-year period.*Psychology of Women Quarterly, 29,* 119–128.

Dion, K. K., & Dion, K. L. (1993). Individualistic and collective perspectives on gender and the cultural context of love and intimacy.*Journal of Social Issues, 49*(3), 53–69.

Dunne, G. A. (1997).*Lesbian lifestyles: Women's work and the politics of sexuality.* Toronto: University of Toronto Press.

Dunne, G. A. (1998).*Living "difference": Lesbian perspectives on work and family life.* New York, NY: Harrington Park Press.

Elizur, Y., & Mintzer, A. (2003). Gay males' intimate relationship quality: The roles of attachment security, gay identity, social support, and income.*Personal Relationships, 10,* 411–435.

Eskridge, W. N. (2001).*Equality practice: Civil unions and the future of gay rights.* New York, NY: Routledge.

Gochros, J. S. (1989).*When husbands come out of the closet.* New York, NY: Harrington Park Press.

Gottman, J. M. (1979).*Marital interaction: Experimental investigations.* New York, NY: Academic.

Gottman, J. M. (1994).*What predicts divorce?*Hillsdale, NJ: Erlbaum.

Gottman, J. M., Levenson, R. W., Swanson, C., Swanson, K., Tyson, R., & Yoshimoto, D. (2003). Observing gay, lesbian and heterosexual couples' relationships: Mathematical modeling of conflict interaction.*Journal of Homosexuality, 45*(1), 65–91.

Green, R. J., Bettinger, M., & Zacks, E. (1996). Are lesbian couples fused and gay male couples disengaged? Questioning gender straightjackets. In J. Laird & R.J. Green (Eds.),*Lesbians and gays in couples and families: A handbook for therapists* (pp. 185–230). New York, NY: Jossey-Bass.

Green, R. J., & Mitchell, V. (2002). Gay and lesbian couples in therapy: Homophobia, relational ambiguity, and social support. In A.S. Gurman & N.S. Jacobson (Eds.),*Clinical handbook of couple therapy* (pp. 546–568). New York, NY: Guilford.

Harkless, L. E., & Fowers, B. J. (2005). Similarities and differences in relational boundaries among heterosexuals, gay men, and lesbians.*Psychology of Women Quarterly, 29*(2), 167–176.

Herek, G. M. (1994). Assessing heterosexuals' attitudes toward lesbians and gay men: A review of empirical research with the ATLG Scale. In B. Greene & G.M. Herek (Eds.),*Lesbian and gay psychology: Theory, research, and clinical applications*(pp. 206–228). Thousand Oaks, CA: Sage.

Hickson, F. C. I., Davies, P. M., Hunt, A. J., Weatherburn, P., McManus, T. J., & Coxon, A. P. M. (1992). Maintenance of open gay relationships: Some strategies for protection against HIV.*AIDS Care, 4,* 409–419.

Johnson, S. (1991).*The ship that sailed into the living room: Sex and intimacy reconsidered.* Palo Alto, CA: Wildfire Books.

Jordan, K. M., & Deluty, R. H. (2000). Social support, coming out, and relationship satisfaction in lesbian couples.*Journal of Lesbian Studies, 4,* 145–164.

Kaufman, P. A., Harrison, E., & Hyde, M. L. (1984). Distancing for intimacy in the lesbian relationship.*American Journal of Psychiatry, 141,* 530–533.

Krestan, J. A., & Bepko, C. S. (1980). The problem of fusion in the lesbian relationship.*Family Process,19,* 277–289.

Kurdek, L. (1988a). Perceived social support in gays and lesbians in cohabiting relationships.*Journal of Personality and Social Psychology, 54*(3), 504–509.

Kurdek, L. (1988b). Relationship quality of gay and lesbian cohabiting couples.*Journal of Homosexuality, 15*(3/4), 91–118.

Kurdek, L. (1989). Relationship quality in gay and lesbian cohabiting couples: A 1-year follow-up study.*Journal of Social and Personal Relationships, 9,* 39–59.

Kurdek, L. (1992). Relationship stability and relationship satisfaction in cohabiting gay and lesbian couples: A prospective longitudinal test of the contextual and interdependence models.*Journal of Social and Personal Relationships, 9,* 125–142.

Kurdek, L. (1993). The allocation of household labor in gay, lesbian, and heterosexual married couples.*Journal of Social Issues, 49*(3), 127–130.

Kurdek, L. (1994). Areas of conflict for gay, lesbian, and heterosexual couples: What couples argue about influences relationship satisfaction.*Journal of Marriage and the Family, 56*, 923–934.

Kurdek, L. (1998). Relationship outcomes and their predictors: Longitudinal evidence from heterosexual married, gay cohabiting, and lesbian cohabiting couples.*Journal of Marriage and the Family, 60*, 553–568.

Kurdek, L. (2003). Differences between heterosexual-nonparent couples and gay, lesbian, and heterosexual-parent couples.*Journal of Family Issues, 22*(6), 727–754.

Kurdek, L. (2004). Are gay and lesbian cohabiting couples *really* different from heterosexual married couples?*Journal of Marriage and Family, 66*, 880–900.

Kurdek, L., & Schmitt, J. P. (1987a). Partner homogamy in married, heterosexual cohabiting, gay, and lesbian couples. *The Journal of Sex Research, 23*, 212–232.

Kurdek, L., & Schmitt, J. P. (1987b). Perceived emotional support from family and friends in members of homosexual, married, and heterosexual cohabiting couples. *Journal of Homosexuality, 14*(3/4), 57–68.

Laumann, E. O, Gagnon, J. H, Michael, R. T, & Michaels, S. (1994). *The social organization of sexuality: Sexual practices in the United States*. Chicago, IL: University of Chicago Press.

Lochhead, C. (November 19, 2003). Massachusetts court allows gay marriage. *San Francisco Chronice*, A15, A22.

Lund-Andersen, I. (2001). The Danish Registered Partnership Act, 1989: Has the Act meant a change in attitudes? In R. Wintemute & M. Andenaes,*Legal recognition of same-sex partnerships: A study of national, European and international law*. Oxford: Hart.

Mackey, R. A., Diemer, M. A., & O'Brien, B. A. (2004). Relational factors in understanding satisfaction in the lasting relationships of same-sex and heterosexual couples.*Journal of Homosexuality, 47*(1), 111–136.

Mays, V. M., Chatters, L. M., Cochran, S. D., & Mackness, J. (1998). African American families in diversity: Gay men and lesbians as participants in family networks.*Journal of Comparative Family Studies, 29*(1), 73–87.

Mays, V. M., Cochran, S. D., & Rhue, S. (1993). The impact of perceived discrimination on the intimate relationships of Black lesbians.*Journal of Homosexuality,25*(4), 1–14.

McCandlish, B. M. (1982). Therapeutic issues with lesbian couples.*Journal of Homosexuality, 7*, 71–78.

McCormick, N. B. (1994). Sexual salvation: Affirming women's sexual rights and pleasures. Westport, CT: Praeger.

Morris, J. F., & Rothblum, E. D. (1999). Who fills out a "lesbian" questionnaire? The interrelationship of sexual orientation, years out, disclosure of sexual orientation, sexual experience with women, and participation in the lesbian community.*Psychology Of Women Quarterly, 33*, 537–557.

Morton, S. B. (1998). Lesbian divorce.*American Journal of Orthopsychiatry, 68*(3), 410–419.

Munson, M., & Stelboum, J. (Eds.). (1999).*The lesbian polyamory reader*. New York, NY: Haworth.

Murphy, B. C. (1989). Lesbian couples and their parents: The effects of perceived parental attitudes on the couple.*Journal of Counseling and Development,68*(September–October), 46–51

Noack, T., Seierstad, A., & Weedon-Fekjaer, H. (2005). A demographic analysis of registered partnerships (legal same-sex unions): The case of Norway.*European Journal of Population, 21*, 89–109.

Oerton, S. (1998). Reclaiming the "housewife"? Lesbians and household work.*Journal of Lesbian Studies, 2*(4), 69–83.

Peplau, L. A., Cochran, S. D., & Mays, V. M. (1997). A national survey of the intimate relationships of African American lesbians and gay men: A look at commitment, satisfaction, sexual behavior, and HIV disease. In B. Greene & G. Herek (Eds.),*Psychological perspectives on lesbian and gay issues: Ethic and cultural diversity among lesbians and gay men* (pp. 11–38). Newbury Park, CA: Sage.

Peplau, L. A., Cochran, S., Rook, K., & Padesky, C. (1978). Loving women: Attachment and autonomy in lesbian relationships.*Journal of Social Issues, 34*(3), 7–27.

Peplau, L. A., Fingerhut, A., & Beals, K. P. (2004). Sexuality in the relationships of lesbians and gay men. In J. Harvey, A. Wenzel, & S. Sprecher (Eds.),*Handbook of sexuality in close relationships* (pp. 349–369). Mahwah, NJ: Erlbaum.

Peplau, L., Padesky, C., & Hamilton, M. (1982). Satisfaction in lesbian relationships.*Journal of Homosexuality, 8*, 23–35.

Peplau, L. A., Veniegas, R. C., & Campbell, S. M. (1996). Gay and lesbian relationships. In R.C. Savin-Williams & K.M. Cohen (Eds.),*The lives of lesbians, gays, and bisexuals* (pp. 250–273). Fort Worth, TX: Harcourt Brace College.

Porche, M. V., Purvin, D. M., & Waddell, J. M. (2005).*Tying the knot: The context of social change in Massachusetts.* Working Paper No. 432, Wellesley Centers for Women, Wellesley, MA.

Reilly, M. E., & Lynch, J. M. (1990). Power-sharing in lesbian partnerships. *Journal of Homosexuality, 19*(3), 30.

Rosenfeld, M. J., & Kim, B. (2005). The independence of young adults and the rise of interracial and same-sex unions.*American Sociological Review, 70*, 541–562.

Roth, S. (1985). Psychotherapy with lesbian couples: Individual issues, female socialization, and the social context.*Journal of Marriage and Family Therapy, 11*, 273–286.

Rothblum, E. D. (1994). "I only read about myself on bathroom walls": The need for research on the mental health of lesbians and gay men.*Journal of Consulting and Clinical Psychology, 62*, 213–220.

Rothblum, E. D. (2004). Same-sex marriage and legalized relationships: I do, or do I?*Journal of GLBT Family Studies, 1*, 21–31.

Rothblum, E. D., Balsam, K. F., & Mickey, R. M. (2004). Brothers and sisters of lesbians, gay men, and bisexuals as a demographic comparison group: An innovative research methodology to examine social change.*The Journal of Applied Behavioral Science, 40*, 283–301.

Rothblum, E. D., Balsam, K. F., Solomon, S. E., & Factor, R. J. (2005). Siblings and sexual orientation: Products of alternative families or the ones who got away?*Journal of GLBT Family Studies, 1*, 71–87.

Rothblum, E. D., & Brehony, K. A. (1993).*Boston marriages: Romantic but asexual relationships among contemporary lesbians.*Amherst, MA: University of Massachusetts Press.

Rothblum, E. D., & Factor, R. J. (2001). Lesbians and their sisters as a control group: Demographic and mental health factors.*Psychological Science, 12*(1), 63–69.

Rust, P. C. (1995). Bisexuality and the challenge to lesbian politics: Sex, loyalty, and revolution. New York, NY: New York University Press.

Savin-Williams, R. C. (2005).*The new gay teenager.* Boston: Harvard University Press.

Schreurs, K. M. G., & Buunk, B. P. (1996). Closeness, autonomy, equity, and relationship satisfaction in lesbian couples.*Psychology of Women Quarterly, 20*, 577–592.

Soland, B. (1998). A queer nation? The passage of the gay and lesbian partnership legislation in Denmark, 1989.*Social Politics, spring*, 48–69.

Solomon, S. E., Rothblum, E. D., & Balsam, K. F. (2004). Pioneers in partnership: Lesbian and gay male couples in civil unions compared with those not in civil unions, and heterosexual married siblings.*Journal of Family Psychology, 18*, 275–286.

Solomon, S. E., Rothblum, E. D., & Balsam, K. F. (2005). Money, housework, sex, and conflict: Same-sex couples in civil unions, those not in civil unions, and heterosexual married siblings.*Sex Roles, 52*, 561–575.

Strock, C. (2000).*Married women who love women.* New York, NY: Alyson.

Testa, R. J., Kinder, B. N., & Ironson, G. (1987). Heterosexual bias in the perception of loving relationships of gay males and lesbians.*The Journal of Sex Research, 23*(2), 163–172.

Todosijevic, J., Rothblum, E. D., & Solomon, S. E. (2005). Relationship satisfaction, affectivity, and gay-specific stressors in same-sex couples joined in civil unions.*Psychology of Women Quarterly, 29*, 158–166.

Waaldijk, K. (2001). Small change: How the road to same-sex marriage got paved in the Netherlands. In R. Wintemute & M. Andenaes (Eds.),*Legal recognition of same-sex partnerships: A study of national, European and international law.* Oxford: Hart.

Weinstock, J. S. (2004). Lesbian FLEX-ibility: Friend and/or Family connections among Lesbian Ex-lovers.*Journal of Lesbian Studies, 8*(3/4), 193–238.

Wintemute, R., & Anderaes, M. (2001). Legal recognition of same-sex partnerships: A study of national, European and international law. Oxford: Hart.

Wockner, R. (1997). New statistics on Danish gay marriage. http://gaytoday.badpuppy.com/garchive/world/040497wo.htm.

Wyers, N. L. (1987). Homosexuality in the family: Lesbian and gay spouses.*Social Work, 32*(2), 143–148.

Yep, G. A., Lovaas, K. E., & Elia, J. P. (2003). A critical appraisal of assimilationist and radical ideologies underlying same-sex marriage in LGBT communities in the United States.*Journal of Homosexuality, 45*(1), 45–64.

Lesbian and Gay Parents and their Children: A Social Science Perspective

Charlotte J. Patterson

At the current moment in history, the extent to which relationships among lesbian and gay parents and their children are recognized in law or respected in practice is in tremendous flux. For many years, the family relationships of lesbian and gay parents and their children were not legally recognized in most parts of the United States, or in most countries of the world. Today, these relationships are recognized in some jurisdictions, and the matter is under active debate in others. With regard to the social and legal status of lesbian and gay relationships, we are living in a time of tremendous and rapid change.

In view of the rapidly shifting legal and policy environments, my aims in this chapter are threefold. First, I hope to summarize the current status of legal and policy issues as well as conceptual and theoretical issues relevant to lesbian and gay parents and their children in the United States today. Second, I hope to provide an overview of research evidence about these families, with special emphasis on the development of children living within them. This overview will emphasize work I have undertaken in this area with colleagues and students over the last 15 years, but will also seek to place this work in the context of related research. Finally, I hope to summarize the implications of research findings for both theoretical concerns relevant to our conceptualizations of human socialization, and for practical concerns relevant to law and family policy.

Current Contexts of Sexual Minority Family Lives

Lesbian and gay parents and their children in the United States today are the subjects of considerable controversy. Thus, an overview of the legal and policy contexts in which these families live in the United States today will be a useful tool for understanding their situations. In this section, we consider very briefly the legal status of lesbian and gay parents and their children, with regard to legal recognition of couple relationships, child custody and visitation, adoption and foster care.

D.A. Hope (ed.), *Contemporary Perspectives on Lesbian, Gay, and Bisexual Identities*,
DOI: 10.1007/978-0-387-09556-1, © Springer Science+Business Media, LLC 2009

Legal Status of Lesbian and Gay Parents and their Children

Consideration of the legal status of lesbian and gay parents and their children involves three interrelated areas of law. The first involves legal recognition of same-sex couple relationships, which may take the form of marriage, civil union, or domestic partnership. The second involves the status of parental sexual orientation in disputes about custody of and visitation with minor children. The third involves the role of parental sexual orientation in adoption and foster care proceedings. Our review of the legal situation of lesbian and gay parents in different jurisdictions within the United States reveals a patchwork of varied legal arrangements and shows how rapidly situations are changing in many parts of the country.

Legal Recognition of Same-Sex Couples

Although the right to marry and the right to rear children as one sees fit are regarded by American law as fundamental, these rights have not been extended to lesbian or gay Americans. The rights to marry (Loving v. Virginia, 1967), to procreate (Skinner v. Oklahoma, 1942), and to rear children (Meyer v. Nebraska, 1923) have long been held by the United States Supreme Court to be fundamental, and as such, have been seen as guaranteed by the Constitution. However taken for granted these rights may be by the majority of Americans, they have often been denied to lesbian and gay Americans (Herek, 2006).

At the time of this writing, legal recognition of same-sex marriage has occurred in only one jurisdiction within the United States. Even in Massachusetts, where same-sex couples now have their marriages recognized under state law, they nevertheless must struggle with the fact that their marriages are not recognized under federal law. Under the mandates of the oddly named Defense of Marriage Act, same-sex marriages that are entirely legal in Massachusetts are not recognized at all in federal law. For this reason, same-sex couples are still subject to discrimination in taxation, social security, immigration, veterans' benefits, and a host of other areas. In short, although a same-sex couple may be legally married in Massachusetts, they are not legally married in any other state, nor are they legally married under federal law.

In other states, civil unions or domestic partnerships may provide some or all of the rights and responsibilities of marriage under state (but again, not under federal) law. For instance, same-sex couples may undertake civil unions in Vermont, Connecticut, New Jersey, and New Hampshire. Same-sex couples may register domestic partnerships in California, Maine, Oregon, Washington, and the District of Columbia. They may also register as reciprocal beneficiaries in Hawaii. In some states, such as Vermont, many state-level rights and responsibilities accrue to those in civil unions or domestic partnerships; in other states, such as Maine, fewer rights and responsibilities are entailed. At the time of this writing, a number of cases are in the courts. In many states, the legal situation for same-sex couples is in rapid flux (Herek, 2006).

Child Custody and Visitation Involving Lesbian Mothers and Gay Fathers

The extent to which a parent's sexual identity is considered relevant in deciding a child's best interest, for purposes of child custody and visitation, varies from state to state. In many states, parental sexual orientation is considered relevant to custody and visitation disputes only if it can be shown to have an adverse impact on the child. Before parental sexual orientation can be considered as a factor relevant to the child's best interests, in these states, a connection, or *nexus*, must be demonstrated between a person's sexual orientation, on the one hand, and a negative outcome for the child, on the other. For instance, in S.N.E. v. R.L.B. (1985), an Alaska court awarded custody to a lesbian mother, noting that there was "no suggestion that (her sexual orientation) has or is likely to affect the child adversely." Similar rulings have emerged recently in a number of states. For instance, in a Maryland visitation case (Boswell v. Boswell, 1998), the court refused to limit children's visitation with their gay father in the presence of his same-sex partner because there was no evidence of harm to the children from such visitation.

At the other end of the spectrum, some states have in place presumptions against lesbian or gay parents. Even though these may not any longer rise to the level of per se rule against parental fitness among lesbian and gay adults, they may nevertheless remain influential. In the Bottoms v. Bottoms (1995) case, for example, the Virginia Supreme Court reiterated its earlier holding that a lesbian mother is not per se unfit, but included the mother's sexual orientation among factors considered to make her an undesirable parent (Bottoms v. Bottoms, 1995, p. 108).

The legal standards for custody in a number of states fall somewhere between these two extremes. In one recent case (Burgess v. Burgess, 1999), the Indiana Supreme Court denied a gay father's request for review of a lower court's decision that denied him custody of his son. Indiana law does not allow parental sexual orientation to be considered as a determinative factor in placement of a child, but the court noted in its decision that the father's sexual orientation "raises the specter of an aberrant lifestyle" (Burgess v. Burgess, 1999). In another recent North Carolina case, a gay father was denied custody of his two sons because of the court's concern about his long-term relationship with a male partner, who was helping to care for the boys (Pulliam v. Smith, 1998). Despite legal progress in many states, child custody and visitation for lesbian and gay parents after the break-up of heterosexual marriages continue, in some jurisdictions, to be adjudicated in an atmosphere of antigay prejudice.

Adoption and Foster Care

Legal adoptions of minor children by lesbian and gay adults can be seen as falling into one of two types (Patterson, 1995c). When biological parents are unable or unwilling to care for a child, and an adoptive parent who is not related to the biological parents offers to provide that child with a home, the result is called a *stranger adoption*. In such cases, the courts dissolve existing legal bonds, and create a new legal relationship between the child and the adoptive parent. *Second-parent adoptions* are pursued by lesbian and gay couples who raise a child together, although only one member of the couple — the biological parent or legal adoptive parent — is viewed as a parent in law. These couples seek legal recognition of the relationship between the other parent and the child. In recent years, both types of adoptions have been completed by openly lesbian and gay individuals in the United States (Polikoff, 1990; Patterson, 1995c).

Like laws on custody and visitation, those governing adoption vary considerably across the states (Patterson, 2007). At the time of this writing, adoption of minor children by lesbian or gay adults is specifically barred by statute in Arkansas, Florida, Mississippi, and Utah. New Hampshire had a statute barring lesbian and gay individuals from becoming adoptive parents until recently, but the Legislature repealed it in 1999. In other states, such as New York and Massachusetts, the law allows adoptions by openly lesbian and gay prospective adoptive parents. For example, in a landmark New York second-parent adoption case, In re Adoption of Evan (1992), the court noted that "(t)he fact that the petitioners here maintain an open lesbian relationship is not a reason to deny adoption... A parent's sexual orientation or sexual practices are presumptively irrelevant..." (In re Adoption of Evan, 1992, pp. 1001–1002).

Even though state adoption laws vary, both stranger adoptions and second-parent adoptions by openly lesbian and gay adults have occurred in numerous jurisdictions. Openly lesbian or gay adults have completed stranger adoptions in many states, including California, Ohio, and the District of Columbia. Many more strange adoptions have no doubt been accomplished by lesbian or gay adults in other states without their sexual orientation becoming a topic of public discussion. Second-parent adoptions have been granted in 17 states and in the District of Columbia. State supreme courts in Massachusetts, Vermont, and Wisconsin have ruled on the legality of second-parent adoptions, and two of the three — Massachusetts (Adoption of Tammy, 1993) and Vermont (Adoptions of B.L.V.B. & E.L.V. B., 1993) have affirmed them.

Summary

Across the United States today, the legal and policy landscape for lesbian and gay parents and their children is remarkably varied. At one end of the spectrum, in a state such as Massachusetts — in which same-sex marriage is legally recognized, in which parental sexual orientation is considered irrelevant to child custody and visitation proceedings, and in which the State Supreme Court has affirmed the legality of second-parent adoptions — the legal climate for lesbian and gay parents and their children is generally positive. At the other end of the spectrum, in a state such as Virginia — in which same-sex marriages are not recognized by the law, in which lesbian and gay parents are disadvantaged in custody and visitation proceedings by negative presumptions about their parental fitness, and in which second-parent adoptions have not yet been reported — the legal atmosphere for lesbian and gay parents and their children is less desirable. Although the pace of change may vary from state to state, the direction of movement over time during the last 50 years is clearly toward provision of greater legal recognition of the many different family types formed by lesbian and gay adults.

Theoretical Issues Relevant to Lesbian and Gay Parents and their Children

Theories of psychological development have traditionally emphasized distinctive contributions of both mothers and fathers to the healthy personal and social development of their children. As a result, many theories predict negative outcomes for children who are raised in environments that do not provide these two kinds of inputs. An important theoretical question thus concerns the extent to which such predictions are sustained by results of research on children of gay and/or lesbian parents.

For instance, psychoanalytic theory places heavy weight on the Oedipal drama, in which children experience very different reactions to their mothers and to their fathers (Bronfenbrenner, 1960). From the psychoanalytic perspective, healthy psychological development is believed to require the child's eventual resolution of Oedipal issues. Factors which inhibit or distort this process are therefore thought to be detrimental to the child's development. Some writers in the psychoanalytic tradition (e.g., Chodorow, 1978) also emphasize different influences of male and female parents in the socialization of children. From psychoanalytic perspectives, then, when one or more parents are either absent and/or homosexually oriented, disruptions of personality development for their children could be anticipated.

From the point of view of social learning approaches to personality development (e.g., Huston, 1983), children are seen as learning distinctive lessons from the examples and the rewards offered by both male and female parents. For example, fathers are thought to model and reward masculine behavior among sons, and mothers to model and reward feminine behavior among daughters. Predictions based on social learning suggest negative outcomes for children brought up in families that do not provide conventional models or rewards for the acquisition of sexual identities.

There have been significant challenges to these theoretical positions, especially from cognitive developmental theory (Kohlberg, 1966) and from gender schema theory (Bem, 1983), neither of which in principle requires that a child's home environment include both heterosexual male and heterosexual female parents in order to support favorable development. Advocates of cognitive developmental and gender schema theory have not, however, discussed the assumption that children's development is best fostered in families that contain both male and female parents, nor have they challenged the premise that development is optimal in families where the parents are heterosexual.

In short, psychoanalytic and social learning theories of personal and social development during childhood emphasize the importance of children having both heterosexual male and heterosexual female parents, and they predict generally negative outcomes for children whose parents do not exemplify these qualities. Although cognitive developmental theory and gender schema theory do not require such assumptions, proponents of these views have not challenged them. As a result, these perspectives on individual differences in personal and social development are commonly believed to predict difficulties in development among children of lesbian and gay parents. Empirical research with such children thus provides an opportunity to evaluate anew these theoretical assumptions.

Social Science Research on Lesbian and Gay Parents and their Children

How do the results of social science research address legal and policy issues raised by child custody, visitation, and adoption by lesbian and gay parents? And how do they bear on the theoretical issues? In this section, we provide an overview of studies focused on children of lesbian and gay parents. For other recent reviews of this material, see Patterson (2000, 2005, 2006), Perrin (2002), Stacey and Biblarz (2001) and Tasker and Patterson (2007).

Early Research

The most visible group of nonheterosexual parents may be lesbian mothers. Many lesbian mothers conceived and gave birth to children within the context of heterosexual relationships, but assumed a lesbian identity later in life (Kirkpatrick, 1996). More recently, observers have commented upon the growing numbers of women who have chosen to have children after assuming a lesbian identity, and this trend has sometimes been referred to as a "lesbian baby boom" (e.g., Patterson 1994; Weston, 1991). Similar trends can be observed among gay fathers, but perhaps because of their prominence in child custody cases (Patterson, Fulcher, & Wainright, 2002), lesbian mothers have generally drawn more attention from researchers.

To determine if being reared by lesbian parents results in different outcomes for children, as has often been assumed in the legal system, researchers designed studies that examined the social and personality development of such children. A few studies have focused on the normative development of children born to or adopted by women who already identified as lesbians (Flaks, Ficher, Masterpasqua, & Joseph, 1995; Gartrell et al., 1996, 1999; Gartrell, Banks, Reed, Hamiliton, & Deck, 2000; Gartrell, Deck, Rodas, Peyser, & Banks, 2005; McCandlish, 1987; Patterson, 1995a,b; Patterson, Hurt, & Mason, 1998; Steckel, 1987). Overall, these studies indicated that children of lesbian mothers were developing much like children of neterosexual mothers.

Similarities were revealed between the children of lesbian and heterosexual parents across a wide array of assessments of cognitive and behavioral functioning (Patterson, 2002; Perrin, 2002). More recently, Gartrell and colleagues (1996, 1999, 2000, 2005) have analyzed data from a longitudinal study of 84 lesbian-headed families who conceived their children via donor insemination. By the age of five, they reported that the children were developing normally; and in most cases, both parents were actively involved in the child's upbringing (Gartrell et al., 2000). These findings provide valuable information about the development of children born to lesbian mothers, as well as about the adjustment of such families over time, yet many questions remain in need of study.

One important issue concerns parental division of family labor and partners' satisfaction with their division of labor. In many families headed by heterosexual couples, mothers are responsible for the bulk of household and child-care labor (Cowan & Cowan, 1992). Lesbian couples, on the other hand, are more likely to report dividing household and child-care labor equally between partners (Kurdek, 1993; Peplau, Veniegas, & Campbell, 1996). Lesbian couples also report generally high satisfaction with division of labor arrangements in their households (Flaks et al., 1995; Koepke, Hare, & Moran, 1992). If lesbian couples with children maintain equal division of labor, and if they are satisfied with these arrangements, then parents' satisfaction with these arrangements may be associated with positive outcomes for their children.

Another important issue concerns the nature and extent of children's social networks. In particular, grandparents can contribute to the healthy development of their grandchildren on many levels, both directly and indirectly. Until recently very little information has been available about the social networks of lesbian mothers and their children (Allen & Demo, 1995; D'Augelli & Patterson, 1995; Laird 1993; Patterson, 1998). In the absence of research, it has sometimes been assumed that lesbians may be estranged from their families of origin. For instance, informal reports suggest that grandparents may be less likely to remain in contact with children being reared by lesbian daughters as compared to those being reared by heterosexual daughters (Patterson, 1996; Saffron, 1996). Some anecdotal reports suggest that such stereotypes are incorrect (Laird, 1993; Lewin, 1993; Weston, 1991), but empirical research has been limited.

In order to examine these and other related issues, Patterson designed the Bay Area Families Study (Patterson, 1994). This study involved 4- to 9-year-old children who were conceived or adopted by a lesbian mother or mothers.. This study examined the mental health of mothers, the mental health of children, division of household labor among parents, parents' relationship satisfaction and the associations among these variables (Patterson, 1994, 1995a, 2001; Patterson et al., 1998).

The results of this study revealed several important findings. Based on results from standardized assessments, both mothers' and children's average levels of adjustment fell within the normal range for all measures (Patterson, 1994, 2001). Lesbian couples who took part in this study reported that they divided household labor and child-care in a relatively even manner (Patterson, 1995a). A third major finding was an association between division of labor and psychosocial outcomes for mothers and their children (Patterson, 1995a). When lesbian couples shared child-care more evenly, mothers were more satisfied and children were more well-adjusted. This suggested that children might benefit from egalitarian divisions of labor.

Finally, contrary to popular stereotypes, Patterson and her colleagues reported that most children of lesbian mothers in their sample were in regular contact with grandparents, relatives, and other adults outside their immediate households (Patterson et al., 1998). Consistent with expectations based on earlier research, children who had more contact with grandparents also showed fewer internalizing behavior problems than did other children (Patterson et al., 1998). Taken together with those of previous studies, results from the Bay Area Families Study suggested that children of lesbian mothers show normal psychosocial development. Although these results were valuable, a number of limitations hindered a clear-cut interpretation of them. Data for the Bay Area Families Study were drawn from a convenience sample of families who lived in a single geographical area. In addition, the study did not include a comparison group of heterosexual families. Clearly, it would be desirable to study a larger, more diverse sample of children with lesbian mothers, and it would be helpful to include a well-matched comparison sample of children with heterosexual parents. The Contemporary Families Study was designed to address these and related issues.

The Contemporary Families Study

The Contemporary Families Study involved a sample of lesbian- and heterosexual-headed families who had conceived children via donor insemination using the resources of a single sperm bank (Chan, Brooks, Raboy, & Patterson, 1998; Chan, Raboy, & Patterson, 1998; Fulcher, Chan, Raboy, & Patterson, 2002). Although all the families were clients of a single sperm bank, they actually resided in many parts of the United States, and so the findings are not limited to a single geographic area. This sample allowed a comparison of heterosexual- and lesbian-headed families drawn from the same population. In addition, among families headed by couples (as opposed to a single parent), regardless of sexual orientation, one parent was genetically related to the child and one was not. This allowed the separation of questions regarding sexual orientation from those regarding genetic relatedness.

In this section, I describe the Contemporary Families Study and its principal results. The demographic and other characteristics of the participating families are described first. Next, assessments of adjustment of both parents and children in heterosexual- as well as lesbian-parented families and according to parental relationship status (i.e., single or coupled) are descibed. In families that were headed by couples, the study also examined key facets of couple functioning (e.g., relationship satisfaction, division of labor), and comparisons by parental sexual orientation are reported next. The study also investigated associations of individual differences in children's adjustment with couple functioning variables. Finally, the study also explored children's contacts with grandparents and other important adults.

Although statistical details are not elaborated below, all findings described as statistically significant were at the $p < 0.05$ level. The methods and findings are summarized briefly, but additional details and commentary are available elsewhere (Chan, Raboy, et al., 1998; Chan, Brooks, et al., 1998; Fulcher et al., 2002; Flucher, Sutfin, Chan, Scheib & Patterson 2005). There were no significant sex differences in the data presented here, so the presentation does not consider this variable.

Description of Participating Families

Families participating in this study were all former clients of The Sperm Bank of California (TSBC, located in Berkeley, California), which has been providing reproductive services to clients regardless of sexual orientation or relationship status since 1982. Clients who had conceived and given birth prior to July 1990 were considered eligible to participate in this research (thus their children were at least 5 years old at the beginning of data collection). Six families who had already participated in Patterson's Bay Area Families Study were excluded to maintain independence of data between the two studies. Also excluded was one family headed by a woman who identified herself as bisexual.

The sample consisted of 80 families — 34 headed by lesbian couples, 21 by lesbian single mothers, 16 by heterosexual couples, and 9 by heterosexual single mothers. Children averaged 7 years of age and genetically related mothers averaged 42 years of age. There were 26 girls and 54 boys. The families were primarily Caucasian and parents were generally well educated, with most holding a college degree and most employed at least part-time. They were relatively affluent, with family incomes well above national averages.

We explored the possibility that demographic differences might exist among the four family types. We found that, on average, lesbian birth mothers had completed more years of education than had heterosexual mothers, and lesbian nonbirth mothers had completed more years of education than had heterosexual fathers. As one would expect, families headed by couples reported higher annual household incomes than did families headed by single parents. Otherwise, no significant demographic differences emerged from these analyses.

Procedure and Results

Each eligible family was initially contacted by a letter from the Executive Director of TSBC. The letter gave a brief explanation of the study and asked each family to consider participation. Telephone calls from TSBC staff members followed these letters to describe the study more fully and to request each family's participation. When a family agreed to participate, a brief, structured telephone interview about family background and current family status was conducted. It was during this interview that parents responded to questions about their child's contact with grandparents and other adults. Remaining materials were then mailed to participating families along with self-addressed stamped envelopes in which the participants were asked to return questionnaires to investigators. In families that consented, a parent gave the child's teacher The Teacher's Report Form (TRF, Achenbach, 1991). Teachers returned the form in a provided self-addressed stamped envelope.

Maternal Mental Health

Parenting stress was measured using the Parenting Stress Index- Short Form (PSI/SF; Abidin, 1995). This short form includes 63 items on 5-point rating scales, scored from strongly agree to strongly disagree. The score reflects stress directly related to the parenting role as well as stress from other life events. Items such as: "I feel trapped by my responsibilities as a parent" are included. Higher scores indicate reports of greater stress. Depressive symptoms among parents were measured with the Center for Epidemiologic Studies Depression Scale (CES-D; Radloff, 1977). On this 20 item self-report measure, respondents indicate how often they felt or behaved in a certain way on a 3-point rating scale (e.g., "I had trouble keeping my mind on what I was doing"). Higher scores indicate more depressive symptoms.

Maternal self-esteem was assessed using the Rosenberg Self-Esteem Scale (Rosenberg, 1979). This scale consists of ten statements, each with four response alternatives, indicating the respondent's degree of agreement with each statement (e.g., "I am able to do things as well as most people"). Results were tabulated to obtain total scores, based upon the recommendations contained in Rosenberg (1979). Higher scores indicate higher self-esteem.

Our results indicated that the parents participating in this study were well adjusted when compared to available norms. Very few parents in this sample showed symptoms of serious depression or low self-esteem. There was no difference in parental adjustment between parents who were coupled or single. Likewise, there were no significant differences in reported stress, depressive symptoms or self-esteem in birth mothers as a function of sexual orientation. In families headed by couples, there were also no significant differences in adjustment measures between fathers and nonbirth mothers. In summary, parents were generally well-adjusted, and there were no significant differences in adjustment as a function of parental sexual orientation.

Couple Functioning

In order to get an overall indication of couple functioning, we assessed couples' division of labor and marital satisfaction. The measures of couple functioning were only given to parents who described themselves as being involved in a coupled relationship. To assess division of labor in the household, as well as satisfaction with the division, Cowan and Cowan's (1990) Who Does What? was used. This instrument was designed to measure parents' perceptions of the current and ideal distribution of labor within the family, as well as each parent's satisfaction with their arrangements.

The Who Does What? instrument is divided into three sections: division of household tasks, decision-making and child-care within a family. Minor wording changes were made in order to make the measure suitable for lesbian mothers. Each section began by asking respondents to rate, on a scale from 1 to 9, their actual and ideal distribution of certain family tasks (1 = my partner does it all, 5 = we both do this about equally, 9 = I do it all). The first section included 13 household tasks (e.g., meal preparation and cleanup), the second section included 12 family decision-making tasks (e.g., making financial decisions), and the third section included 20 child-care tasks (e.g., bathing the child). Scores around 5 indicated a relatively equal division of labor, while high scores indicated that the respondent reported performing more of the labor. At the end of each section of this instrument, respondents were asked to indicate their overall satisfaction with that specific area of household labor. Finally, in the decision-making and child-care sections, respondents were asked to indicate global ratings of both their own and their partner's influence over family decisions and involvement in child-care.

To assess relationship satisfaction, two instruments were used. The Locke—Wallace Marital Adjustment Test (LWMAT; Locke & Wallace, 1959) was used to indicate overall relationship quality, while the Partnership Questionnaire (Braiker & Kelley, 1979) assessed more specific aspects of couples' relationships. The LWMAT is a 15-item self-report measure that was designed to assess marital adjustment in heterosexual marriages (e.g., "Do you confide in your partner?"). In order to make the instrument suitable for use with lesbian couples as well as with heterosexual couples, minor wording changes were made. Possible scores range from 2 to 158, with higher scores indicating greater satisfaction.

The Partnership Questionnaire (Braiker & Kelley, 1979) is a 25-item instrument designed to assess components of a close relationship. We used two scales: the Love Scale, consisting of ten items relating to caring and emotional attachment (e.g., "To what extent do you love your partner at this stage?"), and the Conflict Scale, consisting of five items concerning problems and arguments (e.g., "How often do you and your partner argue with one another?"). Each partner indicates level of agreement ranging from 1 (not at all or very little) to 9 (very much or very often). Higher scores on these scales indicate more love and more conflict.

For division of labor, the results for lesbian couples indicated that overall, household tasks, family decision-making, and child-care were all seen as being shared relatively equally between the partners. Lesbian birth mothers reported doing almost the same amounts of child-care as their partners. Lesbian parents also divided time spent on work outside the home about equally. Lesbian nonbirth mothers reported working longer hours in paid employment than lesbian birth mothers, but this difference did not reach statistical significance.

There was more variation in scores for heterosexual couples. Heterosexual parents reported sharing household tasks and family decision-making relatively equally. However, for child-care, the results indicated an unequal distribution of labor. Mothers reported doing more child-care and fathers reported doing less child-care. Indeed, heterosexual mothers reported doing more child-care than did lesbian birth mothers and heterosexual fathers reported doing less child-care than did lesbian nonbirth mothers.

Comparisons were also made between actual and ideal divisions of labor. In the areas of household tasks and family decision making, both lesbian and heterosexual respondents reported sharing these responsibilities relatively equally with their partner. They also reported that this matched their ideals. In the area of child-care, however, differences emerged as a function of parental sexual orientation. For ideal distribution of labor, heterosexual mothers indicated that they would prefer a more equitable distribution of child-care labor than they currently experienced. Fathers reported preferring that their wives assume most of the child-care; their actual score on current child-care participation was similar to their report on their ideal amount of responsibility. On the other hand, in addition to reporting the practice of equal child-care, both lesbian birth mothers and their partners reported wanting an equal division of child-care. Overall, both lesbian and heterosexual mothers preferred a more equitable division of child-care than did fathers. For lesbian mothers, this desire was realized in their actual child-care arrangements, but this was not the case for heterosexual mothers.

Regardless of their actual labor arrangements, most parents reported feeling satisfied with their current division of labor. There was no significant difference between heterosexual and lesbian parents in this regard. Likewise, there were no significant differences between birth parents and nonbirth parents and their satisfaction with the division of child-care labor. It seems that regardless of how these couples actually divided labor they were satisfied with their arrangements.

Heterosexual and lesbian couples' scores on the LWMAT (Locke & Wallace, 1959) exceeded mean scores for similar populations, indicating high relationship satisfaction. In addition, heterosexual and lesbian couples reported high levels of love and low-to-moderate levels of conflict on the Partnership Questionnaire (Braiker & Kelley, 1979), suggesting that parents were generally satisfied with their relationships. Overall, lesbian and heterosexual couples reported similar levels of love, conflict, and satisfaction with their relationships.

Children's Adjustment

To assess levels of children's social competence and behavior problems, the Child Behavior Checklist (CBCL, Achenbach & Edelbrock, 1983) and the Teacher Report Form (TRF, Achenbach, 1991) were administered. These scales were particularly useful here because of their ability to discriminate children in the clinical vs. normative range of functioning for both internalizing (e.g., inhibited, overcontrolled behavior) and externalizing (e.g., aggressive, antisocial, or undercontrolled behavior) behavior problems. The CBCL is designed to be completed by parents, and, in families headed by couples, each parent completed a CBCL for the target child. In addition, the CBCL scale measured social competence whereas the TRF measured academic performance and adaptive functioning. The TRF utilized teacher reports. These scales were selected because they are widely used child assessment instruments for which national age and sex norms are available for both clinical and nonclinical populations. Moreover, sex- and age-specific raw scores can be converted to standard T scores that allow comparisons across age and gender groups.

Results showed that, compared to a large group of normal children, children in this sample were well adjusted according to both their CBCL and TRF scores as reported by both parents and teachers. Children's average scores on Externalizing, Internalizing, and Total Behavior Problems scales fell well below clinical cutoffs. Likewise, Social Competence and Academic Performance and Adaptive Functioning scores for these children were well above clinical cutoffs. There was no significant difference in adjustment scores between children of lesbian parents and children of heterosexual parents. Furthermore, there was also no difference in children's adjustment as a function of mothers' relationship status. We found that both parents and teachers reported that children conceived via donor insemination were well adjusted.

Because the family structure variables, parental sexual orientation, and relationship status were not related to children's adjustment in this sample, efforts to predict adjustment focused on other variables. Generally, we report the associations of family interactions and processes with children's adjustment across family types except when interactions are revealed between family type and children's adjustment. We turn next to results from these analyses.

Associations Between Child and Parental Adjustment

Children's adjustment was significantly associated with parental adjustment. When parents reported more parenting distress and more dysfunctional parent—child interactions on the Parenting Stress Index, children were described as showing more behavior problems. When birth mothers reported dysfunctional interactions with their children, those children had more reported internalizing problems. Likewise birth mothers' reports of greater parental distress and dysfunctional interactions were associated with more reports of their children's externalizing and total behavior problems. A similar pattern emerged for nonbirth parents' reports of parental stress and dysfunctional interactions, which were also associated with children's externalizing and total behavior problems. Teachers' reports of children's behavior problems were most associated with the nonbirth parents' reports of parental distress. There was no relationship between parents' depressive symptom scores and children's behavior scores, probably because parents in this sample showed very few depressive symptoms.

There were also significant associations between children's adjustment scores and parental reports of relationship satisfaction. When couples in this sample reported higher relationship satisfaction and love, their children were less likely to show adjustment problems. For example, when birth mothers reported higher global relationship satisfaction and higher levels of love in their couple relationship, their children showed better adjustment. Nonbirth parents' reports of relationship satisfaction and love were also associated with lower levels of children's reported behavior problems. Birth mothers who reported higher conflict with their partners also reported that their children had more behavior problems. Thus, when parents reported higher levels of relationship satisfaction and love, and lower levels of parental conflict, they also reported that their children had fewer behavior problems.

Association of Parental Division of Labor and Children's Adjustment

We also assessed the relationship between parents' division of labor, satisfaction with the division of labor, and children's adjustment. Overall, nonbirth parents' reports of greater satisfaction with the couple's division of household labor were associated with children's lower externalizing behavior problems as reported by their teachers. However, some associations differed according to parental sexual orientation.

In families headed by heterosexual couples, when fathers reported greater satisfaction with the division of family decision making, but lower levels of satisfaction in the division of household tasks, mothers' reports of children's externalizing problems were lower. In lesbian-headed families, the associations among division of labor and children's adjustment were more complicated. Birth mothers' reports of greater satisfaction with the division of household labor and family decision-making were associated with reports of children's lower levels of externalizing behavior. Nonbirth mothers' reports of greater satisfaction with division of family decision making were associated with their own reports of lower levels of children's externalizing behavior. Finally, in lesbian-headed families, when nonbirth mothers actually participated in more child-care tasks, the children were reported by birth mothers to have fewer externalizing problems. These complicated associations between division of labor and children's adjustment were mediated by parents' satisfaction with the couple relationship. This mediation makes clearer the paths of influence and we examine such associations next.

Parental Relationship Satisfaction, Division of Labor, and Children's Adjustment

We were interested in whether associations between parental division of labor and children's adjustment might be mediated by parents' relationship satisfaction. The results indicated that in lesbian-headed families, nonbirth mothers' reports of their satisfaction with the division of family decision-making were associated with their reports of higher relationship satisfaction and with the description of their children as having fewer externalizing behaviors. Furthermore, the results showed that this association was mediated by nonbirth mothers' satisfaction with the couple relationship. When effects of relationship satisfaction and division of family decision-making satisfaction were considered simultaneously, only parents' relationship satisfaction remained predictive. Thus, the associations between parental division of labor and children's adjustment were mediated by parents' relationship satisfaction. When parents reported higher levels of relationship satisfaction, children were described as showing fewer externalizing behaviors. We conclude that parental satisfaction is more highly associated with child outcomes than any specific division of labor. This finding is consistent with others in the literature that included only heterosexual families which show that associations between children's outcomes and parental division of labor are mediated by parents' level of marital satisfaction (e.g., Cowan & Cowan, 1992). Thus, our main finding was that parents' higher levels of satisfaction in the couple relationship were associated with lower levels of children's behavior problems.

Children's Contacts with Grandparents and Other Adults

During the initial telephone interview, information about contact with grandparents and other adults was collected from the child's birth mother. Mothers reported the amount of contact the target children had with grandparents. Genetic grandparents were identified by the child's birth mother as her parents, and nongenetic grandparents were identified by the child's birth mother as the other parent's parents. Contact was defined as a visit, a telephone call, a card, or e-mail. Contact scores ranged from 1 to 7 (1 = no contact, 2 = less than once a year, 3 = once a year, 4 = every other month, 5 = once a month, 6 = once a week, and 7 = daily contact). If the mother did not list nongenetic grandparents, because she was single or not in contact with a former partner, the family was not included for these comparisons. Data for children whose grandparent had died were not considered in the comparisons for that grandparent. Parents also listed up to five adults, in addition to parents and grandparents who were seen as "important" in the child's life. The adult's gender and relationship to the child (e.g., parent's friend, relative, neighbor, child-care provider, or coach) was recorded as well. Each of these adults was also scored for contact using the scale described earlier.

Most parents reported that their children were in at least monthly contact with their grandparents. There were no significant differences in amount of contact between grandparents and children of lesbian parents vs. children of heterosexual parents. Among couples, this was true for both genetic grandparents and for nongenetic grandparents. However, children of both lesbian and heterosexual parents were in more frequent contact with their genetic grandparents than with their nongenetic grandparents.

The amount of contact between children and other adults also did not differ according to parental sexual orientation. Children of lesbian parents had contact with as many adult relatives as did children of heterosexual parents. Contrary to stereotypes, children of lesbian parents had contact with as many adult men as did children of heterosexual parents. Children of lesbian parents did, however, have significantly more contact with unrelated women than did children of heterosexual parents. Overall, the amount of contact with adults outside the home was similar among children of lesbian and heterosexual parents.

Overview of Results and Implications

The Contemporary Families Study was designed to examine child development and family functioning among families headed by lesbian and heterosexual parents who conceived their children via donor insemination. This sample allowed us to compare parents and children in families headed by lesbian and heterosexual parents, taking into account that only one parent is genetically related to the child.

Our first major finding was that both parents' and children's average levels of adjustment fell clearly within the normative range in both family types. This finding is consistent with results from earlier studies of lesbian parents and their children (Flaks et al., 1995; Steckel, 1985, 1987). Furthermore, there were no significant differences in children's or parents' adjustment scores according to parental sexual orientation. Considering that this result is consistent with findings from other research on lesbian women in general (Gonsiorek, 1991), lesbian mothers in particular (Patterson, 1992, 2002), children of divorced lesbian and gay parents (Patterson, 1992), and children born to lesbian mothers (Flaks et al., 1995; McCandlish, 1987; Steckel, 1985, 1987), this outcome was not surprising. Particularly in light of judicial and popular prejudices against lesbian and gay families that still exist in many parts of the United States, the result is worthy of attention. The present data revealed not only that lesbian mothers' adjustment and self-esteem were within the normative range, but also that their children's development was proceeding in normal fashion.

The second major finding was that both lesbian and heterosexual parents expressed high satisfaction and high levels of love within their couple relationships. There were no differences in satisfaction or warmth between heterosexual and lesbian couples. Although both lesbian and heterosexual parents reported relatively equal contributions to paid labor, household chores, and family decision making, differences did emerge in the division of labor involved in child-care. Lesbian couples divided child-care more evenly than did heterosexual couples. In families headed by heterosexual parents, mothers reported doing more child-care than did their husbands. This is consistent with previous findings on child-care arrangements among heterosexual couples (Cowan & Cowan, 1992; Perry-Jenkins & Crouter, 1990). Parents in both family types reported satisfaction with division of child-care; however, children's adjustment was more strongly related to partners' satisfaction with division of labor than to their reports of actual division of labor. Therefore, in well-functioning families it may be more important for children that parents negotiate a division of labor that is satisfactory to both parents than that they adhere to an egalitarian arrangement.

Another principal finding emerging from these data was that family process variables such as parental adjustment and couple adjustment were more strongly related to children's outcomes than were family structural variables such as parental sexual orientation or relationship status. The family process variables showed the same pattern of associations in families headed by lesbian and heterosexual parents. For example, regardless of parental sexual orientation, elevated parenting stress was associated with more externalizing behavior problems among children. Parents in both family types who reported being less happy with their relationship also reported having children with more behavior problems. Patterns of family interaction were clearly related to children's outcomes, regardless of parental sexual orientation (Patterson, 2002).

Finally, we found that children of lesbian and heterosexual parents who conceived via donor insemination were described by their parents as being surrounded by networks of supportive adults. Children of lesbian and heterosexual parents were described as being in equal amounts of contact with their grandparents. The lineal bridge between child and grandparent seemed to function without regard to parental sexual orientation. Our results suggested that grandparents were not less willing to invest time in grandchildren born in the context of a lesbian relationship than in those born in the context of a heterosexual one. Children were also said to have similar amounts of contact with other adults in addition to grandparents, regardless of parental sexual orientation. The only significant difference was that children with lesbian parents were in regular contact with more unrelated women than children with heterosexual parents. In short, consistent with earlier findings (Patterson et al., 1998), our results showed that children of lesbian parents in this sample were not living in isolation nor were they lacking adult male role models.

Several limitations of this study must be considered when interpreting the results. First, the Contemporary Families Study was cross-sectional in design and so does not afford the opportunity to examine children's development across time. Secondly, because lesbian parents were more likely than heterosexual parents to participate, the sample may be more representative of these families. Finally, the measures used here relied on self-reports and reports from parents and teachers. Future studies that are longitudinal in design, that use representative samples, and that employ observational measures may be better able to clarify causal questions.

The results of the Contemporary Families Study have afforded some insight into families formed by lesbian and heterosexual parents who conceived via donor insemination. The study also raises many questions for further research. Questions about children's development over time would clearly benefit from longitudinal research. Questions about the role of reproductive technology could be clarified by research on lesbian and heterosexual families formed in other ways (e.g., through adoption). Questions about broader aspects of children's social worlds might also be addressed through research on other aspects of children's social development.

In an age in which children are being conceived and raised in families that are growing increasingly diverse, it is important to examine the role that family constellations play in children's development. The family structural variables studied here (e.g., number of parents and parental sexual orientation) were not associated in this sample with children's adjustment or with their frequency of contact with important adults such as grandparents. It was family process variables, such as parental relationship satisfaction, that were associated with children's adjustment. Overall, results of the Contemporary Families Study were consistent with those of other studies on lesbian mothers and their children (Gartrell et al., 2000, 2005; Patterson, 2000; Perrin, 2002; Stacey & Biblarz, 2001; Tasker & Golombok, 1997) in revealing that these families can provide supportive environments in which children can grow and develop. At the same time, additional research would clearly be helpful.

The National Longitudinal Study of Adolescent Health

The Contemporary Families Study focused on the development of young children who had been conceived via donor insemination by lesbian or heterosexual parents. As valuable as the results of this study have been, it would also be useful to know more about the development of older children and adolescents with lesbian or gay parents. Some writers have suggested that caution be used when generalizing the results of research conducted with young children to adolescents (e.g., Perrin 2002). Because adolescence is a time during which issues such as personal identity, peers, and dating become very important, and because of concerns about the possible effects of same-sex parenting during adolescence (e.g., Baumrind, 1995), it is an especially important period in which to examine the development of youth with nonheterosexual parents (Wainright, Russell & Patterson, 2004; Wainright & Patterson, 2006, 2008).

Background

A small body of research has focused on development of adolescent offspring of families headed by lesbian or gay parents. In general, like the literature on children, the research on adolescents has found few differences in adjustment as a function of parental sexual orientation (Gershon, Tschann, & Jemerin, 1999; Huggins, 1989; O'Connor, 1993). For instance, Huggins (1989) reported that the self-esteem of adolescents with lesbian mothers was not reliably different than that among those with heterosexual mothers.

While parental sexual orientation has not emerged as a potent predictor of adolescent outcomes, parenting practices have been implicated as important factors in many studies. A substantial body of research indicates that parenting style influences the effectiveness of parents' efforts to socialize their children (Steinberg & Silk, 2002). In particular, a warm and accepting style of parenting is related to optimal outcomes for adolescents (Rohner, 1999), especially if it is combined with appropriate limit setting and monitoring of adolescent behavior (Steinberg, Lamborn, Dornbusch, & Darling, 1992). Associations between parental warmth and positive outcomes have been found for adolescents from a wide variety of ethnic, cultural, and socioeconomic backgrounds (Khaleque & Rohner, 2002). That these linkages have been found among such a diverse group of adolescents suggests that they might also be expected among the offspring of lesbian and gay parents.

In summary, the research on adolescent offspring of lesbian and gay parents suggests that they are developing in positive ways. However, research has been limited and generally based on small samples, the representativeness of which can be difficult to assess (Stacey & Biblarz, 2001). The research described later is the first to assess development of adolescents living with same-sex parents, using data that are drawn from a large national sample. The sample is drawn from the National Longitudinal Study of Adolescent Health (known as Add Health) which includes participants from many different backgrounds, from many parts of the United States (Bearman, Jones, & Udry, 1997; Resnick et al., 1997).

Examination of the existing research indicates that many studies of the offspring of lesbian or gay parents focus on a single outcome or on a small set of outcomes. The Add Health study assessed adolescent adjustment in many different ways, including various aspects of psychosocial well-being, school functioning, romantic relationships and behaviors, substance use, delinquency, victimization, and the qualities of family and peer relationships. Data from the Add Health study thus afforded a broad overview of adolescent adjustment.

Our research assessed normative levels of adjustment among adolescent offspring of same-sex couples, and also explored factors associated with individual differences in adjustment and behavior within this group. We assessed structural variables such as family type (i.e., whether the parent has a same-sex or other-sex parent), as well as family and relationship variables such as adolescents' perceptions of parental warmth, care from adults and peers, autonomy, and parental perceptions of the quality of their relationships with adolescent offspring. Based on previous findings with children (e.g., Chan, Brooks, et al., 1998; Flaks et al., 1995; Golombok et al., 2003), we expected to find few differences in adjustment between youth living with parents who had same-sex vs. other-sex partners. Consistent with the literature on sources of individual differences among adolescents, however, we did expect to find associations between family and relationship variables and adolescent outcomes. Details of the studies are presented in Wainright et al. (2004) and in Wainright and Patterson (2006, 2008).

Description of Participating Families

Participating families were drawn from a large national sample of adolescents in the United States collected by Quality Education Data for the National Longitudinal Study of Adolescent Health (Bearman et al., 1997). Add Health is a school-based study of the health-related behaviors of adolescents in grades 7–12. A sample of 80 eligible high schools was initially selected. Schools were stratified to ensure that this sample was representative of US schools with respect to region of country, urbanicity, school type, ethnicity, and school size. More than seventy percent of the originally sampled high schools were recruited by AddHealth. If a high school refused to participate, a replacement school within its stratum was selected. Participating schools provided rosters of their students and, in most cases, agreed to administer an In-school Questionnaire during one class period. They also assisted in identifying their feeder schools (i.e., those schools that include seventh grade and send their graduates to that high school). The final sample consisted of a pair of schools in each of 80 communities, with the exception of some high schools that spanned grades 7–12, and therefore functioned as their own feeder schools (Bearman et al., 1997).

All students who completed an In-school Questionnaire plus those who did not complete a questionnaire but who were listed on a school roster were eligible for selection into the core in-home sample. Students in each school were stratified by grade and sex, and approximately 17 students were randomly chosen from each stratum so that a total of approximately 200 adolescents were selected from each of the 80 pairs of schools. A total core sample of 12,105 adolescents was interviewed.

Most interviews were conducted in 1995 in the participants' homes. All data were recorded on laptop computers. For less sensitive sections, the interviewer read the questions and entered the respondent's answers. For more sensitive sections, the respondent listened to pre-recorded questions through earphones and entered the answers directly.

A parent, preferably the resident mother, of each adolescent respondent interviewed in Wave I of data collection was asked to complete a questionnaire covering topics including, among others, parents' marriages and marriage-like relationships; neighborhood characteristics; involvement in volunteer, civic, or school activities; health-affecting behaviors; education and employment; household income and economic assistance; and parent—adolescent communication and interaction.

Data employed in the present study were collected through the in-home interviews and surveys, as well as in-school surveys of students (collected in 1994–1995) and through the in-home questionnaires of parents. Offspring of same-sex couples were identified through a two-step process. We first identified families in which parents reported being in a marriage or marriage-like relationship with a person of the same sex. Because no data had been collected on parents' sexual identities, per se, families headed by gay, bisexual, or lesbian parents who did not report that they were in a marriage or marriage-like relationship at the time of data collection could not be identified. In the second step, the consistency of parental reports about gender and family relationships was examined. To guard against the possibility that some families may have been misclassified due to coding errors, we retained only those cases in which parental reports of gender and family relationship were consistent (e.g., a parent reported being female and described her relationship to the target adolescent as "biological mother"). Any families in which parental reports of gender and family relationships did not make sense or did not fit our criteria (e.g., a parent reported being female and described her relationship to the target adolescent as "biological father") were discarded. This procedure was designed to ensure that, insofar as possible, only adolescents whose parents reported being involved in a marriage or marriage-like relationship with a person of the same sex were selected for further study. The number of families headed by *male* same-sex couples was very small ($n = 6$). Results of preliminary analyses that included these families were nearly identical to those including only families headed by female same-sex couples. To simplify interpretation of results, we excluded these six families from the final sample.

The focal group of families identified through this process consisted of 44 adolescents, 23 girls, and 21 boys. Approximately 68% of the adolescents identified themselves as European-American or white, and 32% identified themselves as nonwhite or as biracial. On average, the adolescents were 15 years of age, with a range of 12–18 years of age. Average household income for families in the focal group was approximately $45,500 per year.

The resources of the Add Health database allowed the construction of a well-matched comparison group of adolescents. Each of the offspring of same-sex parents was matched with an adolescent from the Add Health database who lived with other-sex parents. This matching was accomplished by generating a list of adolescents from the Add Health database who matched each target adolescent on the following characteristics: sex, age, ethnic background, adoption status (identified via parent reports), learning disability status, family income, and parent's educational attainment. The first matching adolescent on each list was chosen as the comparison adolescent for that target adolescent. The final sample included 88 families, including 44 families headed by mothers with female partners and 44 comparison families headed by other-sex couples.

To assess the degree to which our focal group of 44 families with same-sex parents was representative of the overall population from which it was drawn, we compared the demographic characteristics of the focal group with those for the entire Add Health core sample ($n = 12,105$). We compared adolescent age, parent age, household income, adolescent gender, racial identification, adoption status, and parental education in the two groups. For the entire Add Health core sample, average age of adolescent participants was 15 years and parent's average age was 42 years. Average household income was $47,400 per year. The sample was 52% female, 38% nonwhite, 1 % adopted, and 42% of parents were college-educated. None of these comparisons was statistically significant. Thus, the focal group of 44 families was demographically similar to the population from which it was drawn.

We also explored a more stringent approach to identification of families with same-sexed parents. In this approach, we used the two principal criteria described earlier (1) parent described as being in a "marriage or marriage-like relationship" and (2) parental report data about gender and family relationships were clear and consistent; in addition we required that (3) the responding parent reported being unmarried, and (4) the adolescent reported no other-sex parental figure in his/her household. The fourth criterion required that if an adolescent reported living with his biological mother, he reported no male figure (e.g., biological father, stepfather) as residing in the household.

Because there was no way for adolescents to indicate that they lived in more than one household (e.g., in joint custody situations), we believe that application of the more stringent criteria effectively eliminated from the sample many adolescents from divorced families in which one or both parents were currently involved in same-sex relationships. Thus, use of the more stringent criteria had the disadvantage of failing to include many families of interest, but had the advantage of including only very clear cases in which adolescents described themselves as living only with two same-sex adults, and in which parents described themselves as unmarried, and as involved in a "marriage or marriage-like relationship" with a person of the same sex. In short, these families conformed in every particular to an idealized image of lesbian mother families. We identified 18 such families, and completed all analyses with this sample and a matched comparison group of 18 families (in which parents reported being involved in other-sex relationships). Results were essentially identical to those reported later, revealing few group differences, but much within-group variation in outcomes that was significantly associated with the quality of family relationships. The data from the larger sample are presented later, however, because it more nearly represents the real (rather than the idealized) variety of families in which parents are involved in same-sex relationships.

We examined data from Add Health regarding various aspects of adolescent adjustment and adolescent relationships with parents. Composite variables were created from the Add Health Home Interviews and In-School Questionnaires for adolescents' self-reported levels of depressive symptoms, anxiety, self-esteem, school grades, trouble at school, and school connectedness. Composite variables were also formed for adolescents' reports of their perceptions of parental warmth, caring from adults and peers, their integration into their neighborhood, and their autonomy. Adolescents' romantic attractions, relationships, and behaviors were assessed with individual items.

Procedures, Materials, and Results

In this section, the procedures, materials, and results are described. We begin with assessments of adolescent adjustment and school functioning, then go on to romantic and sexual behavior, family and relationship variables, substance use, delinquency and victimization, and adolescent peer relations. The varied array of assessments provides a comprehensive overview of adolescent outcomes in the two groups of families. Further details can be found in Wainright et al. (2004) and in Wainright and Patterson (2006, 2008).

Adolescent Psychosocial Adjustment and School Functioning

Adolescent depressive symptoms were assessed with a 19-question version of the CES-D (Radloff, 1977) scale from the In-Home Interview. This scale of depressive symptoms included questions about the frequency of symptoms such as feeling depressed, feeling too tired to do things, and feeling lonely. Possible scores on this scale, based on the sum of the 19 items, ranged from 0 to 57, with higher scores indicating greater levels of depressive symptoms.

Adolescent anxiety was measured with a 7-item scale from the In-Home Interview that included questions about the frequency of symptoms such as feeling moody or having trouble relaxing. Items were measured on a scale of 0 (never) to 4 (every day), with scores ranging from 0 to 28, and higher scores indicating higher levels of anxiety.

Self-esteem was assessed using a 6-item scale from the In-School Questionnaire that included items such as feeling socially accepted and feeling loved and wanted. Items were measured on a scale of 1 (strongly disagree) to 5 (strongly agree), with scores ranging from 6 to 30, and higher scores indicating higher self-esteem.

School outcomes measured included grade point average (GPA), school connectedness, and trouble in school, all assessed in the In-Home Interview. GPA was measured on a 4-point scale where 4 = A, 3 = B, 2 = C, and 1 = D, or lower. Following Scal, Ireland, and Borowsky (2003), it was assessed by taking the mean of grades received in four school subjects (English, Mathematics, History/Social Studies, and Science) in the current or most recent school year.

School connectedness was measured using a 5-item scale that assessed respondents' feelings of integration into their school. Items, which were averaged to form the adolescent's score, included the degree to which adolescents felt close to other students, felt like part of their school, felt safe in their school, felt that teachers treated students fairly, and were happy at their school. Possible scores ranged from 1 (strongly disagree) to 5 (strongly agree).Adolescents' trouble at school was assessed with a 4-item scale that included items such as problems getting homework done and problems in getting along with classmates. Items were measured on a scale of 0 (never) to 4 (every day) and the mean of the four items was taken, with higher scores indicating more trouble in school.

Results showed that, overall, adolescents reported positive psychosocial outcomes, with low levels of depressive symptoms ($M = 10.73$, on a scale of 0–57) and anxiety ($M = 0.82$, on a scale of 0–4), and high levels of self-esteem ($M = 4.02$, on a scale of 1–5). Similarly, adolescents reported positive school outcomes, with fairly high GPAs ($M = 2.81$, on a scale of 1–4), high levels of school connectedness ($M = 3.69$, on a scale of 1–5), and low levels of trouble in school ($M = 1.05$, on a scale of 0–4). Higher scores indicated greater levels of that outcome for all variables.

As expected, there were no significant differences in adolescents' psychosocial adjustment, which included depressive symptoms, anxiety, and self-esteem, between offspring of same-sex couples and offspring of comparison families headed by other-sex couples. We found a significant multivariate effect for family type for school outcomes, which was significant in the univariate analyses for school connectedness. Adolescents with same-sex parents were more connected at school than were those living with other-sex parents. We found no differences as a function of gender for psychosocial adjustment or school functioning, and no significant interactions between gender and family type for psychological adjustment or school outcomes. Overall, adolescent psychosocial and school adjustment did not differ as a function of family type or adolescent gender.

Adolescent Romantic Relationships, Attractions, and Behaviors

Adolescents' romantic attractions were assessed with two yes/no questions, "Have you ever been attracted to a female?" and "Have you ever been attracted to a male?" Female adolescents who answered yes to the first question and male adolescents who answered yes to the second question were classified as having had a same-sex attraction. To assess dating behavior, adolescents were asked three yes/no questions: whether they had had a romantic relationship in the past 18 months, whether they had had a same-sex romantic relationship in the past 18 months, and whether they had ever engaged in sexual intercourse.

Analyses of adolescents' reports of romantic attractions and behaviors revealed no difference between the groups in the percentage of adolescents who reported ever having engaged in sexual intercourse (34% of adolescents with same-sex parents and 34% of those with other-sex parents). There was also no significant difference between the groups in the percent of adolescents who had had a romantic relationship in the past 18 months (68% of adolescents with same-sex parents and 59% of those with other-sex parents, *ns*). Fewer than ten adolescents reported same-sex attractions and same-sex romantic relationships in the past 18 months, so under stipulations that permit use of these data, group comparisons are not presented. Reports of romantic relationships, attractions, and behaviors did not differ as a function of age or gender except that older adolescents were more likely than younger ones to report having had a romantic relationship in the past 18 months.

Family and Relationship Variables

Parental warmth toward the adolescent was assessed using the mean of five items from adolescent reports collected during the In-Home Interview. Self-report items included adolescents' perceptions of parents' warmth and caring toward adolescent, perceived level of family's understanding and attention, and adolescents' feelings of closeness to parents. For questions in which adolescents were asked about each of their parents, we used the response for the parent who was described as more warm and loving. Scores ranged from 1 (not at all) to 5 (very much), with higher scores indicating greater warmth.

Adolescents' perceptions of their integration into the neighborhood in which they lived were measured using a scale of three yes/no (1 = yes, 0 = no) items taken from the In-Home Interview. Items included whether adolescents know people in their neighborhood, talk with neighbors, or feel that their neighbors look out for each other. The three items were summed, and possible scores ranged from 0 to 3, with higher scores indicating greater neighborhood integration.

Adolescents' perceived autonomy was assessed with a scale of 7 yes/no (1 = yes, 0 = no) items that addressed the extent to which adolescents are allowed to make decisions about aspects of their lives such as food, bedtime, TV viewing, and friends. The seven items were summed, and possible scores ranged from 0 to 7, with higher scores indicating greater autonomy. Adolescents' perceived care from adults and friends was measured with three items regarding how much the adolescent believed that adults, teachers, and friends care about them. The mean of the three items was taken as the adolescent's score, and possible scores ranged from 1 (not at all) to 5 (very much), with higher scores indicating perceptions of more caring. Parents' perceptions of the quality of their relationship with their child were assessed with a scale of six items from the parent's in-home interview. Items included questions about the parent's assessment of trust, understanding, communication, and the general quality of their relationship with their child, and were measured on a scale of 1–5, with scores ranging from 6 to 30, and higher scores indicating closer relationships.

Results showed that overall, adolescents reported positive family relationships. Adolescents' reports of parental warmth were high. On a scale of 1–5, with higher scores indicating greater warmth, the mean for the entire sample was 4.36, with a range of 2.80–5.00. Very few youngsters reported low-quality relationships with parents. In fact only one adolescent in the focal group and nobody in the comparison group had scores lower than 3 on the scale. Similarly, adolescents' perceptions of others' (teachers, adults, and friends) care for them were high ($M = 4.07$), with a range of 2.33–5.00. Adolescents also reported relatively high levels of autonomy ($M = 5.26$, $Range = 1.00–7.00$) on a scale of 1–7, with higher scores indicating more autonomy. Their average assessment of their integration into their neighborhoods was 2.30 on a scale of 0–3, with higher scores indicating greater integration. Parents' perceptions of the quality of the parent—child relationship were also high, with a mean of 4.20 on a scale of 1–5, with higher scores indicating more positive relationships.

Consistent with results for psychosocial and school outcomes, there were no differences in adolescent reports of family and relationship processes, including parental warmth, care from others, personal autonomy, or neighborhood integration, as a function of family type.

Comparisons with Add Health Core Sample

To what degree did outcomes for adolescents in our focal and comparison samples differ from those for the population from which the samples were drawn? To explore this question, we obtained mean scores (or percentages for categorical variables) for each of the dependent variables. Using one-sample t tests and X^2 tests, as appropriate, we compared means for our focal sample to those for the entire Add Health core sample. None of these comparisons was statistically significant. Thus, outcomes for adolescents with same-sex parents in our focal sample did not differ significantly from those for a representative group of American adolescents.

Associations among Family Relationships and Outcome Variables

Having found almost no associations between family type and adolescent adjustment, we wanted to explore possible associations between processes in the adolescent's environment and adolescent outcomes. In particular, we examined correlations among adolescents' perceptions of parental warmth, care from adults and peers, autonomy, and neighborhood integration; parents' perceptions of the quality of the parent—child relationship; and measures of adolescent adjustment. We also conducted simultaneous multiple regression analyses to determine whether these family and relationship variables were significant predictors of adolescent adjustment, while controlling for family type, adolescent gender, and socioeconomic status. Regression analyses were conducted separately for adolescents' depressive symptoms, anxiety, self-esteem, GPA, school connectedness, and trouble in school. Family type, adolescent's gender, parental education, and family income were also included as predictors. We did not examine romantic attractions and behavior because of the small number of adolescents in either group reporting same-sex attractions or romantic relationships.

Results showed that, as expected, quality of family relationships was significantly associated with many adolescent outcomes, including school connectedness, anxiety, and trouble in school. The association between adolescents' depressive symptoms and parental report of the quality of the parent—adolescent relationship was not statistically significant. Adolescents' anxiety was associated with adolescent gender, with being male associated with less anxiety. Adolescents' reports of trouble in school were associated with the quality of the parent—child relationship and level of parental education; less trouble in school was associated with more positive relationships with parents and having parents with higher levels of education. School connectedness was associated with family type, the quality of the parent—child relationship, and care from adults and peers, with a significant interaction between family type and care from adults and peers. Greater school connectedness was associated with having same-sex parents, reporting higher levels of care from adults and peers, and having parents who reported a more positive parent—child relationship. Adolescents' perceived care from adults and peers had a stronger effect on school connectedness for adolescents living with same-sex parents than for those living with other-sex parents. Adolescents' GPAs were not associated with any family and relationship variable or SES variable. In summary, adolescents' reports of family and relationship processes such as quality of the parent—child relationship and care from adults and peers were associated with several measures of adolescent functioning, and were better predictors of adolescent adjustment than were family type or adolescent gender.

Substance Use

Adolescents' use of tobacco was assessed with a composite variable (Sieving et al., 2000) that uses four items to classify adolescents into one of seven levels of tobacco use (1 = "never smoked," 3 = "currently smoking 1–2 cigarettes per day," 5 = "currently smoking 6–10 cigarettes per day," 7 = "currently smoking >20 cigarettes per day"). Friends' use of tobacco was assessed by asking how many of three best friends smoke at least 1 cigarette per day.

Use of alcohol was assessed with three variables from the adolescent interviews. We used a composite variable (Sieving et al., 2000), which uses two items to create an eight-level variable about adolescents' use of alcohol in their lifetime and in the past 12 months (1 = "2–3 drinks lifetime," 3 = "drank alcohol on 1 or 2 days in the past 12 months," 5 = "drank 2–3 days a month in the past 12 months," 7 = "drank 3–5 days a week in the past 12 months," 8 = "drank every day or almost every day in the past 12 months"). Adolescents were instructed to exclude "a sip or taste of someone else's drink." Individual items measured how often in the past 12 months adolescents had binged on alcohol (5 + drinks in a row) and had gotten drunk. Scores for these items ranged from 1 (never) to 7 (every day or almost every day).

Lifetime and current marijuana use were assessed with a composite variable (Sieving, et al., 2000), which uses two survey items from the Adolescent IHI to form a seven-level variable (1 = "never used marijuana," 3 = " > 3 times in lifetime, no use in past 30 days," 5 = "2–3 times in past 30 days Adolescents' risky use of alcohol and drugs was assessed with a scale of eight items (1 = yes, 0 = no) from the adolescent interviews that asked whether the adolescent had driven a car, gone to school, gotten into a fight, or carried a weapon while consuming alcohol or drugs. The sum of the eight items was taken, with higher scores indicating more risky use.

Relationship and physical problems caused by adolescents' use of alcohol were assessed with a scale of nine items from the adolescent interviews asking about the frequency of being hung over, sick, in a fight, in a situation that was later regretted, or in trouble with parents, school, or friends or dates because of alcohol use in the past 12 months. Items were measured on a scale of 0 (never) to 4 (5 or more times) and the mean of the nine items was taken, with higher scores indicating more problems.

Adolescents' joint occurrences of substance use and sexual activity were assessed using a scale of six items (1 = yes, 0 = no) from the adolescent interviews, asking whether the adolescent had used drugs, alcohol, or been drunk the first time (three items) or most recent time (three items) he or she had sexual intercourse The sum of the six items was taken, and higher scores indicated more joint occurrences.

Results showed that, overall, adolescents reported positive outcomes. They reported moderate use of cigarettes and alcohol, with 25% reporting that they had ever smoked regularly and 44% reporting that they had drunk alcohol when they were not with their parents. Reports of adolescents' frequency of alcohol use ($M = 2.91$) and tobacco use ($M = 1.94$) were low. Adolescents also reported low levels of alcohol abuse, including binging ($M = 1.82$) and getting drunk ($M = 1.81$). Their reports of physical and relationship problems because of alcohol use ($M = 0.24$) were low, as were their reports of risky use of drugs and alcohol ($M = 0.53$) and reports of joint occurrences of sexual activity and drug or alcohol use ($M = 0.23$).

As expected, we did not find a statistically significant difference in adolescents' reports of their frequency of alcohol, tobacco, or marijuana use as a function of family type. In addition, our analyses revealed no significant difference in the number of three best friends who smoke or frequency of getting drunk or binge drinking. Consistent with results for the substance use, we found no significant difference in problems arising from alcohol or drug use (relationship and physical problems, risky use of alcohol and drugs, and sex while under influence of alcohol or drugs) as a function of family type.

Delinquent Behavior and Victimization

Adolescent delinquent behavior was assessed with ten items from the portion of the adolescent interviews in which adolescents listened to questions through headphones and recorded their answers on a laptop computer. These items ask about the occurrence of activities such as damaging others' property, shoplifting, and getting into fights in the past 12 months. Scores on this scale were the sum of the ten items (1 = yes, 0 = no), with higher scores indicating more delinquent behaviors.

Adolescents' experiences as victims and witnesses of violence were assessed with five items from the adolescent interviews asking how often adolescents had been shot at, cut, or jumped, had a gun or knife pulled on them, or had seen someone shot or stabbed. Scores were the sum of five items (1 = yes, 0 = no). Higher scores indicated more victimization.

Results showed that, overall, adolescents reported low levels of delinquent behavior ($M = 1.81$) and victimization ($M = 0.39$). Analyses also revealed no difference in adolescents' delinquent behavior between offspring of same-sex couples and offspring of comparison families headed by different-sex couples. Similarly, we found no difference in adolescents' experiences as victims or witnesses of violence as a function of family type.

Associations Among Family Relationships, Substance Use, Delinquency, and Victimization

Having found no associations between family type and adolescent risk behavior, we explored possible associations between processes in the adolescent's environment and adolescent outcomes. We conducted regression analyses separately for use of tobacco, alcohol, and marijuana, as well as victimization and delinquent behavior. Family type, gender, parental education, and family income were included as predictors. Variables and interactions that were not statistically significant predictors were removed from the models.

Results showed that, as expected, quality of family relationships was significantly associated with many adolescent outcomes. Adolescents' tobacco use was associated with parental report of the quality of the parent—adolescent relationship and with adolescents' reports of caring from adults and peers. As expected, greater perceived care from others and more positive relationships were associated with lower levels of tobacco use.

Adolescents' use of alcohol, use of marijuana, and delinquent behavior were associated with parental report of the quality of the parent—adolescent relationship, with more positive relationships associated with less use of alcohol and marijuana and less delinquent behavior. Interactions between family type and predictor variables were not significant. In summary, adolescents' reports of family and relationship processes such as quality of the parent—child relationship and care from adults and peers were associated with several measures of adolescent outcomes, and were better predictors of adolescent risk behavior than was family type.

Adolescent Peer Relations

Another important dimension of adolescent adjustment is peer relations. To explore experiences with peers among the offspring of same-sex and other-sex couples, we studied not only the adolescents' self-reported friendships but also their popularity among their peers, as described by their peers.

Adolescents' reports of the quality of their peer relationships were measured with a scale of nine items, including questions about how much the adolescent feels friends care about him or her, feels close to people at school, and feels like a part of their school; as well as frequency of trouble getting along with other students, feeling that people were unfriendly, getting into any physical fights or serious physical fights, and being jumped. Negative items were reverse-coded. These items were standardized and the sum was taken, with higher scores indicating more positive relationships.

The adolescent's perceived support from, and amount of time spent with his or her five best male friends and five best female friends were measured with 10 yes/no items (three items each about time with male friends and time with female friends; two items each about support from male friends and support from female friends). The support items asked whether the adolescent had talked to the friend about a problem or talked to the friend on the telephone during past seven days. The time items asked whether the adolescent had gone to the friend's house, hung out with the friend during the past 7 days, or spent time with the friend during the past weekend. The three support items were summed for all five friends of each gender, and possible scores ranged from 0 to 15. The two time items were summed for all five friends of each gender, and possible scores ranged from 0 to 10. Higher scores indicated more support from or time spent with friends.

Adolescents' self-report data on their friendship networks were available for a subset ($n = 56$) of adolescents in our sample. Analyses revealed that this subset of adolescents did not differ on family income or parental education from those adolescents for whom these data were not available. Our analyses of network variables are limited to this smaller sample.

The number of friends the adolescent reported having in his or her school was measured as the number of friendship nominations (up to 10) the adolescent made for students in his or her school. The presence of a best female friend was assessed with a yes/no item indicating whether the adolescent nominated a female friend in the school as his or her best friend. Similarly, the presence of a best male friend was assessed with a yes/no item that indicates whether the adolescent nominated a male friend in his or her school as a best friend. Peer-report network data were available to augment the information provided by adolescents regarding their friendship networks. As with the adolescent self-report network data, analyses of these data are limited to the subset of adolescents ($n = 56$) for whom network data were available. Variables constructed by Add Health staff (Carolina Population Center, 1997) from peer-report data include adolescent popularity, network centrality, network density, network heterogeneity, and several network traits.

Adolescents' popularity was calculated as the number of times an adolescent was nominated as a friend by other students in his or her school, with higher scores indicating greater popularity in the adolescent's network. Adolescents' centrality within their friendship network (Bonacich, 1987; Carolina Population Center, 1997) assesses whether adolescents are located in prominent positions within their friendship network and connected to many peers in their peer group. Higher numbers indicate greater centrality.

The density of adolescents' friendship networks, including students who were nominated by the adolescent as a friend and students who nominated the adolescent as a friend, assesses how many interconnections exist among students in the peer group, which is related to how likely adolescents are to know others in their school (Haynie, 2000). Higher numbers indicate greater network density.

In order to assess the degree of diversity in adolescents' friendship networks, which included students who were nominated as friends by the adolescent and students who nominated the adolescent as a friend, we used heterogeneity measures of grade, age, and race computed by Add Health staff. Higher numbers indicate greater diversity in a trait. We assessed two characteristics of adolescents' friendship networks with the mean value on that characteristic or behavior for students in the adolescent's peer network. These characteristics included grades and number of extracurricular activities. Higher scores indicate higher grades or more activities (Carolina Population Center, 1997). Adolescents' perceived care from adults and friends was measured with three items regarding how much the adolescent believed that adults, teachers, and friends care about them. The mean of the three items was taken as the adolescent's score, and possible scores ranged from 1 to 5, with higher scores indicating perceptions of more caring.

Perceived parental warmth toward the adolescent was assessed using the mean of five items from adolescent reports. Self-report items included adolescents' perceptions of parents' warmth and caring toward adolescent, perceived level of family's understanding and attention, and adolescents' feelings of closeness to parents. For questions in which adolescents were asked about each of their parents, the response for the parent who was described as more warm and loving was used. Scores ranged from 1 to 5, with higher scores indicating greater warmth. Cronbach's Alpha for the parental warmth scale was 0.70 for this sample.

Adolescents answered 8 yes/no items describing activities adolescents sometimes engage in with their mothers. Adolescents reported whether or not they had engaged in each of the activities with their resident mother in the past 4 weeks. These items included going shopping, playing a sport, talking about someone the adolescent is dating, going to the movies, discussing a personal problem, talking about grades, talking about a school project, and talking about other things going on in school. The eight items were summed, with possible scores ranging from 0 to 8. Parents' perceptions of the quality of their relationship with their adolescent were assessed using a scale made up of six items, with higher scores indicating closer relationships.

Analyses of the data were conducted in two major steps. The first set of analyses evaluated the degree to which adolescents living with same-sex couples differed in their family relationships and peer relations from the comparison group, and they employed two-way (family type: same- vs.other-sex parents X gender of adolescent) ANOVAs and MANOVAs. The second set of analyses explored associations of adolescent peer relations with assessments of family and relationship processes. Simultaneous multiple regression analyses were used to determine whether these processes were significant predictors of adolescent adjustment, while controlling for family type, adolescent gender, and socioeconomic status. We expected that family type would be less important than family relationships and processes in accounting for variation in the quality of adolescent peer relations, and that processes related to positive outcomes for adolescents would be similar, regardless of family type, and that no interactions between family type and relationship processes would emerge.

Adolescents also reported that they spent time with between one and two male friends and between one and two female friends, on average, in the past week engaging in activities such as going to the friend's home, hanging out, and talking on the phone.

As expected, there were no differences in the number of friends that adolescents nominated in their school nor in the quality of their peer relations as a function of family type. Girls rated the quality of their peer relations slightly more positively than did boys, but this comparison did not reach statistical significance. There was no significant difference between groups in the percentage of adolescents who reported having a best male friend; 64% of adolescents with same-sex parents and 68% of those with other-sex parents reported this. Adolescents who reported having a best female friend (68% of adolescents with same-sex parents and 40% of adolescents with other-sex parents, *ns*) were somewhat more likely to be living with same-sex couples, but this difference did not reach statistical significance. Analyses of adolescents' reports of time spent with and support received from male and female friends also revealed no significant differences as a function of family type. There was, however, a significant effect for gender; girls reported more support from female friends than did boys. All of the analyses were run again with family income and parent's education as covariates. As the results did not differ between the two analyses and as the influence of demographic characteristics was not a focus of our research, demographic results are not presented here. Overall, adolescent reports of peer relations did not differ as a function of family type.

With regard to peer reports of peer relations, adolescents in this sample were nominated as a friend by an average of almost five schoolmates. As expected, analyses of peer reports of the adolescent's peer relations, including popularity, network centrality, and network density, revealed no significant differences as a function of family type. There was, however, a significant effect for adolescent gender, with girls having higher popularity ratings than did boys.

We also used peer report data to calculate the heterogeneity of the adolescent's friendship network with respect to age, race, and school grades. On average, this sample of adolescents had networks that were moderately diverse, and there were no significant differences as a function of family type or adolescent gender. In summary, adolescents living with same-sex parents had friendship networks that were very similar in heterogeneity and member characteristics to those of adolescents living with other-sex parents.

Overall, as reported earlier, adolescents reported positive family relationships. Adolescents' reports of parental warmth were high. With regard to time spent with their parents, adolescents reported an average of more than three activities with their mother in the past four weeks. As described, adolescents' perceptions of others' care for them were high, as were parents' perceptions of the quality of the parent—adolescent relationship.

In line with our expectations, there were no significant differences in adolescent reports of family and relationship processes, including parental warmth, activities with mother, or care from others as a function of family type. Girls did, however, report higher levels of care from adults and peers, and greater participation in activities with their mothers, than did boys.

In order to assess the degree to which outcomes for adolescents in our focal and comparison samples differed from those for the population from which the samples were drawn, we obtained mean scores from the Add Health Core Sample for each of the dependent variables. Using one-sample t-tests and chi-squared tests, we compared means for our focal sample to those for the entire Add Health core sample. None of these comparisons was statistically significant. Thus, peer relations for adolescents with same-sex parents in our focal sample did not differ significantly from those of a nationally representative group of American adolescents.

We also explored possible associations between processes in the adolescent's environment and adolescent peer relations. Simultaneous multiple regression analyses were used to determine whether these family and relationship variables were significant predictors of adolescent peer relations, while controlling for family type, adolescent gender, and socioeconomic status. Regression analyses were conducted separately for adolescents' reports of the quality of their peer relations and the number of friends nominated by the adolescent as friends, as well as for peer reports of popularity, network centrality, and network density. Family type, adolescent's gender, parental education, and family income were also included as predictors, with family type and adolescent gender remaining in all models for comparison. Demographic variables and family and relationship variables that were not statistically significant predictors were removed from the models.

Results showed that, as expected, family and relationship variables were significantly associated with many measures of adolescent peer relations. Adolescents' reports of the quality of their peer relations were significantly associated with parents' reports of the quality of the parent—adolescent relationship and with the adolescents' reports of caring from adults and peers, with more positive parent—adolescent relationships and more perceived care from adults and peers associated with more positive peer relations. Similarly, the number of school friends reported by adolescents was associated with the quality of the parent—adolescent relationship and the number of activities done with mother, with more positive parent—adolescent relationships and more activities with mother associated with having more friends at school.

Peer reports of adolescent peer relations were also significantly associated with family and relationship variables. Peer reports of adolescents' popularity were significantly associated with the number of activities with mother, with more activities with mother associated with greater popularity. Adolescents' centrality in their peer networks was associated with the quality of the parent—adolescent relationship; more positive relationships were associated with greater network centrality. There was also a significant association between network centrality and parental education, with higher levels of parental education associated with greater network centrality. There were no significant associations among the density of adolescent's peer networks and family and relationship variables.

In summary, adolescent peer relations were associated in expected ways with several family and relationship variables. Adolescent reports of care from adults and peers and number of activities with mother, as well as parental reports of the quality of the parent —adolescent relationship, were significantly associated with numerous measures of adolescent peer relations. Also as predicted, family type was not significantly associated with any measure of adolescent peer relations, but several associations were found among these measures and adolescent gender. Overall, these results suggest that family and relationship process variables are more important predictors of adolescent peer relations than is family type.

Summary of Results

The results of this research showed that, across a diverse array of assessments, including measures of adolescent adjustment, school functioning, delinquent behavior, victimization, substance abuse, and qualities of family and peer relationships, adolescents with female same-sex parents did not differ significantly from a matched group of adolescents living with different-sex parents. Regardless of family type, adolescents were more likely to report positive outcomes when they had close relationships with parents. Consistent with results from research with younger children, it was qualities of adolescent—parent relationships rather than family composition that was significantly associated with adolescent adjustment (Golombok, 1999).

Confidence in the present findings is bolstered by the strengths of the Add Health study (Bearman et al., 1997), which allowed for examination of important outcomes among adolescents living with female same-sex parents, compared with a well-matched sample of adolescents living with different-sex parents, using data from a large national sample. Results of our current study add significantly to those from earlier studies, which were most often smaller in their size, less representative in their sampling, and less comprehensive in their assessment of adolescent outcomes (Stacey & Biblarz, 2001). The clarity of results from our broad array of assessments, however, strengthens our confidence that adolescents living with same-sex parents were functioning well in many domains, both at home and at school. Despite many strengths of this research, however, there were also limitations. For instance, parents were not asked directly about their sexual identities, and we were thus forced to rely on indirect assessments (e.g., parents' reports of being in a "marriage or marriage-like relationship" with a person of the same sex). As a result, we were unable to identify or study adolescents who lived in households headed by single or divorced mothers. The sample size of the current study is larger than those of much of the previous research with this population, but the finding of no group differences would be strengthened by replication in larger samples.

An unexpected aspect of our results was the finding that adolescents' feelings of connectedness at school varied as a function of family type. Adolescents living with same-sex parents reported feeling more connected to school than did those living with other-sex parents. Inasmuch as school connectedness among adolescents has been associated with fewer problem behaviors and with greater emotional well-being (Resnick et al, 1997), this finding suggests that adolescents with same-sex parents might be expected to show more favorable adjustment. For measures of adjustment such as self-esteem and depressive symptoms, however, we found no effects of family type. Consequently, the best interpretation of this intriguing finding remains unclear.

With only one exception, *processes* linked to positive outcomes for adolescents were similar across family type. Only one interaction of family type and relationship processes emerged as statistically significant. This single significant interaction revealed that adolescents' perceived care from adults and peers was a better predictor of feelings of connectedness at school for adolescents with same-sex as compared to other-sex parents. While greater caring from adults and peers may be more tightly linked with school connectedness for the offspring of same-sex parents, it is not clear why that would be true of school connectedness but no other outcome. Pending replication in other samples, this result should be viewed with caution. Overall, the family relationships and processes associated with positive adjustment were remarkably similar for adolescents with same-sex and other-sex parents.

General Discussion and Implications

The research summarized above suggests several substantive conclusions. In the section that follows, conclusions suggested by the research are enumerated briefly. This is followed by a discussion of their implications for theories of social development, and by an overview of their implications for family law and policy. The section concludes with a discussion of future directions for research.

Overview of Research Findings

The results of our research revealed that, on nearly all of a large array of variables related to school and personal adjustment, children and adolescents with same-sex parents did not differ significantly from carefully matched groups of those living with other-sex parents. Regardless of family type, youngsters were more likely to show favorable adjustment when they perceived more caring from adults and when parents described close relationships with them. Thus, it was the qualities of parent—child and parent—adolescent relationships, rather than the structural features of families (e.g., same- vs. other-sex parents), that were significantly associated with child and adolescent adjustment (Golombok, 1999; Patterson, 2000, 2006). These results are important both for their relevance to theories of development (Golombok & Tasker, 1994) and for their potential bearing upon laws and policies relevant to families headed by lesbian and gay parents (Patterson et al., 2002; Stacey & Biblarz, 2001).

Although family type was not related to most child or adolescent outcomes in this research, youngsters' adjustment was clearly linked with the qualities of relationships within the family. These results were consistent with expectations based on earlier work with children and adolescents in the population at large (Khaleque & Rohner, 2002; Steinberg & Silk, 2002). We found that, regardless of family type, when parents reported more satisfying relationships with their children and adolescents, these youngsters were likely to be developing in positive ways. In other words, adjustment was not linked with family type (e.g., same- vs. other-sex parents), but was strongly associated with the qualities of relationships within the family.

These results have emerged from research that involves many different groups of participants, living in many different parts of the United States. Both child and adolescent samples have been studied. Both white and nonwhite children and teenagers have participated. The results have emerged from our work and also from that of many other researchers. All of these factors add to confidence in the results.

These results have also emerged with great consistency from studies using a wide variety of research methods. Some research has employed survey and questionnaire methods to obtain self-report data from participants. Other studies have employed parents, teachers, and peers as informants. Still others have drawn on archival data such as school records. In all these cases, the convergence of findings obtained from divergent methodological approaches has been noteworthy.

Thus many concerns that were expressed about the early research in this area are no longer as compelling as they might once have been. Whereas early studies were based on convenience samples, much recent work employs stronger sampling methods. Whereas early studies relied heavily on self-reports, current research includes many other methodological approaches. Whereas early studies focused largely on upper-middle-class white samples, current studies involve a much wider array of participants. Thus, one can have greater confidence than ever before in the conclusions based on findings of empirical research in this area.

Implications for Theories of Socialization

Major theories of human development have often been interpreted as predicting that children and adolescents living with same-sex parents would encounter important difficulties in their adjustment. This has been seen as especially true during adolescence (Baumrind, 1995). The fact that results from research fail to confirm such views leads to questions about the extent to which predictions of the theories have been disconfirmed (Patterson, 2000). In particular, results of recent research on children and adolescents who are not living with other-sex parents (e.g., Patterson, 2000; Stevens et al., 2002) suggest that theorists may need to reconsider the importance of different-sex parents for personal and social development (Silverstein & Auerbach, 1999).

A number of different approaches might be examined. It might be argued that certain kinds of family interactions, processes, and relationships are beneficial for children's development, but that parents need not be heterosexual to provide them. In other words, variables related to family processes (e.g., qualities of relationships) may be more important predictors of child adjustment than are variables related to family structure (e.g., sexual orientation, number of parents in the home). This approach has been taken in much research on other nontraditional family forms (Patterson & Hastings, 2006).

Many theoretical perspectives are compatible with an emphasis on function. For instance, attachment theory (Ainsworth, 1985a, b; Bowlby, 1988) emphasizes the functional significance of sensitive parenting in creating secure relationships, but does not stipulate the necessity of any particular family constellation or structure. Similarly, self-psychology (Kohut, 1971, 1977, 1984) describes the significance of mirroring and idealizing processes in human development, but does not insist on their occurrence in the context of any specific family structure. Perspectives such as attachment theory and self-psychology would appear to be compatible with an emphasis on functional rather than structural aspects of family life, and hence to provide possible interpretive frameworks within which to conceptualize further research in these directions.

Implications for Law and Policy

Our findings also have implications for public policies that involve children of lesbian parents (Patterson, 2007; Patterson et al., 2002). Inasmuch as the results of research suggest that children and adolescents living with same-sex parents develop in much the same ways as do those living with other-sex parents, they provide no justification for limitations on child custody or visitation by lesbian parents, nor do they provide justification of any kind for discrimination in regards to adoption or foster care (Wald, 2006). Our findings provide no warrant for legal or policy discrimination against adolescents with same-sex parents (Patterson et al., 2002).

As Pawelski and colleagues (2006) have shown, legal recognition of same-sex couple relationships is likely to prove beneficial both to same-sex couples and to their children (see also Wolfson, 2004). Through the financial benefits of same-sex marriage, domestic partnership or civil union, couples are likely to attain greater economic stability. Through social and emotional benefits, couples are likely to obtain greater happiness, support, and psychological security. Children of such couples are also likely to benefit. Results of the research described provide no reasons to deny such equal benefits to same-sex couples or to their children.

The results of research described also give no reason to discriminate in any way against lesbian or gay parents in matters relating to child custody or visitation (Patterson, 2007). When heterosexual parents divorce and one assumes a lesbian or gay identity, the other may attempt to use this in order to gain advantage in court. Inasmuch as the data reveal no reasons to believe that sexual orientation is important in parenting, there is no warrant for such discriminatory behavior.

Finally, the research results provide no support for denial or abridgement of the rights of lesbian or gay adults in matters relating to adoption or foster care. The results of research give no reason to consider sexual orientation of prospective foster or adoptive parents. On the contrary, the accumulated data suggest that lesbian and gay adults may represent a relatively untapped resource for children needing foster care or adoptive homes (Wald, 2006).

Overall, the results of research in this area can play an important role in legal and policy debates. By providing empirical evaluation of widely held ideas about lesbian and gay parents and their children, research can provide valuable information for use in the policy process. The availability of accurate information can help make it possible for law and policy to support all families.

Future Directions

Research on lesbian and gay parents and their children has been fruitful, but much remains to be learned. Sexual orientation and family life is a large topic, and it has only recently become the focus of research. There are many useful directions for future research to take.

There are a number of topics in need of greater study. We need to know more about the process of family formation among lesbian and gay individuals, especially about the ways in which stigma and discrimination may enter into the process. Adoptive families and families formed via surrogacy in the lesbian and gay community are in need of study. We need to know more about family processes, as they unfold over time, in different environments.

We need to learn more about how lesbian and gay parents and their children cope with prejudice and discrimination, both institutionalized and otherwise.

What are the costs and benefits to different approaches that families can take? How do individuals and families remain resilient, even in the face of massive discrimination? And how do the characteristics of environments make a difference, in this regard?

From a methodological perspective, many options for future research can also be discerned. For instance, much could be learned from detailed behavioral observations or from diary studies of lesbian and gay parented families. Longitudinal work (such as that conducted by Gartrell and her colleagues, 1999, 2000, 2005) is very much needed in order to understand changes in family processes over time. Physiological assessments have yet to be well integrated with other assessment techniques in this area, but much could be gained from the effort to do so.

In conclusion, research on lesbian and gay parents and their children has already made many contributions. Research in this area has challenged significant theoretical traditions and informed legal and policy debates. Despite the progress of recent years, many avenues exist for researchers to pursue. Much remains to be learned about sexual orientation and family lives.

Acknowledgments I wish to thank the graduate students and others who have been my collaborators in the research described in this chapter: Raymond Chan, Megan Fulcher, Susan Hurt, Chandra Mason, Barbara Raboy, Stephen Russell, Joanna Scheib, Erin Sutfin, and Jennifer Wainright. Grateful acknowledgment is due to the Society for Psychological Study of Social Issues for support of the Bay Area Families Study, and to the Lesbian Health Fund of the Gay and Lesbian Medical Association for support of the Contemporary Families Study. Thanks also to all of the participating families whose invaluable contributions have made the research possible. Finally, special thanks to Debra Hope and her colleagues at the University of Nebraska for their many efforts in organizing the symposium for which this chapter was written.

References

Abidin, R. R. (1995). *Parenting stress index: Professional manual* (3rd ed.). Odessa, FL: Psychological Assessment Resources.

Achenbach, T. M. (1991). Manual for the Teacher's Report Form and 1991 profile. Burlington, VT: University of Vermont, Department of Psychology.

Achenbach, T. M., & Edelbrock, C. (1983). *Manual for the child behavior checklist and revised child behavior profile*. Burlington, VT: University of Vermont, Department of Psychiatry

Adoption of Tammy, 416 Mass. 205, 619 N.E.2d 315 (MA., 1993).

Adoptions of B.L.V.B. & E.L.V.B. , 628 A.2d 1271 (Vt. 1993).

Ainsworth, M. D. S. (1985a). Patterns of infant—mother attachments: Antecedents and effects on development. *Bulletin of the New York Academy of Medicine, 61*, 771–791.

Ainsworth, M. D. S. (1985b). Attachments across the life span. *Bulletin of the New York Academy of Medicine, 61*, 792–812.

Allen, K.R., & Demo, D.H. (1995). The families of lesbians and gay men: A new frontier in family research. *Journal of Marriage and the Family 57*, 1–17.

Baumrind, D. (1995). Commentary on sexual orientation: Research and social policy implications. *Developmental Psychology, 31*, 130–136.

Bearman, P. S., Jones, J., & Udry, J. R. (1997). The National Longitudinal Study of Adolescent Health: Research Design. Available via internet at: http://www.cpc.unc.edu/addhealth.

Bem, S. L. (1983). Gender schema theory and its implications for child development: Raising gender-aschematic children in a gender-schematic society. *Signs: Journal of Women in Culture and Society, 8*, 598–616.

Bonacich, P. (1987). Power and centrality: A family of measures. *American Journal of Sociology, 92*, 1170–1182.

Boswell v. Boswell, 352 Md. 204; 721 A.2d 662 (1998).

Bottoms v. Bottoms, No. 941166 (Va. 1995).

Bowlby, J. (1988). *A secure base: Parent—child attachment and healthy human development*. New York: Basic.

Braiker, H. B., & Kelley, H. H. (1979). Conflict in the development of close relationships. In R. L. Burgess & T. L. Huston (Eds.), *Social exchange in developing relationships* (pp. 135–168). New York, NY: Academic.

Bronfenbrenner, U. (1960). Freudian theories of identification and their derivatives. *Child Development, 31*, 15–40.

Burgess v. Burgess, 708 N. E. 2d 930; 1999 Ind. App. LEXIS 300.

Carolina Population Center University of North Carolina at Chapel Hill (1997). *National longitudinal study of adolescent health: Wave I network variables code book*. Retrieved on March 23, 2004, from http://www.cpc.unc.edu/projects/addhealth/codebooks/wave1.

Chan, R. W., Brooks, R. C., Raboy, B., & Patterson, C. J. (1998). Division of labor among lesbian and heterosexual parents: Associations with children's adjustment. *Journal of Family Psychology, 12*, 402–419.

Chan, R. W., Raboy, B., & Patterson, C. J. (1998). Psychosocial adjustment among children conceived via donor insemination by lesbian and heterosexual mothers. *Child Development, 69*, 443–457.

Chodorow, N. (1978). *The reproduction of mothering: Psychoanalysis and the sociology of gender*. Berkeley, CA: University of California Press.

Cowan, C. P., & Cowan, P. A. (1990). Who does what? In J. Touliatos, B. F. Perlmutter, & M. A. Straus (Eds.), *Handbook of family measurement techniques* (pp. 447–448). Newbury Park, CA: Sage.

Cowan, C. P., & Cowan, P. A. (1992). *When partners become parents: The big life change for couples*. New York, NY: Basic.

D'Augelli, A.R., and Patterson, C.J. (Ed.) (1995). *Lesbian, gay and bisexual identities over the lifespan: Psychological persspectives New York: Oxford University Press*.

Flaks, D. K., Ficher, I., Masterpasqua, F., & Joseph, G. (1995). Lesbians choosing motherhood: A comparative study of lesbian and heterosexual parents and their children. *Developmental Psychology, 31*, 105–114.

Fulcher, M., Chan, R. W., Raboy, B., & Patterson, C. J. (2002). Contact with grandparents among children conceived via donor insemination by lesbian and heterosexual mothers. *Parenting: Science and Practice, 2*, 61–76.

Fulcher, M., Sutfin, E. L., Chan, R. W., Scheib, J. E., & Patterson, C. J. (2005). Lesbian mothers and their children: Findings from the contemporary families study. In A. Omoto & H. Kurtzman (Eds.), *Recent research on sexual orientation, mental health, and substance abuse* (pp. 281–299). Washington, DC: American Psychological Association.

Gartrell, N., Banks, A., Hamiliton, J, Reed, N., Bishop, H., & Rodas, C. (1999). The national lesbian family study: 2. Interviews with mothers of toddlers. *American Journal of Orthopsychiatry, 69*, 362–369.

Gartrell, N., Banks, A., Reed, N., Hamiliton, R. C., & Deck, A. (2000). The national lesbian family study: 3. Interviews with mothers of five-year olds. *American Journal of Orthopsychiatry, 70*, 542–548.

Gartrell, N., Deck, A., Rodas, C., Peyser, H., & Banks, A. (2005). The national lesbian family study: 4. Interviews with the 10-year-old children. *American Journal of Orthopsychiatry, 75*, 518–524.

Gartrell, N., Hamilton, J., Banks, A., Mosbacher, D., Reed, N., Sparks, C. H.,et al. (1996). The national lesbian family study: 1. Interviews with prospective mothers. *American Journal of Orthopsychiatry, 66*, 272–281.

Gates, G. J., Badgett, M. V. L., Macomber, J. E., & Chambers, K. (2007). *Adoption and foster care by gay and lesbian parents in the United States.* Los Angeles, CA: The Williams Institute, UCLA Law School.

Gershon, T. D., Tschann, J. M., & Jemerin, J. M. (1999). Stigmatization, self-esteem, and coping among the adolescent children of lesbian mothers. *Journal of Adolescent Health, 24,* 437–445.

Golombok, S. (1999). *Parenting: What really counts?* New York, NY: Routledge.

Golombok, S., Perry, B., Burston, A., Murray, C., Mooney-Somers, J., Stevens, M., et al. (2003). Children with lesbian parents: A community study. *Developmental Psychology, 39,* 20–33.

Golombok, S., & Tasker, F. (1994). Children in lesbian and gay families: Theories and evidence. *Annual Review of Sex Research, 5,* 73–100.

Goodridge v. Department of Public Health, 440 Mass. 309 SJC-08860 (2003).

Gonsiorek, J.C. (1990). The empirical basis for the demise of the illness model of homosexuality. In J.C. Gonsiorek and J.D. Weinrich (Eds.), *Homosexuality: Research implications for public policy.* Beverly Hills: Sage

Haynie, D. L. (2000). *The peer group revisited: A network approach for understanding adolescent delinquency.* Unpublished doctoral dissertation, Pennsylvania State University, Hershey, PA.

Herek, G. M. (2006). Legal recognition of same-sex relationships in the United States: A social science perspective. *American Psychologist, 61,* 607–621.

Huggins, S. L. (1989). A comparative study of self-esteem of adolescent children of divorced lesbian mothers and divorced heterosexual mothers. In F. W. Bozett (Ed.), *Homosexuality and the family* (pp. 123–135). New York, NY: Harrington Park Press.

Huston, A. (1983). Sex typing. In E. M. Hetherington (Ed.) & P. H. Mussen (Series Ed.), *Handbook of child psychology: Volume 4. Socialization, personality, and social development* (pp. 387–487). New York, NY: Wiley.

In Re Adoption of Evan, 583 N.Y.S.2d 997 (Sur. 1992).

Khaleque, A., & Rohner, R. P. (2002). Perceived parental acceptance-rejection and psychological adjustment: A meta-analysis of cross-cultural and intracultural studies. *Journal of Marriage and Family, 64,* 54–64.

Kirkpatrick, M. (1996). Lesbians as parents. In R. P. Cabaj & T. S. Stein (Eds.), *Textbook of homosexuality and mental health.* (pp. 353–370) Washington, DC: American Psychiatric Press.

Koepke, L., Hare, J., & Moran, P. B. (1992). Relationship quality in a sample of lesbian couples with children and child-free lesbian couples. *Family Relations, 41,* 224–229.

Kohlberg, L. (1966). A cognitive-developmental analysis of children's sex-role concepts and attitudes. In E. E. Maccoby (Ed.), *The development of sex differences* (pp. 82–173). Stanford, CA: Stanford University Press.

Kohut, H. (1971). *The analysis of the self.* Madison, CT: International Universities Press.

Kohut, H. (1977). *The restoration of the self.* Madison, CT: International Universities Press.

Kohut, H. (1984). *How does analysis cure?* Chicago, IL: University of Chicago Press.

Kurdek, L. (1993). The allocation of household labor in homosexual and heterosexual cohabiting couples. *Journal of Social Issues, 49,* 127–139.

Laird, J. (1993). Lesbian and gay families. In F. Walsh (Ed.), *Normal family processes* (2nd ed.), (pp. 282–328). New York, NY: Guilford.

Lewin, E. (1993). *Lesbian mothers: Accounts of gender in American culture.* Ithaca, NY: Cornell University Press.

Locke, H., & Wallace, K. (1959). Short marital adjustment and prediction tests: Their reliability and validity. *Marriage and Family Living, 21,* 251–255.

Loving v. Virginia, 388 U.S. 1 (1967).

McCandlish, B. (1987). Against all odds: Lesbian mother family dynamics. In F. W. Bozett (Ed.), *Gay and lesbian parents* (pp. 23–38). New York, NY: Praeger.

Meyer v. Nebraska, 262 U.S. 390 (1923).

O'Connor, A. (1993). Voices from the heart: The developmental impact of a mother's lesbianism on her adolescent children. *Smith College Studies in Social Work, 63,* 281–299.

Patterson, C. J. (1992). Children of lesbian and gay parents. *Child Development, 63,* 1025–1042.

Patterson, C. J. (1994). Children of the lesbian baby boom: Behavioral adjustment, self-concepts, and sex-role identity. In B. Greene & G. Herek (Eds.), *Contemporary perspectives on lesbian and gay psychology: Theory, research and application* (pp. 156–175). Beverly Hills, CA: Sage.

Patterson, C. J. (1995a). Families of the lesbian baby boom: Parents' division of labor and children's adjustment. *Developmental Psychology, 31*, 115–123.

Patterson, C. J. (1995b). Lesbian mothers, gay fathers, and their children. In A. R. D'Augelli & C. J. Patterson (Eds.), *Lesbian, gay and bisexual identities over the lifespan: Psychological perspectives* (pp. 262–290). New York, NY: Oxford University Press.

Patterson, C.J. (1995c). Adoption of minor children by lesbian and gay adults: A social science perspective. *Duke Journal of Gender Law and Policy, 2*, 191–205.

Patterson, C. J. (1996). Contributions of lesbian and gay parents and their children to the prevention of heterosexism. In E. D. Rothblum & L. A. Bond (Eds.), *Preventing heterosexism and homophobia* (pp. 184–201) Thousand Oaks, CA: Sage.

Patterson, C. J. (1998). Family lives of children with lesbian mothers. In C. J. Patterson & A. R. D'Augelli (Eds.), *Lesbian, gay and bisexual identities in families: Psychological perspectives* (pp. 154–176). New York, NY: Oxford University Press.

Patterson, C. J. (2000). Sexual orientation and family life: A decade review. *Journal of Marriage and the Family, 62*, 1052–1069.

Patterson, C. J. (2001). Families of the lesbian baby boom: Maternal mental health and child adjustment. *Journal of Gay and Lesbian Psychotherapy, 4*, 91–107.

Patterson, C. J. (2002). Lesbian and gay parenthood. In M. H. Bornstein (Ed.), *Handbook of parenting* (2nd ed.), (pp. 317–338). Hillsdale, NJ: Erlbaum.

Patterson, C. J. (2005). Lesbian and gay parents and their children: summary of research findings. In *Lesbian and gay parenting: A resource for psychologists* (2nd ed.). Washington, DC: American Psychological Association. Available online at: http://www.apa.org/pi/lgbc/publications/lgparenthome.html.

Patterson, C. J. (2006). Children of lesbian and gay parents. *Current Directions in Psychological Science, 15*, 241–244.

Patterson, C. J. (2007). Lesbian and gay family issues in the context of changing legal and social policy environments. In K. J. Bieschke, R. M. Perez, & K. A. DeBord (Eds.), *Handbook of counseling and psychotherapy with lesbian, gay, bisexual and transgender clients* (2nd ed.) Washington, DC: American Psychological Association.

Patterson, C. J., Fulcher, M., & Wainright, J. (2002). Children of lesbian and gay parents: Research, law, and policy. In B. L. Bottoms, M. B. Kovera, & B. D. McAuliff (Eds.), *Children, social science and the law* (pp. 176–199). New York, NY: Cambridge University Press.

Patterson, C. J., & Hastings, P. (2006). Socialization in context of family diversity. In J. Grusec & P. D. Hastings (Eds.), *Handbook of socialization* (pp. 328–352). New York, NY: Guilford Press.

Patterson, C. J., Hurt, S., & Mason, C. D. (1998). Families of the lesbian baby boom: Children's contact with grandparents and other adults. *American Journal of Orthopsychiatry, 68*, 390–399.

Pawelski, J.G., Perrin, E.C., Foy, J.M., Allen, C.E., Crawford, J.E. et al. (2006). The effects of marriage, civil union, and domestic partnership on the health and wellbeing of children. *Pediatrics, 118*, 349–364.

Peplau, L. A., Veniegas, R. C., & Campell, S. M. (1996). Gay and lesbian relationships. In R. C. Savin-Williams & K. M. Cohen (Eds.), *The lives of lesbians, gays, and bisexuals: Children to adults* (pp. 250–273). Fort Worth, TX: Harcourt Brace.

Perrin, C. E. (2002). Technical report: Coparent or second-parent adoption by same-sex parents. *Pediatrics, 109*, 341–344.

Perry-Jenkins, M., & Crouter, A.C. (1990). Men's provider-role attitudes: Implications for household work and marital satisfaction. *Journal of Family Issues, 11*, 136–156.

Polikoff, N. (1990). This child does have two mothers: Redefining parenthood to meet the needs of children in lesbian mother and other nontraditional families. *Georgetown Law Journal, 78*, 459ff.

Pulliam v. Smith, 348 N. C. 616; 501 S. E. 2d 898 (1998)

Radloff, L. S. (1977). The CES-D Scale: A self-report depression scale for research in the general population. *Applied Psychological Measurement, 1*, 385–401.

Resnick, M. D., Bearman, P., Blum, R. W., Bauman, K. E., Harris, K. M., Jones, J. et al. (1997). Protecting adolescent from harm: Findings from the National Longitudinal Study of Adolescent Health. *Journal of the American Medical Association, 278* (10), 823–832.

Rohner, R. P. (1999). Acceptance and rejection. In D. Livinson, J. Ponzetti, & Jorgenson (Eds.), *Encyclopedia of human emotions* (Vol. 1, pp. 6–14). New York, NY: Macmillan.

Rosenberg, M. (1979). *Conceiving the self*. New York, NY: Basic.

Saffron, L. (1996). *What about the children?: Sons and daughters of lesbian and gay parents talk about their lives*. New York, NY: Cassell.

Scal, P., Ireland, M., & Borowsky, I. W. (2003). Smoking among American adolescents: A risk and protective factor analysis. *Journal of Community Health, 28*, 79–97.

Sieving, R. E., Beurhing, T., Resnick, M. D., Bearinger, L. H., Shew, M., Ireland, M., et al. (2000). Development of adolescent self-report measures from the National Longitudinal Study of Adolescent Health. *Journal of Adolescent Health, 28*(1), 73–81.

Silverstein, L. B., & Auerbach, C. F. (1999). Deconstructing the essential father. *American Psychologist, 54*, 397–407.

Skinner v. Oklahoma, 316 U.S. 535 (1942).

S.N.E. v. R.L.B., 699 P.2d 875 (Alaska 1985).

Stacey, J., & Biblarz, T. J. (2001). (How) does the sexual orientation of parents matter? *American Sociological Review, 66*, 159–183.

Steckel, A. (1987). Psychosocial development of children of lesbian mothers. In F. W. Bozett (Ed.), *Gay and lesbian parents* (pp. 75–85). New York, NY: Praeger.

Steinberg, L., Lamborn, S. D., Dornbusch, S. M., & Darling, N. (1992). Impact of parenting practices on adolescent achievement: Authoritative parenting, school involvement, and encouragement to succeed. *Child Development, 63*, 1266–1281.

Steinberg, L., & Silk, J. S. (2002). Parenting adolescents. In M. H. Bornstein (Ed.), *Handbook of parenting, Volume 1: Children and parenting* (2nd ed.). Mahwah, NJ: Lawrence Erlbaum Associates.

Stevens, M., Golombok, S., Beveridge, M., & the ALSPAC Study Team (2002). Does father absence influence children's gender development? Findings from a general population study of preschool children. *Parenting: Science and Practice, 2*, 47–60.

Tasker, F. L., & Golombok, S. (1997). *Growing up in a lesbian family: Effects on child Development*. New York, NY: Guilford Press.

Tasker, F., & Patterson, C. J. (2007). Research on gay and lesbian parenting: Retrospect and prospect. *Journal of Gay, Lesbian, Bisexual and Transgender Family Issues, 3*, 9–34.

Wainright, J. L., & Patterson, C. J. (2006). Delinquency, victimization, and substance use among adolescents with female same-sex parents. *Journal of Family Psychology, 20*, 526–530.

Wainright, J. L., & Patterson, C. J. (2008). Peer relations among adolescents with female same-sex parents. *Developmental Psychology, 44*, 117–126.

Wainright, J. L., Russell, S. T., & Patterson, C. J. (2004). Psychosocial adjustment, school outcomes, and romantic relationships of adolescents with same-sex parents. *Child Development, 75*, 1886–1898.

Wald, M. S. (2006). Adults' sexual orientation and state determinations regarding placement of children. *Family Law Quarterly, 40*, 381–434.

Weston, K. (1991). *Families we choose: Lesbians, gays, kinship*. New York, NY: Columbia University Press.

Wolfson, E. (2004). *Why marriage matters: America, equality and gay people's right to marry*. New York, NY: Simon & Schuster.

Love, Marriage, and Baby Carriage Among Sexual Minorities- and Bias: Discussion of the 54th Nebraska Symposium on Motivation

Marvin R. Goldfried

One of the benefits of being the discussant is that it allows me to be somewhat unconstrained and freewheeling in commenting on the other chapters. I have fully taken advantage of this benefit, and my comments are personal, empirical, professional, and political. After describing how I came to be interested in LGB issues, I go on to discuss the heterogeneity of those individuals who are included in the "LGB" label, and the complications that sometimes exist in defining who is gay. These labels, although more sociopolitically than scientifically rooted, nonetheless are associated with discrimination and bias – in society at large and within psychology as well. I also comment on some of the issues associated with same-sex unions and parenting, the change in attitudes toward sexual minorities, and the importance of closing the gap between the LGB and mainstream psychological literature. Let me start with the personal.

My Involvement in LGB Issues

After many years of silence, I have decided to come out professionally. Not as a gay man, but as the father of a gay son. My son is now in his mid-30s, and my wife and I knew that he was probably gay when he was seven. I had read the work of Green (1974) on gender atypicality, and saw that my son shared many of the characteristics in young boys who eventually identified themselves as being gay (e.g., preferring to play with girls, dislike of rough-and-tumble games). We consulted some professionals about what we should do, and the advice they gave us was to wait. It was a long wait. We did what we could to place him in safe circumstances and encouraged him to go to a college that we knew to be gay-affirmative. He finally came out to us during his freshman year.

This was all personal and did not become professional for me until several years later. One major turning point occurred as my wife and I were watching the Gay Pride parade in New York City. As the Parents, Family and Friends of Lesbians and Gays (PFLAG) contingent marched by, we decided that we would join them and lend them our support. It soon became evident that they did not need our support. We were carrying signs reading "You will always have a home at PFLAG" and

D.A. Hope (ed.), *Contemporary Perspectives on Lesbian, Gay, and Bisexual Identities*,   183
DOI: 10.1007/978-0-387-09556-1, © Springer Science + Business Media, LLC 2009

"We love our gay and lesbian children," and the reactions of the onlookers were electrifying. The younger people watching the parade were excited as we marched by and enthusiastically cheered us on. There was a very different reaction by the older men and women, who had a look of sadness and despair – reflecting a never-to-be-obtained longing. This was a transforming moment for me. I knew that I wanted to do something, but did not know what.

The next event that helped me to become better aware of what I needed to do occurred at the meetings of the Association for Advancement of Behavior Therapy (AABT). I was attending a very crowded panel discussion on conversion therapy, which was dealing with the issue of whether therapists should make any attempt to have sexual minority clients become more attracted to or involved in sex with members of the opposite sex. One of the presenters was a friend and colleague, Jerry Davison, who in his presidential address at AABT some years earlier argued that it was never ethical to try to change the sexual behavior of LGB individuals (Davison, 1976). I had disagreed with him back then – I believe that exceptions can at times be made on this issue – and disagreed with him at this panel discussion. Although I wanted to say something during the discussion period, I was concerned that what I had to say might be construed as being anti-gay. I finally decided that I would preface my comments by stating my credentials, saying: "One of my two favorite sons is gay, and I am a dues-paying member of PFLAG. Now let me disagree with Jerry." At the end of the meeting, he came over to me and said: "That was very courageous of you." I responded: "You mean for disagreeing with you?" He then said: "No. You just came out!" Without realizing, I indeed had.

My professional activities up until that time involved the integration of different schools of therapy (Goldfried, 1982). Since my professional coming out, I have expanded this interest from psychotherapy integration to the integration of LGB issues into mainstream psychology (Goldfried, 2001). I will say more about this after commenting on the other chapters.

The Heterogeneity of Lesbian, Gay, and Bisexual Individuals

A theme that runs through the chapters in this volume deals with the heterogeneity of LGB individuals. The more we learn about sexual behavior and identity, the more we realize that our conceptions need to be updated. Savin-Williams (2008) set the stage by addressing the question: Who is gay? How we answer that question has very important behavioral and psychological implications. He notes that a person's sexual orientation may be defined by *sexual identity* – how one views him or herself. There is also *sexual behavior* – the gender of those with whom one has sexual contact. As we know from other aspects of our lives, the two do not necessarily coincide (e.g., one's religious identity may not be consistent with one's religious practices). Savin-Williams added a third criterion – *attraction* – which can be *romantic* and/or *sexual*.

In his discussion of sexual attraction, Bailey (2008) broke it down in still a different way: a person's subjective *preference* – with whom we state we would prefer to have sexual contact – and one's sexual *orientation*, as measured by sexual arousal. Bailey's research on measuring sexual arousal physiologically indicates that using it to define sexual orientation seems to hold better for men than it does for women. The lack of correspondence among verbal statement of sexual attraction, physiological measures of arousal, and actual behavior is seen not only in the case of determining sexual orientation, but has also been found to occur in other area of human functioning as well, such as in Lang's (1968) observation that subjective, physiological and behavioral measures of anxiety do not always correspond.

Bailey's finding that women who identify themselves as heterosexual manifest sexual arousal to lesbian as well as heterosexual encounters fits with Diamond's research on the sexual plasticity in women (Diamond, 2003a,b). Her biobehavioral model of female sexuality addresses the differences and potential association between *affectional bonding* and *sexual desire*. At times, the boundary between the two can become blurred. Related to this distinction between affectional and sexual bonding, Yoneda and Davila (2006) found that with a sample of seventh and eighth grade girls, emotional attraction was positively correlated with psychological well-being, but that same-sex sexual attraction correlated negatively with psychological well-being and social competence. Somehow, at least in the case of adolescent girls, once they cross the line, they encounter problems.

In her discussion of the variation among women who are involved romantically and sexually with other women, Rothblum (2008) acknowledges that "Being a lesbian is not a homogeneous experience" (p. 109). The label "lesbian" can include a variety of women who differ in the degree to which they identify as a lesbian, the number of years in which they have been out, the degree of outness, the proportion of same- to opposite-sex experiences they have had, and the extent to which they are involved in the lesbian community. Moreover, being lesbian is not necessarily a stable identity. In her longitudinal study of young lesbians, Diamond (2003b) found that 25% of them shifted their identity to heterosexual 5 years later. One of the predictors of this shift was the strength of their original attraction to women, in that if this attraction was less strong, there was greater fluidity.

A latent theme that runs through many of the chapters is that there are different ways in which we can categorize people and relationships. As reflected in the contributions to this volume, one of the major ways in which we classify people is on the basis of gender. Indeed, this volume can be considered the summary of a conference on gender and gender differences as well as on sexual orientation. At birth – and even before birth – we are interested in knowing: "Is it a girl, or is it a boy?" A classification is made.

However, as reflected in Diamond's work on attraction and close relationships of an emotional, romantic nature and of a sexual nature, it appears that there are some people – particularly some women – who do not make that primary male-female distinction when close relationship and sexual attraction are concerned. They seem to operate from a different starting point, namely, what someone is as a person. Is this a caring, warm, giving individual, or is this an uncaring, cold, self-centered person? Once they make that categorization, they may decide to become involved with the nicer person. That can allow them to make a strong bond, which can sometimes result in the blurring of the line between emotional and sexual attraction. Although this is more likely to occur among women than men, Savin-William's (2008) prediction that this same phenomenon will one day occur more frequently in the case of men is intriguing and remains to be seen. At present, sexual behavior between men is based more on sexual than emotional attraction.

In conducting research on "lesbians," "gay men," and "bisexuals," the heterogeneity within each label creates problems, which are only increased once we combine these to form the larger "LGB" category. Adding to this those individuals who identify themselves as "transgender" or "queer" to form "LGBTQ" results in even further heterogeneity. LGB or LGBTQ represents more of a sociopolitical category than a scientific category. It is not a variable, but rather a useful way that individuals can bind together to protect themselves from a common enemy. If we are interested in conducting research in this area, we need to focus more on the mediators and moderators that are associated with the difficulties or benefits of being a sexual minority.

Although some people may object to the term "sexual minority," in some ways it is a useful label. Because it does not communicate much information, it is therefore less likely to be associated with the stereotypes we may have about lesbians, gay men, bisexuals, and transgender individuals. It is difficult to make generalizations about sexual minorities; one needs more information to understand what it is to be a sexual minority. One member of a sexual minority might be a 37-year-old, partnered professional male who came out at age 19 to parents who were very accepting of his sexual orientation, and another might be a 17-year-old, homeless Latino whose parents threw him out of the house upon learning of that he was gay. The details are clearly much more informative than the general label.

Labels and Bias

Most heterosexuals – including heterosexual psychologists, social workers, and psychiatrists – are unaware of the heterogeneity of the LGB label. A result of that is that it increases the likelihood that stereotyping and bias might occur (see Ritter & Terndrup, 2002). There are two examples of such bias that my students and I have studied. One is the tendency to diagnose sexual minorities as borderline personality disorders (Eubanks-Carter & Goldfried, 2006), and the other is the tendency to diagnose them as having social anxiety disorder (Pachankis & Goldfried, 2006).

The study on borderline personality disorder was based on the possibility that individuals who were undergoing a sexual identity crisis could appear to be borderline (Eubanks-Carter & Goldfried, 2006). We constructed a vignette of a 20-year-old client coming from a religious family who was having identity concerns, relationship problems, being anxious and depressed, having suicidal thoughts, and using alcohol to excess. We varied the gender and sexual orientation of the person described in the vignette, and gave a different vignette to different groups of psychologists, asking them to make judgments of various sorts, including offering a diagnosis. Although each vignette depicted the exact same clinical description, we found that if the person in the vignette was viewed as being a gay man, he was more likely to be diagnosed as having a borderline personality disorder. Although this might instead have been viewed as a young man who was struggling with his sexual identity and the coming out process, the person instead was seen as having a clinical disorder. Hopefully, educating mental health professionals about such LGB issues could influence this bias in diagnosis.

The second study we conducted was on social anxiety (Pachankis & Goldfried, 2006). Lily Tomlin once commented that in the 50s, no one was gay – they were just shy. Such "shyness" is now likely to be diagnosed as a social anxiety disorder, which is typically associated with unrealistic concerns about being negatively evaluated by others. The premise of this study was that much of the interpersonal inhibition sometimes seen in gay men is not the result of a social anxiety disorder, but rather realistic concerns about the negative reactions of other people. We compared gay and heterosexual college men and found that the gay students scored higher on measures of social anxiety and fears of being negatively evaluated by others. Although the gay participants were found to be more anxious in interpersonal situations, they did not differ from heterosexuals in performance anxiety. Thus they were no more anxious about giving a speech or eating in public, but are more apprehensive about interactions with others. Moreover, we found that gay participants who were less out and less secure about their sexual orientation scored higher on interpersonal anxiety.

We also compared the heterosexual and gay participants' anxiety reactions to certain situations that might seem innocuous to heterosexual, but might realistically be aversive for gay men. Included among these situations was an extended family gathering where someone asks you if you have a girlfriend, and being around heterosexual men who are talking about sports. Not surprisingly, gay college students were more anxious in such situations. Although their reactions may have been due to concerns about the negative reactions of others concerns – that may be the effect of direct and indirect discrimination, harassment, and abuse – it would be erroneous to conclude that this was the result of a social anxiety disorder. Interestingly enough, the one situation in which heterosexual men were more anxious involved making eye contact with a gay professor – more likely reflecting homophobia than social anxiety disorder.

Herek (2008) has indicated that the term "homophobia" originally referred to both to a fear of and a prejudice against homosexuals. From a psychodynamic point of view, one might say that this combined reaction occurs because of a person's denial of their latent homosexual attractions. Or, from a sociological point of view (Kimmel, 1997), the fear might be that of being labeled by others as being a homosexual. From the point of view of a cognitive-behavior therapist and someone who had been involved in the profeminist, progay men's movement in the 1970s, I believe that something else is involved. This men's movement was spearheaded by straight men trying to adjust to the strain in gender roles in their heterosexual partnerships that were brought about by the feminist movement, and by gay men who wanted to examine the negative impact that men's gender roles had on their lives. As part of this men's movement, there were dialogs between heterosexual and gay men, which very clearly revealed that a major fear that straight men had was that gay men would make sexual overtures to them. In short, they are phobic and most likely unrealistically so. As a result of having repeated interactions with gay men who do not make sexual overtures, heterosexual men can become desensitized, and this fear can diminish. Thus such exposure not only can reduce prejudice (Herek, 2008), but can also help heterosexual men to be less phobic. If Herek is correct that prejudice can sometimes be a way of reducing anxiety, and given the contributions of behavior therapy in reducing unrealistic fears and phobias, then these contributions may have relevance in improving the relationship that some heterosexual men can have with gay men.

What also came out of these men's movement dialogues was the heterosexual men's view of gay men as being obsessed with having sex, which is seen as the predominant motive in their lives. However, this interest in sex is more likely a function of gender than sexual orientation, and gay men are probably no more obsessed with sex than are heterosexual men. The primary difference is that gay men are more likely to have willing and available sexual partners than are heterosexual men.

Herek's decision to replace the term homophobia with "sexual prejudice" can not only help to reduce the confusion that may exist in understanding negative reactions to LGB individuals, but can hopefully also provide a better connection that the literature on sexual minorities has with the mainstream literature on the causes and cures of prejudice.

Another term that I have some difficulty with is "heterosexism," referring to a cultural prejudice against same-sex relationships. Although heterosexism clearly exists, it sometimes is used to characterize a societal reaction that is somewhat different, namely, "heterocentrism." Whereas heterosexism refers to a stigmatization of same-sex relations, heterocentrism is a manifestation of an implicit assumption that romantic/sexual relationships involve members of the opposite sex. For example, the questionnaire that we have been administering to clients in the Psychology Department clinic at Stony Brook had a question about "marital status" and name of "spouse." Only in more recent years have we noticed that and changed it to add "partnership" and "partner." As research on how one can help individuals overcome problems in close relationships has recognized that some of these relationships involve same-sex partners, the term "marital therapy" is being replaced by "couples therapy." Thus the term heterocentrism, which has less of an accusatory tone, can better characterize the limitations sometimes associated with our world views, pointing to the need for consciousness-raising interventions.

From Love to Marriage and the Baby Carriage

In her research on same-sex marriage and civil unions, Rothblum (2008) has creatively dealt with the perennial problem associated with research on sexual minorities, namely, the reliance on convenience, rather than representative samples. Her use of heterosexual siblings of sexual minorities is particularly helpful in controlling for demographic and other variables, and represents a significant methodological advancement. Rothblum's ability to obtain actual populations rather than convenience samples to study represents another important step forward methodologically. With regard to the differences that she found between same-sex couples who were united in civil unions, those who were not, and married heterosexual couples, it was not possible to determine if this reflected a self-selection issue or was the result of the type of relationship. Hopefully the follow-up findings will be able to shed light on this question. Rothblum also notes that the prospect of having laws regarding marriage for same-sex couples has clearly created considerable controversy in this country, which hardly leads the way internationally in legalizing same-sex unions.

On the topic of same-sex marriage, I would like to become personal again, as I have some problematic emotional reactions to it. Having been raised in a society where marriage has been between a man and a woman, the figures of a bride and groom on the wedding cake has been my default image. I have no objections to same-sex marriage on moral or religious terms, but – because of my earlier conditioning – I nonetheless experience a sense of emotional dissonance in thinking about same-sex marriage. I suspect that I am not alone in having this reaction, even among those people who attribute their objections to religious reasons. As I am not very happy in having this emotional reaction, I have been attempting to change it. What works in overriding this reaction is when I think of my gay son and how wonderful it would be if he could become married. I suspect that the growing acceptance of gay marriage among younger people in this country is similarly the result of their caring about the happiness and welfare of gay friends and relatives.

Which brings us to the baby carriage, and Patterson's (2008) research on same-sex parenting. Even though she has needed to make use of a convenience sample, she nonetheless presents findings that contradict the belief that children raised by same-sex parents cannot possibly be well adjusted. It is also interesting that the differences she found in children had more to do with gender than it did with the sexual orientation of the parents. Here again, the theme of gender emerges in research studying LGB issues.

In comparison to opposite-sex relationships, same-sex partnerships have been found to be more egalitarian with regard to occupation, distribution of household chores, and child care (Patterson 2008; Rothblum, 2008). Related to this finding is that one of the differences that seems to have emerged is that children are less stereotyped in their gender roles when raised by same-sex – typically lesbian – parents. If that, in fact, is a reliable phenomenon, then same-sex parenting has been able to achieve what the feminist movement was not able to accomplish.

In their review of the same-sex parenting research that has failed to find that offspring are adversely affected psychologically, Stacey and Biblarz (2001) conclude that...

> "it is time to recognize that the categories "lesbian mother" and "gay father" are historically transitional and conceptually flawed, because they erroneously imply that a parent's sexual orientation is the decisive characteristic of her or his parenting. On the contrary, we propose that homophobia and discrimination are the chief reasons why parental sexual orientation matter at all (p. 177)".

The Change in Attitudes Toward Sexual Minorities

As Herek (2008) has found, individuals who know people who are LGB are more likely to have favorable attitudes toward sexual minorities. Given the fact that more sexual minorities are coming out – and at an earlier age – more heterosexuals are likely to know people who are gay, which can explain the more favorable attitude that younger people in this country have toward sexual minorities.

Because knowing someone who is gay can influence both sexual prejudice and fear, one can readily make the case for the importance of sexual minorities coming out. By extension, one can also argue for the importance of family members coming out. As it is hard to estimate the number of sexual minorities in this country (Savin-Williams, 2008), it is hard to know how many heterosexuals have family members who are LGB. However, consider the possibility that either 3%, 6%, or 9% of the population in the US are sexual minorities. With a current population of approximately 300 million, one may estimate that that there are 9, 18, or 27 million sexual minorities in this country. Assuming that each individual has two parents, one sibling, four grandparents, we have seven immediate family members – which does not include aunts, uncles, nephews, nieces, cousins, and children. Taking the figure of seven family members for illustrative purposes, we have either 63, 126, or 189 million family members who are potential allies of sexual minorities. To the extent that these family allies come out in open support – even simply acknowledging to others that they have an LGB family member – it will further increase the number of individuals in this country who know a sexual minority, and thereby increase the likelihood that they will become more accepting.

On the Invisibility of the LGB Literature

Although there is an extensive psychological literature that deals with LGB issues, it tends to be ignored by mainstream psychology (Goldfried, 2001). After being closeted for many years, LGB professionals are now contributing to the literature on those psychological issues associated with being a sexual minority. Included within this literature are such topics as adolescent development, aging, couple relationships, parenting, family relations, victimization and abuse, and teenage suicide. LGB professionals are now telling, but the rest of psychology has not been listening.

It has been found that LGB individuals are more likely to make use of individual psychotherapy than are heterosexuals (Bieschke, McClanahan, Tozer, Grzegorek, & Park, 2000). This is also the case with same-sex couples, in that approximately half of lesbian couples and close to one-third of same-sex male couples indicate that they have sought professional help for relationship issues (Green, 2000). The more frequent use of therapy by sexual minorities may be explained by the fact that they not only have to deal with the same kind of issues that confront heterosexual individuals, but also need to cope with stigmatization, family rejection, oppression, and discrimination.

What is particularly disconcerting about the invisibility of the LGB literature is that while therapists are called on to provide professional services, they typically have received little or no information about sexual minorities during their training and have acknowledged that they do not feel qualified to work clinically with sexual minorities (Doherty & Simmons, 1996). This often results in less than adequate care and, at times, has unfortunate psychological consequences for LGB individuals undergoing therapy (Garnets, Hancock, Cochran, Goodchilds, & Peplau, 1991).

The invisibility of the LGB literature in mainstream psychology can be illustrated with teenage suicide. A recent meta-analysis of suicide attempts among gay teenagers and young adults has found that, on average, the rate is approximately three times higher among sexual minorities (Burckell, 2006). If one defines being "gay" in terms of the individual's personal identity, the suicide attempt rate is close to 10 times greater. Although one may raise the question of the extent to which these attempts were serious (Savin-Williams, 2001), the fact that mainstream psychology has typically ignored the higher rate of suicide attempts among gay adolescents is nonetheless distressing. The Association for Advancement of Behavior Therapy (1992) publishes factual brochures on a number of topics and erroneously indicated in the one dealing with teenage suicide that "There is no one, typical adolescent suicide." At the Sixth Annual Conference of the Canadian Association for Suicide Prevention, Tremblay (1995) highlighted the practice of overlooking the LGB literature in this area:

> Why have most studies of youth suicide problems not been concerned with identifying sexual orientation, and child sexual abuse in their research? Is this how truly scientific work should be done?… Has it been ethical, given the facts of the case, for suicidologists to have ignored GLB issues? Why did this happen?

Still another example of how findings about suicide attempts among gay adolescents have been absent in the mainstream literature comes from the experience of someone who attended conference on teenage suicide (Mallon, 1997). He reports being at a presentation in which the speaker raised the question: "What secret could be so terrible that you would rather kill yourself than tell?" As neither the presenter nor anyone in the audience offered an answer to the question, Mallon went up to her afterward and asked she why did not say anything about the higher rate of suicide attempts among gay adolescents, to which she replied: "Oh, I never even thought about them." (Mallon, p. 25).

The mainstream psychology practice of ignoring the LGB literature is not only bad for sexual minorities, but it is also bad science. Much of what we know about human behavior is based on research in which gender and sexual orientation have been confounded, and the interpretation of these findings may consequently be erroneous. For example, LaSala (2004) compared men in same-sex relationships who were, and were not monogamous, and found there was no difference in couple satisfaction between these groups, provided that the partners had agreed upon this in advance to have an open relationship, and it was not the result of couple conflict. Current research in mainstream psychology on the consequences of infidelity, or with issues among heterosexual couples who are in open relationships, has tended to overlook findings such as these obtained with same-sex male couples.

Another example of ignored research on couple relationships deals with the demand-withdrawal pattern, where wives approach their husbands to discuss issues, but where husbands withdraw (Julien, Arellano, & Turgeon, 1997). This demand-withdrawal pattern is particularly significant, in that it is associated with marital distress. The fact that the wife typically approaches and the husband withdraws has been interpreted as being the result in gender differences. One of the difficulties with this interpretation is this same demand-withdrawal pattern has been found to exist in same-sex couples (Julien et al.).

Still another example of how the confounding of gender and sexual orientation can lead to limited interpretations comes from the research on domestic violence. Koss and colleagues (Koss et al., 1994) have interpreted the findings on partner abuse within a feminist context, and have linked it to gender role differences between men and women. However, once she became aware of the research on partner abuse within same-sex couples, Koss realized that this interpretation was limited, and that other determinants to abuse in close relationships needed to be considered (M. P. Koss, personal communication, October 19, 2000).

The question is: What other conclusions have mainstream psychology drawn about human behavior that has been based on such methodological limits? This is part of a more general question that has also been raised by others. For example Taylor and colleagues (Taylor et al., 2000) have questioned the well-accepted "fact" that fight-or-flight is how one typically responds to stress. What she and her colleagues point out, however, is that these findings have typically been based on research using male rats. In studying female subjects, the reaction to stress is a very different – one that is better described as "tend and befriend" – where females take steps to protect their young.

Providing a better integration between the LGB and mainstream literature can clearly benefit everyone. As noted by Rothblum (1994) and Stacey and Biblarz (2001), research with both LGB and heterosexual individuals may be thought of as providing us with a natural laboratory for better understanding the role that gender and sexual orientation play in human behavior. However, as noted earlier, the labels "LGB" and "sexual minority" are not scientific variables, and what we need to study are those mediators (e.g., life stressors) and moderators (e.g., parental support) that impact on the lives of individuals, and which of these variables may differ as a function of sexual orientation.

Toward the Integration of the LGB and Mainstream Psychology Literature

As I noted earlier in this chapter, much of what I have been involved in professionally prior to my interest in LGB issues has dealt with the integration of different approaches to psychotherapy. I have more recently extended this interest to the integration of the LGB literature into mainstream psychology. With some exceptions (e.g., Bailey, 2008; Davison, 1976; Hooker, 1957), most of the clinical and research work carried out on LGB issues has been done by those who themselves are sexual minorities. Given the greater interest in LGB by society as a whole, the time may have come for psychologists, regardless of their sexual orientation, to have more of a professional interest in understanding the lives of sexual minorities.

In Vaid's (1995) sociopolitical analysis of the gay rights movement described in her book *Virtual Equality: The Mainstreaming of Gay & Lesbian Liberation*, she argued that true progress could not be made until mainstream society became more aware of sexual minority issues. In light of this, she recommends the following agenda:

> Rather than asking how gay and lesbian people can integrate themselves into the dominant culture, what if, instead, we affirm that our mission is explicitly to assimilate the dominant culture to us?... Defining our movement's goal as the assimilation of our heterosexual families, employers, neighbors, and institutions to the normalcy of gay and lesbian people, we clarify the educational work we need to do (p. 206).

She goes on to say that a partnership needs to be formed with nongay allies, to "focus on the segments of the mainstream where education and transformation are possible" (p. 304). I believe this is starting to happen. After all, what can be more mainstream that the Nebraska Symposium on Motivation – the conference on which this volume is based!

Another example of how mainstream psychology can become better aware of LGB issues is exemplified in an organization of mainstream psychologists that was formed in the year 2000 – AFFIRM: Psychologists Affirming Their Lesbian, Gay, Bisexual, and Transgender Family. At the time of this writing over 850 nongay family allies have joined AFFIRM, coming out in support of their sons, daughters, sisters, brothers, mothers, fathers, grandparents, aunts, uncles, cousins, nieces, and nephews who are sexual minorities. AFFIRM is supportive of clinical and research on sexual minority issues, and is dedicated to closing the gap between LGB and mainstream psychology. Further information about AFFIRM can be found on its Web site (http://www.sunysb.edu/affirm).

Concluding Comment

The status of sexual minorities has changed dramatically since the landmark Stonewall Rebellion over 35 years ago. Although there undoubtedly will be setbacks, the status of sexual minorities will most likely continue to improve. Within psychology, however, much more needs to be done to raise our consciousness, reduce heterosexism and heterocentrism, and extend the limitations of our science. Mainstream psychology needs to become aware of the LGB work carried out in such areas as adolescent development, couple relationships, parenting, family relations, suicide risk and prevention, and psychotherapy. In short, we need to integrate the LGB literature into relevant areas within mainstream psychology. Hopefully the 54th Annual Nebraska Symposium on Motivation will serve as a landmark in this integrative movement.

Acknowledgment I would like to thank Joanne Davila for her comments on an earlier draft of this chapter.

References

Association for Advancement of Behavior Therapy. (1992). *Adolescent suicide*. New York: Association for the Advancement of Behavior Therapy

Bailey, M. (2008). Sexual arousal, sexual orientation and sex differences. In D. A. Hope (Ed.), *Contemporary perspectives on lesbian, gay, and bisexual identities*. New York: Springer.

Bieschke, K. J., McClanahan, M., Tozer, E., Grzegorek, J. L, & Park, J. (2000). Programmatic research on the treatment of lesbian, gay, and bisexual clients: The past, the present, and the course of the future. In R. M. Perez, K. A. DeBord, & K. J. Bieschke (Eds.), *Handbook of counseling and psychotherapy with lesbian, gay, and bisexual clients* (pp.207–223). Washington, DC: American Psychological Association.

Burckell, L. A. (2006). *Suicide attempts in sexual minority and heterosexual youth and young adults: A meta-analysis*. Unpublished manuscript, Stony Brook University.

Davison, G. C. (1976). Homosexuality: The ethical challenge. *Journal of Consulting and Clinical Psychology, 44*, 157–162.

Diamond, L. M. (2003a). What does sexual orientation orient? A biobehavioral model distinguishing romantic love and sexual desire. *Psychological Review, 110*, 173–192.

Diamond, L. M. (2003b). Was it a phase? Young women's relinquishment of lesbian/bisexual identities over a 5-year period. *Journal of Personality and Social Psychology, 84*, 352–364.

Doherty, W. J., & Simmons, D. S. (1996). Clinical practice patterns of marriage and family therapists: A national survey of therapists and their clients. *Journal of Marital & Family Therapy, 22*, 9–25.

Eubanks-Carter, C., & Goldfried, M. R. (2006). The impact of client sexual orientation and gender on clinical judgments and diagnosis of borderline personality disorder. *Journal of Clinical Psychology, 62*, 751–770

Garnets, L., Hancock, K. A., Cochran, S. D., Goodchilds, J., & Peplau, L. A. (1991). Issues in psychotherapy with lesbians an gay men: A survey of psychologists. *American Psychologist, 46*, 964–972.

Goldfried, M. R. (Ed.). (1982). *Converging themes in psychotherapy: Trends in psychodynamic, humanistic, and behavioral practice*. New York: Springer.

Goldfried, M. R. (2001). Integrating gay, lesbian, an bisexual issues into mainstream psychology. *American Psychologist, 56*, 977–988.

Green, R. F. (1974). *Sexual identity conflict in children and adults.* New York: Basic Books.

Green, R.-J. (2000). Lesbians, gays, and family psychology: Resources for teaching and practice. In B. Green, & G. C. Croom (Eds.), *Education, research, and practice in lesbian, gay bisexual, and transgendered psychology: A resource manual* (pp. 207–225). Thousand Oaks, CA: Sage.

Herek, G. (2008) Sexual prejudice and stigma in the United States. In D. A. Hope (Ed.), *Contemporary perspectives on lesbian, gay and bisexual identities.* New York: Springer.

Hooker, E. (1957). The adjustment of the male overt homosexual. *Journal of Projective Techniques, 21,* 18–31.

Julien, D., Arellano, C., & Turgeon, L. (1997). Gender issues in heterosexual, gay, and lesbian couples. In W. K. Halford & H. I. Markman (Eds.), *Clinical handbook of marriage and couples interventions* (pp. 107–127). New York: Wiley.

Kimmel, M. S. (1997). Masculinity as homophobia: Fear, shame and silence in the construction of gender identity. In M. M. Gergen & S. N. Davis (Eds.), *Toward a new psychology of gender* (pp. 223–242). New York: Routledge.

Koss, M. P., Goodman, L. A., Browne, A., Fitzgerald, L. F., Keita, G. P., & Russo, N. P. (1994). *No safe haven: Male violence against women at home, at work, and in the community.* Washington, DC: American Psychological Association.

Lang, P. J. (1968). Fear reduction and fear behavior: Problems in treating a construct. In J. M. Shlien (Ed.), *Research in psychotherapy* (Vol. I, pp. 90–102). Washington, DC: American Psychological Association.

LaSala, M. C. (2004). Extradyadic sex and gay male couples: Comparing monogamous and non-monogamous relationships. *Families in Society, 85,* 405–412.

Mallon, G. (1997). Obstacles to queer research. *In the Family, 2*(4), 25.

Pachankis, J. E., & Goldfried, M. R. (2006). Social anxiety in young gay men. *Journal of Anxiety Disorders, 20,* 996–1015.

Patterson, C. (2008). Families of the rainbow: Lesbian and gay parents and their children. In D. A. Hope (Ed.), *Contemporary perspectives on lesbian, gay and bisexual identities.* New York: Springer.

Ritter, K. Y., & Terndrup, A. I. (2002). *Handbook of affirmative psychotherapy with lesbians and gay men.* New York: Guilford Press.

Rothblum, E. D. (1994). "I only read about myself on bathroom walls": The need for research on the mental health of lesbians and gay men. *Journal of Consulting and Clinical Psychology, 62,* 213–220.

Rothblum, E. D. (2008). Pioneers in partnership: Lesbian and gay male couples in civil unions compared with those not in civil unions, and married heterosexual siblings. In D. A. Hope (Ed.), *Contemporary perspectives on lesbian, gay and bisexual identities.* New York: Guilford Press.

Savin-Williams, R. (2001). Suicide attempts among sexual minority youths: Population and measurement issues. *Journal of Consulting and Clinical Psychology, 69,* 983–991.

Savin-Williams, R. (2008). Who is gay? And are they healthy? In D. A. Hope (Ed.), *Contemporary perspectives on lesbian, gay and bisexual identities.* New York: Guilford Press.

Stacey, J., & Biblarz, T. J. (2001). (How) does the sexual orientation of parents matter? *American Sociological Review, 66,* 159–183.

Taylor, S. E., Klein, L. C., Lewis, B. P, Gruenewald, T. L., Gurung, R. A. R., & Updegraff, J. A. (2000). Biobehavioral responses to stress in females: Tend-and-befriend, not flight-or-flight. *Psychological Review, 107,* 411–429.

Tremblay, P. J. (1995, October). *The homosexual factor in the youth suicide problem.* Paper presented at the Sixth Annual Conference of the Canadian Association for Suicide Prevention, Banff, Alberta, Canada.

Vaid, U. (1995). *Virtual equality: The mainstreaming of gay and lesbian liberation.* New York: Anchor Books.

Yoneda, A. C., & Davila, J. (2006, March). *Same-sex emotional and same-sex sexual attractions: Differing implications for the psychological health of adolescent females.* Poster session presented at the annual meeting of the Nebraska Symposium on Motivation, Lincoln, Nebraska.

Index

A
American National Election Studies
(ANES), 76
Association for Advancement of Behavior
Therapy (AABT), 184
Attitudes Toward Gay Men (ATG), 83
Attitudes Toward Lesbians and Gay Men
(ATLG) scale
condemnation–tolerance factor, 84
OLS regression analyses, 85, 86, 97
policy attitudes, 86, 87
reliability and validity, 83
SDQ-L and SDQ-G versions, 84
Attitudes Toward Lesbians (ATL), 83

B
Bisexuality, 115–116

C
Contemporary Families Study
child adjustment *vs.* parental labor
division, 154
children and grandparents, 155–156
children's adjustment, 152–153
couple involvement, 150–151
findings of study, 156–157
implications of study, 157–158
lesbian *vs.* heterosexual mothers,
151–152
limitations, 157
Locke—Wallace Marital Adjustment Test
(LWMAT), 151
maternal mental health, 150
parental relationship satisfaction, 154–155
parent-child adjustment, 153–154
participating families, 149
Partnership Questionnaire, 151

F
Female sexual orientation
arousal definition
arousal pattern
genital sexual arousal, 54, 56
heterosexuals *vs.* homosexuals, 55, 56
subjective self-reported arousal, 56
vaginal photoplethysmography, 54
vaginal vasocongestion, 54
VPA reliability, 54
VPA *vs.* VBV, 54
stimuli for measurement, 55

G
Gays
history of homosexuality, 6
homosexual demarcation, 6, 7
prevalence rates
adults *vs.* adolescents, 30
bisexual orientation, neglect of, 32
calculations' repurcussions, 32
cohort- based, 31
combination possibilities, 35
degree of measure, 31–32
meaningful measures, use of, 36–37
measure-based statistics, 18–30
researchers' dilemma, 36
sexuality dimension assessment, 34–35
statistical fallacies, 32–34
sexual orientaion
components (expressions), 7–9
definition, 5, 6
General Social Survey
ANES' feeling thermometer, 77–78
attitude trends, 77
sexual prejudice, 77
correlation to, 78
situational and dispositional factors, 78–79

H
Heterosexism
    individual manifestations
        enacted stigma, 68–70
        felt stigma, 70–73
        internalised stigma, 73–79
    sexual minority subjugation, 77
    and sexual prejudice, 79
Heterosexual 'controls'
    survey participants, 116–117
    vs. same-sex couples, 117
Homophobia, 75

L
Lesbian and gay parents
    children
        adoption, 143–144
        Bay Area Families Study, 147–148
        cognitive development theory, 146
        Contemporary Families Study,
            148–149
        current context, 141–142
        custody and visitation, 143
        gender schema theory, 146
        grandparent contribution, 147
        legal status, 141–142
        lesbian *vs.* heterosexual mothers, 146
        male and female parental influence,
            145
        psychoanalytical theory, 145
        social science research, 146
        variation across states, 144–145
LGB literature
    and mainstream psychology
        AFFIRM, the organisation, 193
        virtual equality, 193

M
Male sexual orientation
    arousal definition, 45–46
    arousal pattern
        brain imaging techniques, 46
        erotic stimuli *vs.* neutral stimuli, 47–48
        heterosexual and homosexual, 49
        pedophilia, a case study, 50
        penile plethysmography (PPG), 45
        PPG *vs.* brain imaging, 46–47
        vs. the Kinsey scale, 50–51
    and male bisexuality, 51–52
        minimum genital arousal, 53
        minimum subjective arousal, 52–53

private and public sexual identity, 44
stimuli for measurement, 44–45

N
National Longitudinal Study
    adolescent outcomes
        future directions, 177–178
        law and policy implications, 176–177
        research findings overview, 175
        results summary, 174
        vs. Add health samples, 165
    adolescents
        Add Health database, 161
        adjustment issues, 158–159
        alchohol use, 167
        approach criteria, 161–162
        attraction and behaviors, 164
        delinquent behavior, 168
        environment and peer relations,
            172–173
        family and relationship variables,
            164–165
        friendship networks, 170
        in-school and in-home surveys, 160
        normative levels of adjustment, 159
        and parental warmth, 170
        participating families, 159–161
        and peer relations, 169
        psychosocial adjustment, 162–163
        psychosocial results, 163
        romantic relationship, 164
        victimization, 168
    family relationships
        adolescent adjustment, 173
        and outcome variables, 166
        and substance/alcohol use, 168–169
Nebraska Symposium on Motivation
    baby carriage, 189–190
    heterogeneity of LGBs
        categorization, 185–186
        labels and bias, 186–187
        sexual plasticity in women, 185
    labels and bias
        anxiety reactions, 187
        borderline personality disorder, 186–187
        heterosexism, 188
        homophobia, 187–188
        social anxiety, 187
    LGB issues involvement
        AABT meeting, 184
        PFLAG parade, 183–184
    same-sex marriages, 189

P
Parents, Family and Friends of Lesbians and
     Gays (PFLAG), 183

S
Same-sex couples
     attitude change over time, 122–123
     definition, 113
     legal recognition, 142
     marriage and legal relationships
          countries permitting, 118–120
          current marriage, 122
          general public attitude, 120–121
          issues, 113–114
          long-term couples, 118
          personal wishes, 119
          previous marriages, 121–122
          survey criteria, 117
     research conclusions
          community support, 132
          conflict areas, 129–130
          current knowledge, 133–134
          demographic similarity, 123–124
          ex-lover's role, 133
          family contact, 130–131
          household tasks, 127–128
          monogamy, 125–126
          outness to others, 124–125
          overinvolvement vs. autonomy, 126
          participant choice, 125–126
          power sharing, 129
          relationship termination, 132–133
          research surveys, 126
          sexual activity, 125
          sharing problems, 128
          social support, 131–132
     research subjects, 114
     sexual oreintation
          research, 115
          survey participants, 114–115
          survey results, 114–115
Sexual arousal patterns
     males vs. females, 55–58
     methodological concerns
          female volunteers, 57
          photoplethysmography limitations, 57
          transexuals, 58
          vaginal arousal sensitivity, 58
Sexual minorities
     attitude change, 190
     LGB literature, invisibility
          demand-withdrawal pattern, 192

          integration with mainstream, 192
          psychological issues, 190–191
          teenage suicides, 191–192
     Stonewall Rebellion, 194
Sexual orientaion
     components (expressions)
          romantic attraction, 8, 10
          sexual attraction, 7, 8, 10
          sexual behavior, 8
          sexual identity, 8
     consistency
          adult studies, 14
          in data documentation, 13
          same-sex attraction vs. behavior, 15
          same-sex behavior vs. identity, 14
          same-sex identification vs. attraction, 15
     definition, research, 10–11
     in males
          arousal definition, 45–46
          arousal pattern, 46–51
          and male bisexuality, 51–53
          private and public sexual identity,
               44–45
          stimuli for measurement, 44–45
     males vs. females, 16, 59, 60
     sexual partner choices
          men vs. women, 43
     stability
          longitudinal data sets, 12–13
          retrospective studies, 12
     stability and consistency, causes
          adolescent experiences, 16–17
          real-life developmental experiences, 17
          same-sex sexuality continuum, 17
     types of changes, 16
Sexual orientation
     in females
          bisexuality, 59
          paraphilias, rarity, 60
          partner choices, 60
     gender nonconformity, 60
Sexual prejudice
     equal employment rights, 81
     and heterosexism, 79
     legislation, 80
     marriage rights, 82–83
     measures of, 83
     and public policy attitudes, 79–80, 82
     tolerance levels, 81
     vs. policy attitudes, 79
Sexual stigma
     cultural factors, 88
          civil rights movements, 89

Sexual stigma (*cont.*)
    conservative backlash, 90
    deep rooted prejudices, 92
    education levels, 89
    feminist movements, 89
    gay and lesbian movement, 89
    gay rights proponents, 91
    improved attitudes, 90
    increased tolerance, 91
    overcoming internalisation, 92
    public discussions, 91
    US AIDS epidemic, 90
  definition, 77
  individual manifestations, 68–79
  prejudice reduction
    close friendships, 95, 97
    feeling thermometer scores, 96
    personal contact, 93–94
    social processes, 94–95
  structural manifestations (heterosexism),
    77
Sexual stigma manifestations
  enacted stigma
    AllportÆs conceptualization, 68
    hate crime prevalence, 69
    population prevalence, 69
    violent victimization, 68–70
  enacted stigma-antigay attacks, 68
  felt stigma
    concealment of sexuality, 72
    fear stress, 70
    operational definition, 71

    preemptive reactions, 70
    self preservation strategies, 72
    stereotype threat, 71
    subtle behavior influences, 72–73
  internalised stigma
    affective reactions, 75
    attitudes, 75
    definition, 73
    prevalence, in USA, 75
    self stigma, 73–74
    sexual prejudice, 74–75
    stereotypical ideas, 75
Social Discomfort Questionnaire (SDQ), 84
Stigma
  social definition, 66
Survey studies methodology
  ATLG measure utility, 98
  National telephone survey
    features, 101
    issues addressed, 101
    process, 101
  student questionnaire study
    affective responses, 99–100
    ATL/ATG, attitudes, 99
    policy attitudes, 100

V
Vaginal blood volume (VBV), 54
Vaginal pulse amplitude (VPA), 54
VBV. *See* Vaginal blood volume
VPA. *See* Vaginal pulse amplitude

Printed in the United States
138220LV00002B/1/P

9 780387 095554